The Essentials of
FINANCE *and*
BUDGETING

The Business Literacy for HR Professionals Series

The Business Literacy for HR Professionals Series educates human resource professionals in the principles, practices, and processes of business and management. Developed in conjunction with the Society for Human Resource Management, these books provide a comprehensive overview of the concepts, skills, and tools HR professionals need to be influential partners in developing and executing organizational strategy. Drawing on rich content from Harvard Business School Publishing and the Society for Human Resource Management, each volume is closely reviewed by a content expert as well as by senior HR professionals. Whether you are aspiring to the executive level in your organization or already in a leadership position, these authoritative books provide the basic business knowledge you need to play a strategic role.

Other books in the series:

The Essentials of Managing Change and Transition
The Essentials of Negotiation

The Essentials of
FINANCE *and*
BUDGETING

Harvard Business School Press
Boston, Massachusetts

and

Society for Human Resource Management
Alexandria, Virginia

Library of Congress Cataloging-in-Publication Data

Business literacy for HR professionals : the essentials of finance and budgeting.
   p.   cm. — (Business literacy for HR professionals series)
Includes bibliographical references and index.
ISBN 1-59139-572-0
   1.Personnel departments—Finance. I. Harvard Business School. II. Society
for Human Resource Management (U.S.) III. Harvard business literacy for HR
professionals series.
   HF5549.B923 2005
   658.15'024'6583—dc22

                                                                        2004025560

Contents

Introduction

Familiarity with finance concepts has become increasingly important for anyone who works in the area of human resources—whether you're an executive or a manager in the HR department of a large corporation or the head of an HR services or consulting business. As companies everywhere face stiffening competition, they're demanding that *all* managers understand finance so they can better support the firm's strategic goals, generate the profitability that enables the organization to fulfill its purpose, and make the smartest possible use of limited resources.

The Essentials of Finance and Budgeting explains the basics of this important subject. The book will not make you a finance expert, nor will it qualify you to become a financial analyst, controller, or chief financial officer (CFO). But it *will* explain what you need to know to be an intelligent consumer of financial information. And it will help you use financial concepts to make the wisest decisions for your HR department and your organization.

By reading this book, you're joining the rising numbers of HR professionals who maintain that business knowledge—including understanding how your company delivers value to customers, makes money, and manages costs—has become increasingly crucial for anyone who works in the realm of human resources.

The book uses a fictional manufacturing company throughout to illustrate the concepts introduced. However, the ideas, tools, and techniques you'll find in these chapters are vital in all kinds of companies and industries—whether they make a product or deliver a service.

And though this book treats the subject of finance from the perspective of for-profit companies, managers in not-for-profit organizations can also benefit from the chapters that follow. No organization—whether for-profit or not-for-profit—can survive and fulfill its purpose if it spends more money than it takes in. Thus a solid understanding of finance basics can serve managers in every endeavor. If you work in a not-for-profit organization, note that the standards required and terminology used in your organization's financial statements will differ in some ways from those introduced in this book. You may want to augment your learning by also obtaining and reading resources such as Edward McMillan's *Not-for-Profit Budgeting and Financial Management* and *Not-for-Profit Accounting, Tax and Reporting Requirements*, both published by Jossey-Bass.

The Big Picture of Finance

Reduced to its essentials, finance is about acquiring and allocating resources—how an organization goes about financing the assets it needs to fulfill its purpose and how firms and departments can best make use of their assets. Questions about acquiring assets include the following:

- How will the company acquire and finance intangible assets such as human capital, as well as physical assets such as inventory and equipment?

- Should the firm use the owners' money, borrowed funds, or internally generated cash for these acquisitions? If borrowing makes sense, which are the most appropriate sources of debt capital? How would profitability be affected if the company operated with a larger proportion of borrowed funds?

- How long does it take to collect on the money owed by customers (accounts receivable)?

Now consider the allocation of resources. Here, finance addresses important questions such as these:

- If a company or department had an opportunity to invest in two initiatives, how could it determine which would produce the greatest economic value in the years ahead?

- What return must a new initiative produce to be worth undertaking? And how are returns measured, anyway?

- How many units of a new product or service must the company sell to break even on its investment?

- How can managers determine the profitability of the many different goods and services they produce?

Finance is also an information system. Drawing on the accounting function and its meticulous recording of transactions, finance produces numbers that managers can use to plan and control operations. These numbers take the form of financial statements, budgets, and forecasts. Financial information gives managers the numbers they need to make better decisions—if they interpret and use those numbers correctly. One thing you'll learn here is how to use financial information to determine which of your HR department's efforts and investments are contributing to your firm's profitability and which are not—something that isn't always obvious.

How to Use This Book

Chapter 1 of this book starts things off by explaining why financial literacy is so important to HR professionals. It also outlines the ways in which you can benefit your company by applying financial know-how.

Chapters 2 and 3 are concerned with financial statements: the balance sheet, income statement, and cash flow statement. These are the primary documents of finance. Chapter 2 explains these documents, while chapter 3 shows you how to interpret them.

Chapter 4 introduces the balanced scorecard methodology—a model for measuring activities (such as workforce learning, business-process improvement, and customer-service enhancement) that translate into future financial performance. You'll discover how companies create balanced scorecards for their enterprise overall, and how you can create an HR department scorecard that supports your firm's strategy.

Chapter 5 covers a selected set of important accounting concepts, including accrual versus cash accounting, accounting for inventories and depreciation, the treatment of leases, the principle of historical cost, and cost accounting. This chapter won't make you an accountant, but it will help you understand some concepts that are important for your company or business.

Taxes form the subject of chapter 6. The discussion is limited to business taxes, with particular emphasis on how the different forms of business organizations (proprietorships, partnerships, corporations, etc.) are uniquely taxed. If you're an entrepreneur faced with determining—or changing—how your business will be legally organized, you'll find this material particularly useful.

Both chapters 7 and 8 are concerned with financing operations and growth, and with the sources of debt and equity capital. Chapter 7 describes a typical life cycle of a successful business—from start-up, through growth, and to maturity—and the financing sources that businesses tap at each phase. Chapter 8 describes the money and capital markets that growing businesses turn to as these companies become larger and more credible entities. Initial public offerings (IPOs), the role of investment bankers, and market securities are discussed.

Few enterprises and HR departments function successfully without a good budget, the subject of chapter 9. Budgets are important tools for planning, coordinating, monitoring, and evaluating performance. This chapter provides a practical guide to budgeting, and explains step-by-step how you can create operating and cash budgets for your business unit.

Chapter 10 introduces financial tools you can use to make better decisions about internal and external investments. What is the return on investment in a new HR initiative? How long will it take to recoup that investment?

Chapter 11 shifts focus to a major challenge for companies today: measuring and reporting human capital. This elusive but vital intangible asset has increased in importance as the foundation for business has shifted away from physical assets such as manufacturing plants and equipment. This chapter presents strategies for quantifying human capital and gauging how people contribute to your firm's bottom line.

Chapter 12 presents additional tools for decision making: net present value and internal rate of return. These tools are based on time-value-of-money concepts that you'll find useful in many spheres of analysis and decision making.

In chapter 13, you'll learn about valuation—that is, determining what a business is worth. How would your firm go about estimating the value of an operating unit it planned to buy or sell? How would you do the same if you owned an HR services firm and were considering selling it or acquiring another firm to grow your business? An important and technical subject, valuation is generally the province of experts. But like every important business issue, it is too important to be left solely to the experts. As a manager, you should be familiar with the different valuation approaches, as well as their strengths and weaknesses.

Finally, chapter 14 wraps things up with suggestions for further strengthening and practicing your financial skills. The chapter also sums up how financial savvy can help you serve as a strategic business partner in your firm, forge positive working relationships with your CFO and other finance experts, and position and operate your HR department as a profit center.

The book's appendices offer additional detail on activity-based budgeting, a valuable planning tool, as well as templates that enable you to practice creating and analyzing balance sheets, income statements, cash flow statements, and HR cash and department budgets.

Like every discipline, finance has a unique vocabulary. Part of the challenge of mastering finance is simply understanding this language and becoming familiar with its use. At the back of this book, you'll find a glossary of key terms. Each new term is italicized when first introduced in the text, indicating that you can find its definition in the glossary.

And if you'd like to learn more about any of the topics covered in these chapters, we've provided a For Further Reading section, also at the end of the book. There you'll find references to books, articles, and, occasionally, to Harvard Business School classroom materials that are available at www.hbsp.harvard.edu.

This book's content is based on a number of books, articles, and online productions of Harvard Business School Publishing (HBSP) and the Society for Human Resource Management (SHRM), including class notes, *Harvard Business Review* articles, the online learning series Harvard ManageMentor, *HR Magazine* and *Human Resource Executive* articles, and SHRM surveys and research reports.

The Essentials of
FINANCE *and*
BUDGETING

CHAPTER ONE

Finance and the HR Professional

A Crucial Competency

Key Topics Covered in This Chapter

- *Why finance literacy is important for HR professionals*

- *How HR professionals can provide valuable guidance or assistance on financial issues for their company*

I F YOU FIND BALANCE SHEETS, income statements, ratio analysis, and other financial concepts intimidating, you're not alone. Many HR and other "nonfinancial" professionals feel the same way. But as business grows ever more competitive, managers and employees from every function within organizations must deepen their understanding of basic financial concepts. Why? The more you know about how your company makes money and delivers value to customers and shareholders, the more you can identify ways to boost revenues, contain costs, and contribute to your organization's profitability in other ways.

In this chapter, we'll take a closer look at why financial literacy is so important for HR executives and managers. We'll also consider how you, as an HR professional, can create more value for your company by applying your financial knowledge in the workplace.

Minding Your Business

If you work for a large firm, the company probably has a chief financial officer and other financial and accounting specialists on staff.[1] If you work for a smaller organization, perhaps the company hires an accountant to come in once a month and "do the books." In either case, it can be tempting to assume that, with these experts on board, you and other nonfinancial managers don't need to know much about the books or the numbers. After all, that's what the experts are for, right?

Wrong. Finance involves much more than just columns of figures and spreadsheets. It's about understanding a company's *value chain*— how the firm makes and spends its money, delivers value to customers and shareholders, and measures its ability to carry out its competitive strategy. When HR and other nonfinancial managers and employees grasp how their company's value chain works, they can better see how decisions they make and actions they take every day can save the firm money, boost revenues, and otherwise improve the bottom line.

Financial savvy has other benefits as well. It enables managers and employees to comprehend why their company sometimes has to make difficult and painful decisions, such as initiating layoffs or other cost-cutting measures. When people are familiar with and understand the hard-core numbers that express the business's performance, they realize that management isn't just cutting for the sake of cutting—it's taking needed steps to ensure the firm's survival. Many people develop a whole new appreciation for management once they've deepened their financial knowledge.

Managers and employees who have mastered finance basics are also better able to recognize when something questionable is going on in their organization. If you understand the books, you can more easily detect when someone's "cooking" them. At Enron, for example, managers throughout the ill-fated firm might have realized that questionable dealings were afoot if they had understood more about the company's finances.

You don't need a graduate degree in finance or accounting to begin generating these kinds of benefits for your firm. But you *do* need to take proactive steps to develop a working knowledge of how your company conducts and measures its business. Where do you begin? Taking the time to read books like this one is a good start. Classes on finance basics, such as those offered by the Society for Human Resource Management Academy or other institutions that offer similar learning opportunities, can also be very valuable. In one course offered by Delta Air Lines, facilitators helped participants gain familiarity with balance sheets and other financial statements by having the students create such statements for their own households.

But you can also enhance—and demonstrate—your financial know-how by taking action on the job. Consider these guidelines:

- **Understand key external business trends.** What's happening in your company's industry and markets? Are supply chains, distribution channels, and other major elements of your firm's value chain undergoing major shifts? If so, how might those changes affect the way your company does business? Talk with suppliers, customers, line managers, and executives about what they see happening in the business world. Ask them what they consider the most important implications of these changes.

- **Connect with your company.** Spend time with line managers and employees who work in the functions and departments that make up your firm's internal end-to-end process for creating and delivering customer value. Show interest, ask questions, and find out what keeps these individuals awake at night. Do the same with key suppliers and customers— you'll enrich your knowledge of your firm's business even further.

- **Link HR to the business.** Think about how your HR department might better link its strategy and practices to the overall business. How might you inspire and empower employees to collectively execute the firm's strategy so that customers and shareholders benefit?

Clearly, business knowledge generates crucial value for companies, and many HR professionals seem to understand this. Indeed, in an informal survey of HR professionals conducted by the Society for Human Resource Management during the fall of 2003, 76 percent of the respondents said that understanding the business and industry of their organization was "very important."[2] Yet in the same survey, only 47–48 percent of the respondents described themselves as "proficient" or "very proficient" at understanding their company's business and industry.

Applying Your Financial Knowledge

Once you've strengthened your understanding of finance, you'll find a wealth of opportunities to apply your knowledge on the job. Let's take a closer look at some of these opportunities below.

Turning Your HR Department into a Profit Center

Is your HR department profitable? That is, does it generate a return on your investment in training programs, retention initiatives, and other HR services? As Jack J. Phillips, a consultant for Brown Systems, notes, "Return on investment (ROI) has become one of the most challenging and intriguing issues facing the human resources development . . . field."[3]

Phillips adds that several forces have driven interest in the ROI of human resources investment—including pressure from senior managers to show the value of HR investments and to scrutinize all expenditures. Another factor is the renewed interest in measurement and evaluation sparked by management advances such as total quality management and continuous process improvement. In addition, a general trend has emerged in which companies are demanding greater accountability from all functions.

Though the impact of HR programs is harder to measure in financial terms than that of other business activities, HR professionals must still find ways to demonstrate the value generated by their function's investments. Otherwise, senior managers may conclude that such investments don't in fact add value for the company. Or the company executives may assume that HR professionals don't believe they should be held accountable for their investments.

By enhancing your knowledge of finance, you can better isolate the impact of HR policies and programs on your company's performance—and translate that impact into monetary terms.

Measuring the Value of Human Capital

As one business writer points out: "Among . . . 'intangible assets' . . . the most important is human capital, the ability of employees to do the things that ultimately make the company work and succeed."[4] Yet even though employees account for as much as 80 percent of a corporation's worth, companies find it difficult to assess the employees' contribution to the bottom line in concrete terms.

There *is* an emerging science focused on measuring people's impact on a company's bottom line, yet no one has found a magic formula for doing this. Nevertheless, many companies are complementing traditional accounting measures, such as balance sheets and income statements, with measurements of intangible assets. This approach gives a truer picture of a corporation's worth.

Companies use different approaches for assessing the bottom-line value of employees. But the most effective approaches start with a clear understanding of a firm's strategy—that is, how the company makes money. Managers then identify the cause-and-effect relationships driving business success, using statistical analysis to show how HR practices lead to increased profits and rises in stock value. Even without quantifiable measures, you can still develop valuable data about the impact of human capital. For instance, clarify the corporate strategic objective you're trying to achieve for each HR practice. Is it stronger product or service innovation? More efficient use of limited resources? Customer service that beats rival companies' service? Once you've clarified these objectives, define some measurable outcomes—even if they're only subjective—and examine trends in that outcome. Examples might include changes in recruiting costs over several years for a boost in profits, which enables the company to invest in better customer service or product innovation.

The process isn't easy. But if you approach it systematically—and back up your conclusions with solid data—you generate important forms of value for your firm. To illustrate, whereas traditional accounting measures show how a company has performed in the past, measures of human capital indicate how the business might perform in the future. Thus they serve as *leading indicators* rather than *lagging indicators*. Measuring the value of human capital also enables you to show that your company's workforce is an asset to be leveraged for profit—not an expense to be curtailed. In addition, it helps you make intelligent choices about where to invest HR dollars. Equally important, finding a way to express the financial impact of employees enables you and other HR professionals to expand your role in the company to include strategy-related decisions.

Implementing an HR Balanced Scorecard

Many companies are using a methodology known as the balanced scorecard to "balance" financial measures of corporate performance with nonfinancial measures, such as assessments of the firm's innovation and professional-development abilities, the efficiency of its internal business processes, and the quality of its customer service.[5] Managers use this approach to clarify and test their theories about how improvements in *non*financial areas will lead to better performance in financial areas, as expressed in profitability, shareholder value, and other ways. By examining actual performance on all these dimensions and comparing it with expected performance, managers can then make changes aimed at closing any gaps between the two.

HR can play a vital role in this approach. How? HR professionals can take steps to ensure that their department's own professional development, internal processes, and customer service lead to financial outcomes that reinforce the company's overall strategy and support other unit leaders' efforts to implement that strategy. To build an "HR scorecard," you need to assess the ROI of HR programs and practices as well as systematically measure the impact of your firm's human capital on the bottom line, as discussed above.

Encouraging Ethical Financial Practices and Conduct

Numerous forces are coming together to fuel a desire among some businesspeople to score quick profits for their companies, spur stock-value increases for shareholders, or grab personal gain for themselves. These forces include industry deregulation and un-precedented acquisitions, mergers, and cost-cutting activity, as well as heightening demand from investors for ever more spectacular returns. Couple these forces with the sometimes fuzzy rules of corporate accounting, and the stage is set for downright illegal behavior (at worst) and the *perception* among employees and the public of questionable behavior (at best).

Consider this scenario: You're the vice president of HR, and your friend—who's an accountant at the same company—confides in you that the CFO is planning to have managers take an aggressive stance on sales-revenue reporting. This stance promises to enhance the firm's earnings outlook and raise its stock price. But it also stretches the boundaries of acceptable accounting practices and could raise questions about the organization's methods and integrity.[6]

Or consider a situation in which sales reps are lavishing gifts, gratuities, and entertainment on current and potential customers in an effort to sustain or grow revenues or boost their own bonuses. Or perhaps the reverse is occurring: Employees at your company are accepting inappropriate gifts and entertainment.

Whatever form they take, actual or perceived unethical or illegal financial practices can destroy careers and entire companies—as managers at Enron and all too many other firms have discovered. These practices can also erode goodwill and trust among all of a company's stakeholders—employees, investors, customers, and suppliers. To help protect *your* company from these sorts of damage, you can take several steps:

- **Establish a code of ethics.** Initiate an effort to draft, communicate, and provide training on a code of ethics for your firm.[7] Most ethics policies contain extensive definitions of what constitutes ethical and unethical behavior—including how business transactions must be recorded, what constitutes appropriate gifts and entertainment, and how employees may use the company's assets. Once the code is final, communicate it to prospective, new, and longtime employees. Provide formal training that includes realistic case studies based on the code,

Ethics Facts and Trends

A 2003 survey of HR professionals yielded interesting information about how companies are handling ethics issues. Consider these statistics:

- 79 percent of survey respondents said that their organization has written ethics standards.

- 69 percent agreed that a company's HR department is a primary ethics resource.

- 71 percent believed that HR professionals should be involved in formulating ethics policies.

- 48 percent cited "meeting overly aggressive business/financial objectives" as a principal source of pressure to compromise organizations' ethical standards.

- 82 percent said that they would feel comfortable reporting ethics concerns to management.

- 68 percent said they were most likely to seek advice about ethics concerns from their boss. And 40 percent cited legal counsel as their secondary contact for advice.

SOURCE: Joshua Joseph and Evren Esen, "2003 Business Ethics Survey," SHRM/Ethics Resource Center, April 2003.

as well as free discussion of ethics issues. See the Society for Human Resource Management's Web site (www.shrm.org) for information and tools that can help you develop or refine your company's code of ethics.

- **Educate yourself.** Learn as much as you can about auditing procedures and your organization's possible exposure to liability resulting from various unclear accounting or financial practices.[8] To find out what's considered reasonable behavior, research industry norms governing practices that are open to broad interpretation. These include how to measure and report revenue, how to estimate future costs (such as obsolete inventory), and how to estimate an asset's useful life for the purposes of depreciation, among other practices.[9]

- **Make it safe to discuss business ethics.** Get your company to provide an ethics hotline or ombudsman so that employees can get clarification about an ethics issue without fear of punishment. Some companies house this function within the HR department; others create a separate function.

- **Raise concerns through the proper chains of command.** If you suspect that questionable financial or accounting practices are going on in your company, pursue action through the proper chains of command. Resist any temptation to conclude that you're not responsible for taking action. As an HR professional, you have responsibilities and obligations to your company's stakeholders—including employees and their retirement savings. Go first to your firm's general counsel or compliance or ethics officer. Move through the proper additional channels (such as CEO, board of directors, and outside authorities), if necessary. Invoke attorney-client privilege as soon as possible to protect conversations and written communications. And document everything.[10]

Complying with the Sarbanes-Oxley Act of 2002

In the Unites States, a new law signed by President George W. Bush in 2002—the Sarbanes-Oxley Act—has important implications for corporate financial accountability. The act also affects certain HR responsibilities.[11] Designed to end corporate financial malfeasance, the law established new requirements for corporate executives— and stiff penalties for violating the act's provisions. For example, CEOs and CFOs must certify periodic corporate financial reports, must retain all documents relevant to government investigations, and cannot receive personal loans or extensions of credit from the company. In addition, the act prohibits a company from retaliating against any employee who informs his or her supervisor, a federal regulatory agency, a law enforcement agency, or a member of Congress of violations of the act or the commission of any federal offense. The law also prohibits conflicts of interest between public accounting firms and corporations.

There are several measures you can take to help your company comply with Sarbanes-Oxley's employment-related provisions:

- **Hire officers carefully.** Confirm that a candidate for CEO or CFO has complied with the new act while employed by other companies.

- **Develop a code of ethics for senior financial officers.** Ensure that these employees have received these policies and have attended training on how to comply with the act.

- **Incorporate the new act into existing employment policies.** Make it clear that violations of Sarbanes-Oxley's policies are cause for immediate discharge. If employees violate employment policies, you can fire or discipline them without admitting that they violated the law. (Admitting a violation might increase your company's legal vulnerability.)

- **Train supervisors.** Make sure supervisors understand what constitutes retaliatory behavior against whistle blowing or government informing. Require all supervisors to consult with HR before taking action against an employee who has engaged in what may constitute protected activity under the new act.

- **Help establish a document-retention policy.** If you're settling a suit brought by an employee, don't ask the person to destroy or hand over his or her personal records relating to the dispute. Doing so may violate Sarbanes-Oxley, if the documents relate to a government investigation that falls within the act's document-retention provision.

- **Review executive compensation.** Review and, if necessary, modify all executive compensation programs, such as the use of company credit cards for personal expenses, to ensure compliance with the law.

Helping Your Company Through Bankruptcy

What you've been dreading is now happening: Your company is approaching or filing for *Chapter 11 bankruptcy*—the federally protected legal status that offers some financial breathing room while a struggling company attempts to stabilize its operations and survive.[12] How can you help your firm through this difficult, painful time? And how might you boost the organization's chances of emerging revitalized from bankruptcy? You can take key steps both before and after your firm files for bankruptcy:

- **Before filing:** Most bankruptcies stem from companies' taking on too much debt. Long before your firm needs to file for Chapter 11, you can help look for ways to find enough savings for the company to survive. Cost-cutting options may include switching from a defined benefit pension plan to a more affordable defined contribution plan. Also consider consolidating health-care providers. Meet with lawyers, consultants, and turnaround specialists as early as possible, giving them a full financial snapshot of the company's obligations and liabilities—payroll, benefits, collective bargaining agreements, and so forth. If these steps prove insufficient, weigh more drastic actions, such as cutting staff or benefits. But review labor contracts to see where unilateral layoffs are possible. And don't forget about the Worker Adjustment and Retraining Notification (WARN) Act, the U.S. federal law that requires employers with one hundred or more employees to give sixty days' notice before a plant closing or a mass layoff.

- **Preparing for filing:** Learn as much as you can about the bankruptcy process. Assemble an education packet, and customize it for vendors and employees. To find out more, talk with HR people in other firms that have been through the process. Examine vacation accruals and other unfunded liabilities, looking for other ways to fulfill these obligations to workers.

- **After filing:** When a company's lawyers submit a petition to bankruptcy court for a "First Day Order," they ask the court to authorize management to remain in control as "debtor in possession" and to empower the company to honor commitments essential for continued operation—such as salaries, benefits, and severance pay. All other debts are suspended until the company's creditors and the court approve a workout plan for emergence from bankruptcy. Creditor committees must sign off on all funding requests not in the ordinary course of business—such as bonus plans, raises, or retention plans. HR presents such compensation cases to the committees and the court—so you'll need a sound rationale for whatever you're proposing.

Note: Retention plans are crucial during this time, as valued managers and employees may want to jump ship in search of calmer waters—and as competing firms start wooing your best people. Identify those individuals whom the company needs most to survive. Formulate a strategy for "wedding" them to the firm, and make a convincing case for your retention plan to the credit committees and court.

Also develop and implement a comprehensive communications plan for when the Chapter 11 filing becomes public. Have letters, telephone scripts, and other communications handy so you and others in your firm can readily answer questions from customers, suppliers, investors, retirees, and employees. The more you communicate about the situation, the calmer everyone will remain—which can only be helpful for a company seeking to regain solid financial footing.

With these concepts in mind about why it's important for HR professionals to "mind their business" and how you can help your company by applying your financial savvy, take a look at assessment tool 1-1. This questionnaire can help you identify where you need to focus your attention as you work through the chapters in this book.

Assessment Tool 1-1
Gauge Your Overall
Understanding of Finance

Answer the multiple-choice questions that follow. At the end of the questions, check the accuracy of your answers, and see which chapters you need to focus on to strengthen your knowledge.

1. **What does a company's balance sheet show?**
   A. A snapshot of the firm's assets, liabilities, and owners' equity
   B. Revenues, expenses, and profitability
   C. Increases or decreases in the company's cash during a particular year
   D. None of the above

2. **Which of the following is a profitability ratio?**
   A. Inventory turnover—or cost of goods sold divided by average inventory
   B. Debt ratio—or total debt divided by total assets
   C. Return on assets—or net income divided by total assets
   D. Average day's sales—or net sales divided by 365

3. **Which of the following statements is true?**
   A. Companies using the balanced scorecard approach must start with a corporate-level scorecard showing cause-and-effect links that lead to financial performance.
   B. A balanced scorecard is created using input from managers at various levels of the organization.
   C. Balanced scorecards created for various departments in an organization are derived from the HR scorecard.
   D. The balanced scorecard approach works best for large companies in the high-tech and telecommunications industries.

4. Which of the following statements is false?
   A. As part of generally accepted accounting principles (GAAP), every corporation whose stock is publicly traded in the United States must have an independent certified public accountant audit its financial statements.
   B. Companies can track inventory cost flows using the first-in, first-out (FIFO) method, the last-in, first-out (LIFO) method, or the average cost method.
   C. Depreciation reduces the balance-sheet value of a company's asset over its presumed useful life.
   D. With accrual accounting, businesses record transactions only when money has actually traded hands.

5. Which of the following type of business entity accounts for the majority of sales in the United States?
   A. Sole proprietorships
   B. C corporations
   C. Partnerships
   D. S corporations

6. A company is issuing bonds and follow-on shares, as well as using money-center banking or finance companies. In which of the four stages of growth do these financing moves usually take place?
   A. Start-up
   B. Growth 1
   C. Growth 2
   D. Maturity

7. If your company were interested in funding growth through money markets, which of the following instruments might it consider?
   A. U.S. Treasury bills and certificates of deposit
   B. Bonds
   C. Shares of stock
   D. Dividends

Continued

8. **Which of the following statements describes incremental budgeting?**
   A. An incremental budget begins each new budgeting cycle from a zero base, as though it were being prepared for the first time.
   B. An incremental budget extrapolates from historical figures.
   C. An incremental budget covers a specific time frame—usually one fiscal year.
   D. An incremental budget attempts to incorporate continuous improvement through efforts such as cost reduction.

9. **You're considering proposing a one-day, off-site team-building session for your company's department heads, and you want to conduct a payback period analysis of this potential investment. What do you do?**
   A. Evaluate the nonquantifiable benefits and costs that the session would generate.
   B. Divide the net financial return of the session by the total cost of the investment.
   C. Calculate exactly how much time the company will need to recoup its investment in the session.
   D. Figure out how many units of the company's best-selling product must be sold in order to pay for the investment in the session.

10. **What is human capital?**
    A. The patents and other marketable intellectual property created by a company's managers and employees
    B. The revenues generated directly by the efforts of a company's on- and off-site sales force
    C. The number of individuals who make up a company's full-time, part-time, and temporary workforce
    D. The collective skills, knowledge, life experiences, energy, and enthusiasm that a firm's people choose to invest in their work

11. **What is net present value?**
    A. The present value of one or more future cash flows less any initial investment costs
    B. The monetary value today of a future payment discounted at some annual compound interest rate
    C. The amount to which a present value, or series of payments, will increase over a specific period at a specific compounding rate
    D. None of the above

12. **Your company is considering acquiring another firm, and wants to use an asset-based approach to estimating its value. Which of the following calculations would your company perform?**
    A. Earnings multiple
    B. Equity book value
    C. Discounted cash flow
    D. All the above

13. **Which of the following initiatives would *most* help your HR department become a profit center?**
    A. An affirmative-action plan that follows the letter of the law
    B. A recruiting method that reduces time-to-hire for all new employees
    C. A wage survey that aims to keep the company's normal salary structure competitive
    D. An incentive-pay system that rewards employees for what they produce

Continued

Answers to the Questions

See the following chapters to learn more

1. A. A snapshot of the firm's assets, liabilities, and owners' equity. Chapter 2: Financial Statements
2. C. Return on assets—or net income divided by total assets. Chapter 3: Finding Meaning in Financial Statements
3. B. A balanced scorecard is created using input from managers at various levels of the organization. Chapter 4: From Financial Measures to a Balanced Scorecard
4. D. With accrual accounting, businesses record transactions only when money has actually traded hands. Chapter 5: Important Accounting Concepts
5. B. C corporations. Chapter 6: Taxes
6. D. Maturity. Chapter 7: Financing Operations and Growth
7. A. U.S. Treasury bills and certificates of deposit. Chapter 8: Money and Capital Markets

Summing Up

In this chapter, you learned about why financial literacy among HR professionals is so important—including the increasing pressures on managers from all functions to demonstrate how their actions affect the company's bottom line. You also saw brief previews of the kinds of advantages you can generate for your firm by deepening your knowledge of finance. These benefits include the following:

- Demonstrating the value generated by HR investments

- Measuring the value of human capital

- Implementing an HR balanced scorecard

- Encouraging ethical financial practices and conduct

8. B. An incremental budget extrapolates from historical figures. Chapter 9: Budgeting
9. C. Calculate exactly how much time the company will need to recoup its investment in the session.
    Chapter 10: Practical Tools for Management Decisions
10. D. The collective skills, knowledge, life experiences, energy, and enthusiasm that a firm's people choose to invest in their work. Chapter 11: Measuring and Reporting Human Capital
11. A. The present value of one or more future cash flows less any initial investment costs. Chapter 12: The Time Value of Money
12. B. Equity book value. Chapter 13: Business Valuation Concepts
13. D. An incentive-pay system that rewards employees for what they produce. Chapter 14: Developing and Using Your Financial Know-How

- Reducing embezzlement and other forms of theft by employees

- Complying with new federal regulations, such as the Sarbanes–Oxley Act of 2002

- Helping your company avoid, prepare for, or recover from bankruptcy

Leveraging Chapter Insights: Critical Questions

- How would you describe your overall knowledge of finance?

- In which areas of finance is your knowledge the weakest? In which areas is it the strongest? Based on your responses to this chapter's self-assessment, which chapters in the book do you anticipate concentrating on?

- Which of the applications of financial know-how described in this chapter catch your attention most? Why? As you prepare to work through this book, what early thoughts come to mind regarding how you might best help your company through such applications?

CHAPTER TWO

Financial Statements

The Elements of Managerial Finance

Key Topics Covered in This Chapter

- *Balance sheets*

- *Income statements*

- *Cash flow statements*

- *Financial leverage*

- *The financial structure of the firm*

WHAT DOES YOUR COMPANY OWN, and what does it owe to others? What are its sources of revenue, and how has it spent its money? How much profit has it made? What is the state of your company's financial health? As an HR professional, the more you know about these matters, the better you can see how HR policies and initiatives affect your firm's profitability—and the better you can identify ways to boost the bottom line.

This chapter helps you answer such questions by explaining the three essential financial statements: the balance sheet, the income statement, and the cash flow statement. The chapter also examines some of the managerial issues implicit in these statements. Finally, the chapter broadens your financial know-how through a discussion of two important concepts: financial leverage and the financial structure of the firm.

Why Financial Statements?

Financial statements are the essential documents of business. Executives use them to assess a business's performance and identify ways in which managerial intervention may improve that performance. For example, as an HR executive or manager, you might examine your firm's financial statements to look for opportunities to improve revenues, cut costs, or improve cash flow through hiring, training, and other HR-related decisions. You may also need to prepare mini versions of some financial statements to show the impact on the company's profitability that you estimate a new HR initiative or program might have. And if you're an HR consultant in charge of your own business, you'll want to understand these statements as a way of evaluating how your company is performing overall and what changes, if any, you need to make to improve that performance.

But executives and consultants aren't the only individuals who consider financial statements important. Shareholders use these same statements to keep tabs on how well their capital is being managed. Outside investors use financial statements to identify opportunities to make profitable use of their capital. And lenders and suppliers routinely examine the statements to determine the creditworthiness of the companies with which they deal.

The Securities and Exchange Commission (SEC) requires publicly traded companies to produce financial statements and to make them available to anyone who wants to view them. Companies not publicly traded are under no such requirement. Nevertheless, their private owners and bankers expect to see and evaluate financial statements.

Financial statements follow the same general format from company to company. And though specific line items may vary with the nature of a company's business, the statements are usually similar enough to allow readers to compare one business's performance against another's.

The Balance Sheet

Most people go to a doctor once a year to get a checkup—a snapshot of their physical well-being at a particular time. Similarly, companies prepare *balance sheets* as a way of summarizing their financial positions at a given point in time, usually at the end of the month, the quarter, or the fiscal year.

In effect, the balance sheet describes the assets controlled by the business and how those assets are financed—with the funds of creditors (liabilities), with the capital of the company's owners, or with both. A balance sheet reflects the following basic accounting equation:

Assets = Liabilities + Owners' Equity

In this equation, *assets* are the things in which a company invests so it can conduct business. Examples include cash and other financial instruments, as well as inventories of raw materials and finished goods, land, buildings, and equipment. Assets also include moneys owed to the company by customers and others—an asset category referred to as *accounts receivable*.

Now look at the other side of the equation, starting with liabilities. To acquire its necessary assets, a company often borrows money or promises to pay suppliers for various goods and services. Moneys owed to creditors are called *liabilities*. For example, a computer company may acquire $1 million worth of motherboards from an electronic-parts supplier, with payment due in thirty days. In doing so, the computer company increases its inventory assets by $1 million and its liabilities—in the form of *accounts payable*—by an equal amount. The equation stays in balance. Likewise, if the same company were to borrow $100,000 from a bank, the cash infusion would increase its assets by $100,000 and its liabilities by the same amount.

Owners' equity, also known as shareholders' or stockholders' equity, is what's left over after you deduct total liabilities from total assets. Thus, a company that has $3 million in total assets and $2 million in liabilities would have owners' equity of $1 million—as shown in the following equation.

Assets − Liabilities = Owners' Equity
$3,000,000 − $2,000,000 = $1,000,000

If $500,000 of this same company's uninsured assets burned up in a fire, its liabilities would remain the same. However, its owners' equity—what's left after all claims against assets are satisfied—would be reduced to $500,000:

$$\text{Assets} - \text{Liabilities} = \text{Owners' Equity}$$
$$\$2,500,000 - \$2,000,000 = \$500,000$$

Thus, the balance sheet balances a company's assets and liabilities. Notice, for instance, how total assets equal total liabilities and owners' equity in the balance sheet of Parker & Smith Inc., an office-furniture company whose finances we'll consider in many chapters of this book (table 2-1). The balance sheet also describes how much the company has invested in assets, and where the money is invested. Further, the balance sheet indicates how much of those monetary investments in assets comes from creditors (liabilities) and how much comes from owners (equity). Analysis of the balance sheet can give you an idea of how efficiently a company is utilizing its assets and how well it's managing its liabilities.

Balance sheet data is most helpful when you compare it with the same information from one or more previous years. Look again at table 2-1. Notice how this statement represents the company's financial position at a moment in time: December 31, 2005. A comparison of the figures for 2004 against those for 2005 shows that Parker & Smith is moving in a positive direction: The company has increased its total owners' equity by nearly $100,000.

Assets

You should understand some details about this particular financial statement. The balance sheet begins with a list of the assets most easily converted to cash. These include cash on hand and marketable securities, receivables, and inventory. These are called *current assets*. Generally, current assets are those that can be converted into cash within one year.

Next, the balance sheet tallies other assets that are tougher to convert to cash—for example, buildings and equipment. These are

TABLE 2-1

Parker & Smith Balance Sheet as of December 31, 2005

	2005	2004	Increase (Decrease)
Assets			
Cash and marketable securities	$355,000	$430,000	$(75,000)
Accounts receivable	$555,000	$512,000	$43,000
Inventory	$835,000	$755,000	$80,000
Prepaid expenses	$123,000	$98,000	$25,000
Total current assets	$1,868,000	$1,795,000	$73,000
Gross property, plant, and equipment	$2,100,000	$1,900,000	$200,000
Less accumulated depreciation	$333,000	$234,000	$(99,000)
Net property, plant, and equipment	$1,767,000	$1,666,000	$101,000
Total assets	$3,635,000	$3,461,000	$174,000

	2005	2004	Increase (Decrease)
Liabilities and Owners' Equity			
Accounts payable	$450,000	$430,000	$20,000
Accrued expenses	$98,000	$77,000	$21,000
Income tax payable	$17,000	$9,000	$8,000
Short-term debt	$435,000	$500,000	$(65,000)
Total current liabilities	$1,000,000	$1,016,000	$(16,000)
Long-term debt	$750,000	$660,000	$90,000
Total liabilities	$1,750,000	$1,676,000	$74,000
Contributed capital	$900,000	$850,000	$50,000
Retained earnings	$985,000	$935,000	$50,000
Total owners' equity	$1,885,000	$1,785,000	$100,000
Total liabilities and owners' equity	$3,635,000	$3,461,000	$174,000

Source: Harvard ManageMentor (HMM) Finance.

called plant assets or, more commonly, *fixed assets* (because it's hard to change them into cash).

Most fixed assets (except land) depreciate—that is, they become less valuable over time. For this reason, a company must reduce the stated value of these fixed assets by something called accumulated depreciation. Gross property, plant, and equipment minus accumulated depreciation equals the current book value, or net value, of property, plant, and equipment.

Some companies list *goodwill* among their assets. If a company has purchased another company for a price above the fair market value of the purchased company's assets, that so-called goodwill is recorded as an asset. Goodwill may also represent intangible things such as brand names or the acquired company's excellent reputation. These less tangible assets may have real value. So too can other intangible assets, such as patents.

Where Are the Human Assets?

As they look to financial statements to gain insights about companies, many people are questioning the traditional balance sheet's ability to reflect the value of human capital and profit potential. This is particularly true for knowledge-intensive companies, for which workforce know-how, intellectual property, brand equity, and customer relationships are the real productive assets. Unfortunately, these intangible assets don't show up on the balance sheet.

The growing inability of balance sheets to reflect real value prompted Federal Reserve Board Chairman Alan Greenspan to complain in January 2000 that accounting failed to track investments in "knowledge assets." Former SEC chairman, Arthur Levitt, echoed Greenspan's concern: "As intangible assets grow in size and scope, more and more people are questioning whether the true value—and the drivers of that value—are being reflected in a timely manner in publicly available disclosure." Indeed, a study by Baruch Lev of New York University found that 40 percent of the market valuation of the average company was missing from its balance sheet. For high-tech firms, that figure reached more than 50 percent.

Continued

These findings have important implications for HR executives and managers, the entire executive suite, company managers, and investors. Specifically, we must look beyond the bricks and mortar, the equipment, and even the cash that traditionally constitute balance sheet assets and focus on the undisclosed assets that produce the greatest value for shareholders. In most cases, those assets are the people who create the bonds between the enterprise and its customers, who come up with innovations that other people are eager to pay for, and who know how to get others to work together productively. The accounting profession is beginning to debate the pros and cons of including these intangible assets in financial statements. In chapter 11, you'll learn more about the challenges, opportunities, and methods of measuring and reporting human capital.

Finally, we come to the last line of the balance sheet, total assets. This line represents the sum of current and fixed assets.

Liabilities and Owners' Equity

Now let's consider the claims against those assets, beginning with a category called *current liabilities*. Current liabilities represent the claims of creditors and others—claims that typically must be paid within a year. They include short-term IOUs, accrued salaries, accrued income taxes, and accounts payable. This year's repayment obligation on a long-term loan is also listed as short-term debt in table 2-1.

Subtracting current liabilities from current assets gives you the company's *net working capital*. Net working capital is the amount of money the company has tied up in its current (i.e., short-term) operating activities. Just how much is adequate for the company depends on the industry and the company's plans. In its most recent balance sheet, Parker & Smith had $868,000 in net working capital.

Long-term debt are typically bonds and mortgages—debts that the company is contractually obliged to repay, with respect to both interest and principal.

According to the aforementioned accounting equation, total assets must equal total liabilities plus owners' equity. Thus, by subtracting total liabilities from total assets, the balance sheet arrives at a figure for the owners' equity. Owners' equity comprises *retained earnings* (net profits that accumulate on a company's balance sheet after any dividends are paid) and contributed capital (capital received in exchange for shares).

Historical Values

The values represented in many balance-sheet categories may not correspond to their actual market values. Except for items such as cash, accounts receivable, and accounts payable, the measurement of each classification will rarely equal the actual current value shown. This is because accountants must record most items at their historic cost. For example, if Company XYZ's balance sheet indicated land worth $700,000, that figure would represent what the firm paid for the land "way back when." If the land was purchased in downtown San Francisco in 1980, you can bet that it's now worth immensely more than the value stated on the balance sheet.

So why do accountants use historic instead of market values? The short answer is that this practice represents the lesser of two evils. If market values were required on balance sheets, then every public company would have to get a professional appraisal of each of its properties, warehouse inventories, and so forth—every year. And how many people would trust those appraisals? For these reasons, we're stuck with historic values on the balance sheet—at least for now.

Key Balance-Sheet Issues

In most companies, accountants prepare the balance sheet. However, this document represents several important issues for managers. Let's take a closer look at these below.

WORKING CAPITAL AND INVENTORY Financial managers give substantial attention to the level of working capital, which naturally expands and contracts with sales activities. Too *little* working capital can put a company in a bad position: The company may become unable to pay its bills or take advantage of profitable opportunities. Too *much* working capital, on the other hand, reduces profitability. Why? That capital has a carrying cost—it must be financed in some way, usually through interest-bearing loans.

Inventory is one component of working capital that directly affects many nonfinancial managers. As with working capital in general, there's a tension between having too much and too little inventory. Having lots of inventory on hand solves many business problems: The company can fill customer orders without delay, and a robust inventory provides a buffer against potential production stoppages and strikes. The flip side of plentiful inventory is financing cost and the risk of deterioration in the market value of the inventory itself. Every excess widget in the stockroom adds to the company's financing costs, which reduces profits. And every item that sits on the shelf may become obsolete or less salable as time goes by—again hurting profitability.

The personal computer business provides a clear example of how excess inventory can wreck the bottom line. Some analysts estimate that the value of finished-goods inventory melts away at a rate of approximately 2 percent *per day,* because of technical obsolescence in this fast-moving industry. Inventory meltdown hammered Apple during the mid-1990s, before the company dramatically reduced its inventories through operational redesign. Apple had exceptional products and devoted fans, but it finished 1996 with almost $700 million tied up in inventory. Bulging inventories wreaked havoc on Apple's bottom line, as obsolete components and finished goods had to be dumped onto the market at huge discounts. By comparison, Apple's rival Dell operated with *no* finished-goods inventory and with negligible stocks of components. Dell's success formula? An ultrafast supply-chain system that quickly assembled PCs to customer specifications as those orders came in. Dell built nothing until it had a specified customer order in hand.

Finished Dell PCs didn't end up on stockroom shelves for weeks at a time, but went directly from the assembly line into waiting delivery trucks. The profit lesson to managers is clear: Shape your operations to minimize or eliminate inventories.

FINANCIAL LEVERAGE You've probably heard or read the expression "It's a highly leveraged situation." But what does "leveraged" mean in the financial sense? *Financial leverage* refers to a company's use of borrowed money to acquire an asset. We say that a company is highly leveraged when the percentage of debt on its balance sheet is high relative to the capital invested by the owners. For example, suppose you paid $400,000 for an asset, using $100,000 of your own money and $300,000 in borrowed funds. For simplicity's sake, we'll ignore loan payments, taxes, and any cash flow you might get from the investment. Four years go by, and your asset has appreciated to $500,000. You decide to sell it. After paying off the $300,000 loan, you end up with $200,000 in your pocket (your original $100,000 plus a $100,000 profit). That's a gain of 100 percent on your personal capital, even though the asset increased in value by only 25 percent. Financial leverage made this possible. In contrast, if you had financed the purchase entirely with your own funds ($400,000), then you would have ended up with only a 25 percent gain. (*Operating leverage*, in contrast, refers to the extent to which a company's operating costs are fixed versus variable. For example, a company that relies heavily on machinery and very few workers to produce its goods has a high operating leverage.)

Financial leverage creates an opportunity for a company to gain a higher return on the capital invested by its owners. In the United States and most other countries, tax policy makes financial leverage even more attractive by allowing businesses to deduct the interest paid on loans. But leverage can cut both ways. If the value of an asset drops (or fails to produce the anticipated level of revenue), then leverage works against the business owner. Consider what would have happened in our example if the asset's value had dropped by $100,000, that is, to $300,000. You would have lost your entire $100,000 investment after repaying the initial loan of $300,000.

FINANCIAL STRUCTURE OF THE FIRM The negative potential of financial leverage is what keeps CEOs, their financial executives, and board members from maximizing their debt financing. Instead, they seek a financial structure that creates a realistic balance between debt and equity on the balance sheet. Although leverage enhances a company's potential profitability as long as things go right, managers know that every dollar of debt increases the risk of the business. That's because of both the danger just cited and the high interest payments that come with high debt. (Such payments must be paid in good times and bad.) Many companies have failed when business reversals or recessions prevented them from making timely payments on their loans.

When creditors and investors examine corporate balance sheets, they look carefully at the debt-to-equity ratio. They factor the risk expressed in the balance sheet into the interest they charge on loans and the return they demand from a company's bonds. Thus, a highly leveraged company may have to pay a higher percentage on borrowed funds than a less leveraged competitor pays. Investors also demand a higher rate of return for their stock investments in highly leveraged companies. They will not accept high risks without an expectation of commensurately large returns.

To practice your balance-sheet skills, use the sample balance-sheet template in appendix B of this book.

The Income Statement

The *income statement* indicates the results of a company's operations over a *specified period*. Those last two words are important. Unlike the balance sheet, which is a snapshot of the enterprise's position at one *point in time,* the income statement indicates cumulative business results within a defined time frame. It tells you whether the company is making a profit—that is, whether it has positive or negative net income (net earnings). This is why many people also refer to the income statement as the *profit-and-loss statement,* or P&L. This statement shows a company's profitability at the end of a particular time—typically at the end of the month, the quarter, or the company's fiscal year. It also tells you how much money the company spent to make that profit—from which you can determine the firm's *profit margin*.

As we did with the balance sheet, we can represent the contents of the income statement with a simple equation:

Revenues – Expenses = Net Income (or Net Loss)

An income statement starts by showing the company's *revenues*: the amount of money that resulted from selling products or services to customers. A company may have other revenues as well. In many cases, these additional revenues derive from investments or interest income from the firm's cash holdings.

Various costs and expenses—from the costs of making and storing a company's goods, to depreciation of plant and equipment, to interest expense and taxes—are then deducted from revenues. The bottom line—what's left over—is the *net income,* or *net profit* or *net earnings,* for the period covered by the income statement.

Consider the meaning of various line items on the income statement for Parker & Smith Inc. (table 2-2). The *cost of goods sold* is what it costs Parker & Smith to manufacture its products. This figure includes the cost of raw materials, such as steel and lumber, as well as the cost of turning them into finished goods, including direct labor costs. By deducting the cost of goods sold from sales revenue, we get a company's *gross profit*—the roughest estimation of the company's profitability.

The next major category of cost is *operating expenses*. Operating expenses include administrative employee salaries, rents, sales and marketing costs, and other costs of business not directly attributed to the cost of manufacturing a product. The materials for making office furnishings would *not* be included here; the cost of the advertising and the salaries of Parker & Smith's employees would.

Depreciation is counted on the income statement as an expense, even though it involves no out-of-pocket payments. As described earlier, depreciation is a way of estimating the "consumption" of an

TABLE 2-2

Parker & Smith Balance Sheet for the Fiscal Year Ending December 31, 2005

Retail sales	$2,200,000
Corporate sales	$1,000,000
Total sales revenue	$3,200,000
Less cost of goods sold	$1,600,000
Gross profit	$1,600,000
Less operating expenses	$800,000
Depreciation expense	$42,500
Earnings before interest and taxes (EBIT)	$757,500
Less interest expense	$110,000
Earnings before income tax	$647,500
Less income tax	$300,000
Net Income	$347,500

Source: HMM Finance.

asset, or the diminishing value of equipment over time. A computer, for example, loses about a third of its value each year. Thus, the company would not expense the full value of a computer in the first year of its purchase, but as it is actually used over a span of three years. The idea behind depreciation is to lay aside enough money to eventually replace a worn-out asset.

By subtracting operating expenses and depreciation from the gross profit, we get *operating earnings.* These earnings are often called *earnings before interest and taxes,* or EBIT.

We're now down to the last reductions in the path that revenues follow on their way to the bottom line. Interest expense is the interest charged on loans a company has taken out. Income tax, tax levied by the government on corporate income, is the final charge.

What revenues are left are referred to as net income, or earnings. If net income is positive—as it is in the case of Parker & Smith—we have a profit, which is what all for-profit companies live for.

Making Sense of the Income Statement

As with the balance sheet, our analysis of a company's income statement is greatly aided when presented in a multiperiod format. This format enables us to spot trends and turnarounds. Most annual reports make multiperiod data available, often going back five or more years. Parker & Smith's income statement in multiperiod form is depicted in table 2-3.

In this multiyear format, we can see that Parker & Smith's annual retail sales have grown steadily, while its corporate sales have stagnated and even declined slightly. Operating expenses have stayed about the same, however, even as total sales have expanded. That's a good sign that management is holding the line on the cost of doing business. The company's interest expense has also declined, perhaps because it has paid off one of its loans. The bottom line—net income—has shown healthy growth.

TABLE 2-3

Parker & Smith Multiperiod Income Statement for the Period Ending December 31

	2005	2004	2003	2002
Retail sales	$2,200,000	$2,000,000	$1,720,000	$1,500,000
Corporate sales	$1,000,000	$1,000,000	$1,100,000	$1,200,000
Total sales revenue	$3,200,000	$3,000,000	$2,820,000	$2,700,000
Less cost of goods sold	$1,600,000	$1,550,000	$1,400,000	$1,300,000
Gross profit	$1,600,000	$1,450,000	$1,420,000	$1,400,000
Less operating expenses	$800,000	$810,000	$812,000	$805,000
Depreciation expense	$42,500	$44,500	$45,500	$42,500
Earnings before interest and taxes (EBIT)	$757,500	$595,500	$562,500	$552,500
Less interest expense	$110,000	$110,000	$150,000	$150,000
Earnings before income tax	$647,500	$485,500	$412,500	$402,500
Less income tax	$300,000	$194,200	$165,000	$161,000
Net income	$347,500	$291,300	$247,500	$241,500

Source: HMM Finance.

To practice your income statement skills, use the sample income statement template in appendix C of this book.

The Cash Flow Statement

The *cash flow statement,* the last of the three essential financial statements, is also the least used and understood. This statement details the reasons behind changes in the amount of cash (and cash equivalents) during the accounting period covered by the statement. More specifically, the cash flow statement reflects all changes in cash as affected by operating activities, investments, and financing activities. Like the bank statement you receive for your checking account, the cash flow statement tells how much cash was on hand at the beginning of the period, and how much was on hand at the end. It then describes how the company acquired and spent cash in a particular period. The uses of cash are recorded as negative figures in the cash flow statement, and sources of cash are recorded as positive figures.

If you're an HR manager in a large corporation, changes in the company's cash flow won't typically have an impact on your day-to-day functioning. Nevertheless, it's a good idea to stay up-to-date with your company's cash flow projections, because they may come into play when you prepare your budget for the upcoming year. For example, you will probably want to be conservative in your spending during times when cash is tight. Alternatively, during times when the company is flush with cash, you may have opportunities to make new investments. If you're a manager in a small company or you own and run a small firm, you're probably keenly aware of your cash flow situation and feel its impact almost every day.

The cash flow statement is useful because it indicates whether your company is turning accounts receivable into cash—and that ability is ultimately what will keep your company solvent. *Solvency* is the ability to pay bills as they come due.

As we did with the other statements, we can conceptualize the cash flow statement in terms of a simple equation:

Cash Flow from Profit + Other Sources of Cash − Uses of Cash
= Change in Cash

Again using the Parker & Smith example, we see that in the firm's cash flow statement for 2005, the company generated a positive cash flow of $377,900 (table 2–4). The statement shows that cash flows from operations ($283,900), plus that from investing activities ($92,000) and from financing ($2,000), produced $377,900 in additional cash.

TABLE 2-4

Parker & Smith Cash Flow Statement for 2005

Net income	$347,500
Operating assets and liabilities	
Accounts receivable	$(75,600)
Finished-goods inventory	$(125,000)
Prepaid expenses	$(37,000)
Accounts payable	$83,000
Accrued expenses	$25,000
Income tax payable	$(23,000)
Depreciation expense	$89,000
Total changes in operating assets and liabilities	$(63,600)
Cash flow from operations	$283,900
Investing activities	
Sale of property, plant, and equipment	$267,000
Capital expenditures	$(175,000)
Cash flow from investing activities	$92,000
Financing activities	
Short-term debt increase	$27,000
Long-term borrowing	$112,000
Capital stock	$50,000
Cash dividends to stockholders	$(187,000)
Cash flow from financing activities	$2,000
Increase in cash during year	$377,900

Source: HMM Finance.

The cash flow statement doesn't measure the same thing as the income statement. If there is no cash transaction, then it cannot be reflected on a cash flow statement. Notice, however, that net income at the top of the cash flow statement is the same as the bottom line of the income statement—it's the company's profit. Through a series of adjustments, the cash flow statement translates net income into cash terms.

The cash flow statement's format reflects the three categories of activities that affect cash. Cash can be increased or decreased because of (1) operations, (2) the acquisition or sale of assets (i.e., investments), and (3) changes in debt or stock or other financing activities. Let's consider each in turn, starting with operations:

- **Accounts receivable and finished-goods inventory** represent items the company has produced, but for which it hasn't yet received payment. Prepaid expenses represent items the company has paid for but has not consumed. Increases in these items all get subtracted from cash flow.

- **Accounts payable and accrued expenses** represent items the company has already received or used, but for which it hasn't yet paid. Consequently, increases in these items add to cash flow.

Now let's consider investments. Investment activities include the following:

- Gains realized from the sale of plant, property, and equipment

- Cash that the company uses to invest in financial instruments and plant, property, and equipment (such investments are often shown as capital expenditures)

The cash flow statement shows that Parker & Smith has sold a building for $267,000 and made capital expenditures of $175,000— for a net addition to cash flow of $92,000.

Finally, we come to cash flow changes from financing activities. Parker & Smith has raised money by increasing its short-term debt, by borrowing in the capital markets, and by issuing capital stock, thereby boosting the company's available cash flow. However,

Cash Flow Versus Profit

Many people think of profits as cash flow. Don't make this mistake. For a particular period, profit may or may not contribute positively to cash flow. For example, if this year's profit derives from a huge sale made in November, the sale may be booked as revenues in the fiscal period—thus adding to profit. But if payment for that sale is not received until the next accounting period, it goes on the books as an account receivable, which reduces cash flow.

the dividends that Parker & Smith pays ($187,000) must be paid out of cash flow—thus they represent a decrease in cash flow.

To practice your skills with cash flow statements, use the template in appendix D of this book.

Where to Find Financial Information

As we saw earlier, all firms that trade their shares in U.S. public financial markets are required by the SEC to prepare and distribute their financial statements in an annual report to shareholders. Most annual reports go beyond the basic disclosure requirement of the SEC, providing discussion of the year's operations and the future outlook. Most public companies also issue quarterly reports.

If you are looking for even more information on your company—or on one of your competitors—obtain a copy of the firm's annual Form 10-K. The 10-K often contains abundant and revealing information about a company's strategy, its view of the market and its customers, its products, its important risks and business challenges, and so forth. You can obtain 10-K reports and annual and quarterly reports directly from a company's investor relations department, or online at http://www.sec.gov/edgar/searchedgar/formpick.htm.

Using Financial Statements to Enhance
HR Service Quality

As an HR professional, you can use information from your company's financial statements to take a more strategic approach to
your work and improve the quality of the day-to-day services you
deliver. For example, suppose your firm's income statement over the
past three or four years reveals declining profitability in the form of
steadily decreasing net income. In this case, you would want to
brainstorm ways to help improve your company's bottom line. To
illustrate, you could identify strategies for reducing operating
expenses by improving employee retention—which cuts down on
expensive recruitment campaigns. You can reduce expenses in lots
of other ways as well—such as shopping more carefully for the
most affordable but still high-quality health plans and carefully
evaluating an expensive new HR technology system to determine
whether the payoff in savings will come quickly enough to justify
the expense right now.

Keep in mind, too, that profitability comes from both decreasing expenses *and* boosting revenues. So come up with ideas for supporting increased sales in your company. For instance, perhaps you
could suggest redeploying employees who can help support sales of
a new product line. Or recommend a new bonus plan that you
think will motivate sales reps to push a particularly profitable line
of services or products.

If your firm is having cash flow problems, conduct similar
brainstorming sessions to identify ways to address these concerns.
For example, negotiate agreements with HR consultants such that
payment for their services is spread out over a longer time span
than usual. Or sit down with the employees of the company's
accounts payable department and explain to them which of your
HR vendors might be willing to receive payment for their work
within ninety days rather than sixty or thirty.

The better you understand where the numbers of your firm's
financial statements come from and what they mean, the more
you'll be able to see how your own daily activities and decisions can
either improve or hurt those numbers.

Summing Up

This chapter introduced and explained the balance sheet, income statement, and cash flow statement. These statements offer three perspectives on your company's financial performance. They tell three different but related stories about how well your company is doing financially:

- The balance sheet shows a company's financial position at a specific point in time. That is, the balance sheet gives a snapshot of the company's financial situation—its assets, equity, and liabilities—on a given day.

- The income statement shows the bottom line: It indicates how much profit or loss was generated over a period—a month, a quarter, or a year.

- The cash flow statement tells where the company's cash came from and where it went—in other words, the flow of cash in, through, and out of the company.

Here's another way to look at the interrelationships between these statements: The income statement tells you whether your company is making a profit. The balance sheet tells you how efficiently a company is utilizing its assets and managing its liabilities in pursuit of profits. The cash flow statement tells you how cash has been increased or decreased through operations, the acquisition or sale of assets, and financing activities.

Together, these financial statements shed light on what's going on in your company or any other business. They can point to the general need to improve the numbers on those statements—and inspire you to brainstorm about how HR can support that improvement. In chapter 3, you'll find ways to can gain even more business insights through various forms of analysis.

Leveraging Chapter Insights: Critical Questions

- How familiar are you with your company's financial statements—its balance sheet, income statement, and cash flow statement? What might you do to become more familiar with these documents?

- Based on what you're seeing in your firm's financial statements, as well as discussions you may have participated in about the numbers, what are some actions your HR department might take to improve the company's profitability, use of its assets, or cash flow?

CHAPTER THREE

Finding Meaning in Financial Statements

A Look Behind the Numbers

Key Topics Covered in This Chapter

- *What ratio analysis is, why it is useful, and what its limits are*

- *How various types of ratios work—including profitability, activity, and solvency ratios*

- *How to compare different companies' financial statements*

I N THE LAST CHAPTER, you learned about the three key financial statements and their various components. In chapter 3, you'll discover tools for interpreting those statements and assessing your company's business performance. With this added layer of understanding, you can gain further insights into how your HR department might improve the firm's bottom line.

Ratio Analysis

Many people use financial statements, and often for very different reasons. Lenders want to know if a company seeking funds has the capacity to repay them. Investors are interested in financial stability and profit-generating power and want to evaluate whether earnings are likely to grow or diminish in the future. Many potential employees use financial statements to assess the current performance or financial status of an enterprise before they sign on with a company. Regulatory agencies often use these documents to assess an organization's or industry's financial health and performance.

Each of these uses of financial statements is a form of financial analysis. To conduct a financial analysis, you examine the relationships, or ratios, between items found within and across financial statements.[1] These ratios help describe the financial condition of an organization, the efficiency of its activities, its comparable profitability, and the perception of investors as expressed by their behavior in financial markets. Ratios help an analyst or a decision maker piece together a story about an organization's past decisions and performance, its current condition, and its possible future. For HR professionals, ratio analysis can give you even more insights into your firm's financial performance than you can gain simply by looking at the three financial statements. For example, some ratios suggest whether the company's level of debt is appropriate. Other ratios help you identify changes in the firm's profit performance. Still other ratios reveal how well the organization is using its assets. And when you compare your company's ratios against those of other firms, you gain a clear sense of how well the organization is doing compared with its competitors.

In most cases, the story told by each of these ratios is incomplete. However, when you piece those stories together, you get a fuller picture of how your company is doing. And the fuller your picture and deeper your understanding of your firm's financial performance, the greater your ability to ensure that HR contributes to—rather than detracts from—that performance.

The ratios that follow are relevant across a wide spectrum of industries, but are most meaningful when compared against the same measures for other companies in the same industry. There are dozens and dozens of financial ratios to choose from, but we'll explore thirteen of the more common ratios in the sections below. We'll also cluster the thirteen ratios into three categories: profitability, activity, and solvency.

Profitability Ratios

Profitability ratios associate the amount of income earned with the resources used to generate it. Ideally, a firm should produce as much income as possible from a given amount of resources. As the following sections show, managers can use profitability ratios to identify areas where performance is being inhibited—so they can take corrective action. Investors also use profitability ratios to gauge a company's future earning power.

In the pages that follow, you'll learn about numerous profitability ratios: *return on assets* (ROA), *return on equity* (ROE), return on investment (ROI), *operating margin, earnings per share* (EPS), and *profit margin* (or *return on sales,* ROS).

RETURN ON ASSETS (ROA) This ratio relates net income (revenues less expenses less taxes) to the company's total asset base and is figured as follows:

$$\text{ROA} = \frac{\text{Net Income}}{\text{Total Assets}}$$

ROA relates net income to the investment in all the financial resources at the command of a company's management. The ratio is most useful as a measure of the effective use of resources—without regard to how those resources were obtained or financed. Analysts and investors often compare the ROA of one company to the ROA of its peer group of key competitors to assess the effectiveness of top management. For example, if company A has an ROA of 12 percent and company B has 8 percent, then this says something positive about company A's management.

RETURN ON EQUITY (ROE) This ratio relates net income to the amount invested by shareholders. It is a measure of how efficiently management has used the shareholders' stake in the business. You calculate ROE as follows:

$$\text{ROE} = \frac{\text{Net Income}}{\text{Shareholders' Equity}}$$

RETURN ON INVESTMENT (ROI) This phrase is often used in business discussions that involve profitability. For example, expressions like "We aim for an ROI of 12 percent" are common. Unfortunately, there is no standard definition of ROI, since "investment" may be construed from many perspectives. For example, in various companies, investment might represent the assets committed to a particular activity, the shareholders' equity involved, or invested assets minus any liabilities generated by a company's taking on of a project. ROI might also refer to the internal rate of return, a very specific calculation of return described in chapter 10. So, when you or someone else uses the term "return on investment," *always* clarify precisely how investment is defined and calculated.

OPERATING MARGIN Also known as the earnings-before-interest-and-taxes (EBIT) margin, the operating margin is used by many analysts to gauge the profitability of a company's operating activities. This ratio removes from the equation the interest expenses and taxes over which current management may have no control. Thus, operating margin gives a clearer indicator of management performance. To calculate the operating margin, use this formula:

$$\text{Operating Margin} = \frac{\text{EBIT}}{\text{Net Sales}}$$

EARNINGS PER SHARE (EPS) Corporations generally have many owners, not all of whom own an equal number of shares. For this reason, many firms express earnings on a per-share basis.

The calculation of EPS can grow complicated if there is more than one class of ownership, each with different claims against the income and assets of the firm. (Preferred stock or other securities that are convertible into common shares are often treated as common stock equivalents in making this calculation. We'll discuss these different classes of ownership and securities in chapter 8.)

The EPS ratio must be presented in published reports, often in several variations. Here's a simplified formula that contains all the elements for determining EPS:

$$\text{EPS} = \frac{(\text{Net Income} - \text{Preferred Stock Dividends})}{(\text{Number of Common Shares} + \text{Equivalents})}$$

PROFIT MARGIN The profit margin—sometimes called return on sales, or ROS—indicates a rate of return on sales. It tells us what percentage of every dollar of sales makes it to the bottom line. Calculate the profit margin as follows:

$$\text{Profit Margin} = \frac{\text{Net Income}}{\text{Net Sales}}$$

Both managers and investors watch changes in profit margin closely. A rising percentage indicates either that customers are accepting higher prices or that management is doing a better job of controlling costs and expenses—or both. On the other hand, a declining profit margin may signify that management is losing control of its costs, or that the company is having to "give away the store" in the form of discounts to sell its products or services.

As seen in the hypothetical numbers below, the profit margin trend for our fictional company, Parker & Smith, shows a precipitous drop in year 2005:

2005	10.9 percent
2004	20.1 percent
2003	17.4 percent
2002	17.3 percent

Why did the company's margin drop almost in half between 2004 and 2005? One way to narrow down possible answers is to determine which categories of cost or expense—or taxes—have increased relative to sales revenues. (See chapter 6 for more information on taxes.) For instance, examination of the company's income statements, along with a little calculating, indicates that the company paid more taxes relative to sales in 2005 than in the previous year (9.4 percent versus 6.5 percent). We could also look at the cost of goods sold or operating expenses with the same methodology in seeking the answer. These, unlike taxes, represent areas over which management has significant control.

Activity Ratios

Activity ratios reveal how well an organization utilizes its assets. The efficient use of assets minimizes the need for investment by lenders and owners. Less investment means both lower risk and lower cost. Two activity ratios that many managers must deal with regularly are *days receivables outstanding* and *inventory turnover.*

DAYS RECEIVABLES OUTSTANDING Sometimes called the collection period, days receivable outstanding tells us the average time it takes to collect on sales made by the company. As discussed, a longer collection period means that more working capital is required to run the business—working capital, whose interest charges put a drain on profits! We calculate days receivables outstanding through two steps. The first determines the average day's sales:

$$\text{Average Day's Sales} = \frac{\text{Net Sales}}{365}$$

We then use this result to reach our final number:

$$\text{Days Receivables Outstanding} = \frac{\text{Accounts Receivable}}{\text{Average Day's Sales}}$$

As with most forms of ratio analysis, days receivables outstanding provides the greatest insights when we use it (1) to compare one company with another or with its peer group of industry rivals or (2) to examine a trend. For example, Gateway and rival Dell both make personal computers to order. Both sell directly to customers. Their business models are very similar. Thus, a comparison of days receivables outstanding would tell us which company is more effective in collecting the money owed to it. Likewise, we could examine the trend of days receivables outstanding in either or both companies to determine whether the collection period is shortening or lengthening.

INVENTORY TURNOVER Inventory turnover is another ratio that many managers consider important. Determining the number of times that inventory is sold and replaced during the year provides some measure of its liquidity and the ability of the company to convert inventories to cash quickly if that became necessary.

Slow turnover may point to too much capital tied up in inventory. Such capital costs money. And in areas such as technology and apparel, slow turnover can result in inventory obsolescence. Profits improve when you can move inventory out the door quickly.

You can calculate inventory turnover by dividing the cost of goods sold by the inventory cost. If inventory cost has significantly changed from the beginning to the end of the period, you should calculate or estimate an average inventory for the period. Usually you can simply add the beginning and ending inventory amounts and use one-half of that total as the average inventory for the period. Here's the formula:

$$\text{Inventory Turnover} = \frac{\text{Cost of Goods Sold}}{\text{Average Inventory}}$$

What level of inventory turnover represents effective management? There is no universal answer to this question, as inventory turnover is essentially industry-specific. In the retail grocery business, for example, inventory turnover is extremely high—items that come into the receiving dock in the morning usually go out the front door in shopping bags by the end of the same day. An auto dealer, in contrast, may turn his inventory just once every few weeks. A retailer of fine musical instruments may turn her inventory only three or four times each year. Thus, it's again important to examine the turnover rate *trend* and how one enterprise stacks up against its industry rivals.

Solvency Ratios

When an organization can't meet its financial obligations (i.e., when it can't pay its bills), it is said to be insolvent. Because insolvency leads to organizational distress, possibly to bankruptcy, or even to liquidation of the business, investors and creditors closely scrutinize solvency ratios. By measuring a company's ability to meet financial obligations as they become due, solvency ratios give an indication of the firm's liquidity. In finance, the term *liquidity* refers to the extent to which a company can readily turn its assets into cash to meet current obligations. The *current ratio* and *acid-test ratio* are commonly used for this measurement.

CURRENT RATIO The current-ratio formula is simple:

$$\text{Current Ratio} = \frac{\text{Current Assets}}{\text{Current Liabilities}}$$

The size of the current ratio that a healthy company needs to maintain depends on the relationship between inflows of cash and the demands for cash payments. A company that has a continuous and reliable inflow of cash or other liquid assets, such as a public utility or taxi company, may be able to meet currently maturing obligations easily despite a small current ratio—say, 1.10 (which means that the company has $1.10 in current assets for every $1.00 of current liabilities). On the other hand, a manufacturing firm with long product development and manufacturing cycles may need to maintain a larger current ratio.

ACID-TEST RATIO To confirm the absolute liquidity of an organization, an analyst can modify the current ratio by eliminating from current assets all that cannot be liquidated on very short notice. This ratio, called the acid-test ratio, typically consists of the ratio of so-called quick assets (cash, marketable security, and accounts receivable) to current liabilities. Inventory is left out of the calculation. Here's the acid-test ratio calculation:

$$\text{Acid-Test Ratio} = \frac{\text{Quick Assets}}{\text{Current Liabilities}}$$

Paradoxically, a company can have loads of choice assets—office buildings, fleets of delivery trucks, and warehouses brimming with finished-goods inventory—and still risk insolvency if its ratio of current (or quick) assets is insufficient to meet bills as they come due. Creditors don't take payment in used delivery trucks; they want cash.

DEBT RATIOS As discussed earlier, the degree to which the activities of a company are supported by liabilities and long-term debt as opposed to owners' contributions is called leverage. A firm that has a high proportion of debt relative to shareholder contributions is said to be highly leveraged. For owners, the advantage of having high debt is that returns on their actual investments can be disproportionately higher when the company makes a profit. On the other hand, high leverage is a disadvantage when cash flows fall, since the interest on debt is a contractual obligation—it must be paid in bad times and good. A company can be forced into bankruptcy by the crush of interest payments due on its outstanding debt.

The debt ratio is widely used in financial analysis because it reveals the effect of financial leverage. It is calculated in different ways, two of which are illustrated here. The simplest is this:

$$\text{Debt Ratio} = \frac{\text{Total Debt}}{\text{Total Assets}}$$

Alternatively, you can calculate the debt-to-equity ratio by dividing the total liabilities by the amount of shareholders' equity:

$$\text{Debt-to-Equity Ratio} = \frac{\text{Total Liabilities}}{\text{Owners' Equity}}$$

Analysts must use care when interpreting either of these ratios, because there is no absolutely correct debt measure. So when you hear someone say, "The company's debt-to-equity ratio is one-to-two (or 50 percent)," ask what he or she has included as debt. Fully funded debt—that is, all the debt that carries an interest rate charge—is probably the best measure of debt.

In general, as the debt-to-equity ratio increases, the returns to owners are higher, but so too are the risks. Creditors understand this relationship keenly and will often include specific limits on the debt levels, beyond which borrowers may not go without having their loans called in.

TIMES INTEREST EARNED RATIO Creditors also use the times interest earned ratio to estimate how safe it is to lend money to individual businesses. Almost every firm has continuing commitments that must be met by future cash flows if the company is to remain solvent. Interest payments are one of those commitments. The ratio that measures the ability of a company to meet its interest payments is times interest earned. The formula for the ratio is this:

$$\text{Times Interest Earned Ratio} = \frac{\text{Earnings Before Interest and Taxes}}{\text{Interest Expense}}$$

The number of times that interest payments are covered by pretax earnings, or EBIT, indicates the degree to which income could fall without causing insolvency. In many cases, this is not so much a test of solvency as a test of staying power under adversity. For example, if EBIT were to be cut in half because of a recession or another cause, would the company still have sufficient earnings to meet its interest obligations?

Using the Ratios: Another Look at Parker & Smith

Let's look again at Parker & Smith Inc.'s balance sheet and income statement for 2005 (tables 3-1 and 3-2).

Now, see table 3-3 for demonstrations of how we might calculate some of the ratios just described for Parker & Smith Inc.

A Caveat on Ratio Analysis

Though the analyst or decision maker is better informed through ratio analysis, indiscriminate use of financial ratios can be dangerous. Decisions based solely on a specific or minimum level of a ratio can easily lead to missed opportunities or to losses. Even the best ratio is not always indicative of an organization's financial health, status, or performance. Ratios between apparently similar measurements

TABLE 3-1

Parker & Smith's Balance Sheet as of December 31, 2005

Assets

Cash and marketable securities	$355,000
Accounts receivable	$555,000
Inventory	$835,000
Prepaid expenses	$123,000
Total current assets	$1,868,000
Gross property, plant, and equipment	$2,100,000
Less accumulated depreciation	$333,000
Net property, plant, and equipment	$1,767,000
Total assets	$3,635,000

Liabilities and owners' equity

Accounts payable	$450,000
Accrued expenses	$98,000
Income tax payable	$17,000
Short-term debt	$435,000
Total current liabilities	$1,000,000
Long-term debt	$750,000
Total liabilities	$1,750,000
Contributed capital	$900,000
Retained earnings	$985,000
Total owners' equity	$1,885,000
Total liabilities and owners' equity	$3,635,000

Source: HMM Finance.

in financial statements may be affected by differences in accounting practices or by deliberate manipulation.

The ease with which ratios can be manipulated and the danger in using them as criteria lead many analysts to concentrate on ratio trends. When you observe a trend in a ratio, you can raise questions about why the trend is occurring. For example, if the quarter-to-quarter current ratio has been steadily increasing, you'll want to know why—and what that trend implies. You can often find the answers to these questions outside the financial statements. Likewise, simply comparing firms on their ratios can encourage erroneous

TABLE 3-2

Parker & Smith Income Statement, 2005

Retail sales	$2,200,000
Corporate sales	$1,000,000
Total sales revenue	$3,200,000
Less cost of goods sold	$1,600,000
Gross profit	$1,600,000
Less operating expenses	$800,000
Depreciation expense	$42,500
Earnings before interest and taxes (EBIT)	$757,500
Less interest expense	$110,000
Earnings before income tax	$647,500
Less income tax	$300,000
Net income	$347,500

Source: HMM Finance.

TABLE 3-3

Parker & Smith Profitability, Activity, and Solvency Ratios

Profitability Ratios	
Return on Assets (ROI) = Net Income/Total Assets	$347,500/$3,635,000 = 9.5%
Return on Equity (ROE) = Net Income/ Shareholders' Equity	$347,500/$1,885,000 = 18%
Operating Margin = EBIT/Net Sales	$757,500/$3,200,000 = 24%
Profit Margin = Net Income/Net Sales	$347,500/$3,200,000 = 11%
Activity Ratios	
Step 1 for Days Receivable Outstanding = Average Day's Sales = Net Sales/365	$3,200,000 / 365 = $8,767.12
Step 2 for Days Receivable Outstanding = Accounts Receivable/Average Day's Sales	$555,000/$8,767.12 = 63.30 days
Inventory Turnover = Cost of Goods Sold/ Average Inventory	$1,600,000/$835,000 = 1.92 times in 2005

Continued

TABLE 3-3, *continued*

Parker & Smith Profitability, Activity, and Solvency Ratios

Solvency Ratios

Current Ratio = Current Assets/Current Liabilities	$1,868,000/$1,000,000 = 1.87
Acid-Test Ratio = Quick Assets/Current Liabilities	$355,000 (cash and marketable securities) + $555,000 (accounts receivable)/$1,000,000 = 0.91
Debt Ratio = Total Debt/Total Assets	$435,000 (short-term debt) + $750,000 (long-term debt)/ $3,635,000 = 0.326
Debt-to-Equity Ratio = Total Liabilities/ Owners' Equity	$1,750,000/$1,885,000 = 0.93
Times Interest Earned Ratio = EBIT/Interest Expense	$757,500/$110,000 = 6.89

conclusions. The diversity inherent in the available accounting practices can mean that the ratios of different organizations are noncomparable—like comparing apples to oranges. You *can* make comparisons between companies—but you must make them with care and with full attention to the underlying differences in accounting methods.

Percentage-Format Financial Statements

To get a better handle on a firm's changing performance over time, and to compare one firm with another, many analysts create financial statements in which the balance sheet and income statements are prepared in a percentage format. In a percentage-format balance sheet, for example, each asset, liability, and owners' equity amount is expressed as a percentage of total assets. In a percentage-format statement of income, sales revenues are set at 100 percent, and each item is expressed as a percentage of sales. For example, cost of goods sold might be expressed as 40 percent of sales; net income might be 10 percent of sales.

Financial statements expressed in percentage form facilitate the comparison of different-sized firms, allowing analysts to focus on the efficiency of operations. To illustrate, in comparing rival firms in the same industry, you can use percentage-format balance sheets to answer several key questions:

- Which firm has the highest percentage of debt to total assets?

- Which firm is holding the greatest amount of inventory relative to total assets?

- Which has a greater percentage of its assets tied up in fixed assets such as land, property, and equipment?

You can make other comparisons of firms using a percentage-format income statement. You may also find it useful to compare the same firm's income statement performance from year to year. For an example, consider the income statement in table 3-4. This

TABLE 3-4

Income Statement in Percentage Format

	2005	2004	2003
Net sales	100.0	100.0	100.0
Cost of goods sold	37.4	36.6	37.8
Gross profit	62.6	63.4	62.2
Selling, general, and administrative expenses	42.4	43.2	42.1
Realignment expense	—	—	4.9
Profit from operations	20.2	20.2	15.2
Nonoperating charges (income)	(0.1)	(0.3)	(0.5)
Interest income	0.8	1.0	1.1
Interest expense	0.4	1.3	2.0
Net other charges	1.1	2.0	2.6
Income before income taxes and cumulative effect of accounting changes	19.1	18.2	12.6
Income taxes	7.0	6.7	4.7
Income before cumulative effect of accounting changes	12.1	11.5	7.9
Cumulative effect of accounting changes	—	—	(2.6)
Net Income	12.1	11.5	5.3

Source: William J. Bruns Jr., "Introduction to Financial Ratios and Financial Statement Analysis," Case 9-193-029 (Boston: Harvard Business School, 1996).

three-year income statement indicates that the company's cost of goods relative to net sales is on an even keel. Its selling, general, and administrative expenses as a percentage of sales are likewise steady over the three-year period.

In making these sorts of analyses, you're looking for indications that something is going very right or very wrong in these numbers—which we don't see in the particular case shown in table 3-4. For example, if the selling, general, and administrative expenses, as percentages, were in an upward trend, then you'd want to know why. As an HR manager, you would want to know the root cause and would want to identify how your group could help reverse the trend.

Summing Up

Financial statements tell a story about a company's strengths and weaknesses, and about various aspects of performance. But the story doesn't jump off the page—you have to dig, compare, and analyze to understand it. This chapter showed you how to use ratios and percentage-format statements to understand the story of company profitability, key operating activities, solvency, and debt structure. In particular, you learned about three types of ratios:

- Profitability ratios, which associate the amount of income earned with the resources used. The ratios include return on assets (ROA), return on equity (ROE), and earnings per share (EPS).

- Activity ratios, which indicate how well a company has used its assets. These ratios include days receivables outstanding and inventory turnover.

- Solvency ratios, which indicate an organization's ability to meet its financial obligations. These ratios include the current ratio, acid-test ratio, debt ratio, debt-to-equity ratio, and times interest earned ratio.

Leveraging Chapter Insights: Critical Questions

- Select several profitability ratios, and calculate them for your company, using the firm's balance sheet and income statement. What do the results tell you about how well the organization is producing income from a given amount of resource?

- Calculate your company's days receivables outstanding and inventory turnover. What do the results suggest about how well your organization is utilizing its assets?

- Select several solvency ratios, and calculate them for your company. What do your results indicate about how well your company is able to pay its bills on time and how quickly it can turn its assets into cash to meet current obligations?

CHAPTER FOUR

From Financial Measures to a Balanced Scorecard

Measuring Activities That Drive
Future Financial Performance

Key Topics Covered in This Chapter

- *Understanding the balanced scorecard methodology*

- *Implementing a balanced scorecard program*

- *Creating and using an HR scorecard*

F INANCIAL MEASURES such as earnings per share and profit margin tell the tale of business performance, and generations of businesspeople have tried to manage their companies using these measures. But these traditional measures aren't buttons that HR and other managers push to make things happen—they represent *outcomes* of dozens of other activities that came before. Thus they are backward-looking, the products of past decisions. Worse, traditional measures can send the wrong signals. For instance, profit measures that look very good this year may be the result of dramatic cuts in new-product development and reductions in employee training. On the surface, such cuts might make the state of affairs look rosy today—while jeopardizing the profits of tomorrow.

This chapter describes an alternative methodology known as the balanced scorecard—which enables you to measure the activities your company engages in today that will exert the most influence on the firm's *future* financial performance. You'll also learn how to use this same methodology to create and implement a balanced scorecard for your HR department.

What Is a Balanced Scorecard?

Frustrated by the inadequacies of traditional performance measurement systems, some managers have shifted their focus from earnings per share and return on equity to the operational activities that produce them. These managers follow the motto "Make operational improvements, and the performance numbers will follow." But which improvements are the most important? And which are the true drivers of long-term, bottom-line performance?

To answer these questions, Robert Kaplan and David Norton conducted research on a number of companies with leading-edge performance measures. From this research, they developed what they call the balanced scorecard, a performance measurement system that gives top managers a fast but comprehensive view of the business. Kaplan and Norton's balanced scorecard includes financial measures that indicate the results of past actions. And it complements those financial measures with three sets of operational measures that relate directly to customer satisfaction, internal processes, and the organization's ability to learn and improve—the activities that drive future financial performance.

Kaplan and Norton have compared the balanced scorecard to the dials and indicators in an airplane cockpit: "For the complex task of navigating and flying an airplane, pilots need detailed information about many aspects of the flight. They need information on fuel, air speed, altitude, bearing, destination, and other indicators that summarize the current and predicted environment. Reliance on one instrument can be fatal. Similarly, the complexity of managing an organization today requires that managers be able to view performance in several areas simultaneously."[1]

Kaplan and Norton's balanced scorecard uses four perspectives to link performance measures and to galvanize managerial action. Collectively, these perspectives give top management timely answers to four key questions:

- How do customers see us? (customer perspective)

- What must we do to excel? (internal perspective)

- Can we continue to improve and create value? (innovation and learning perspective)

- How do we look to our shareholders? (financial perspective)

Use of the Balanced Scorecard Methodology

A November 2002 research report titled "Aligning HR with Organization Strategy Survey," prepared by SHRM and the Balanced Scorecard Collaborative, reveals some interesting statistics about the use of the scorecard methodology:

- Among 1,288 respondents to the online survey, 24 percent said that their entire organization used the balanced scorecard methodology. Twenty-seven percent said that their HR departments used the scorecard.

- The larger an organization, the more likely it is to adopt the scorecard approach for the entire company.

- The scorecard approach is used in all manner of industries. However, leaders in government and in the insurance, manufacturing (nondurable goods), and utilities industries tend to adopt the methodology for their entire companies more than in other industries. Leaders in the construction, mining, oil and gas, education, and high-tech industries tend to adopt the methodology for their entire organizations the least frequently.

- In the manufacturing (durable and nondurable goods), insurance, and telecommunications industries, companies seem particularly interested in adopting the scorecard approach for their HR functions.

A research report titled "Management Tools 2003," prepared by Darrell Rigby and published by Bain & Company, shed additional light on the use of the scorecard methodology:

- Of 708 respondents from around the world, 62 percent said that their companies used the balanced scorecard approach.

- On a scale of 1 to 5, the average satisfaction rating of respondents from companies that use the scorecard was 3.88.

FIGURE 4-1

The Balanced Scorecard Links Performance Measures

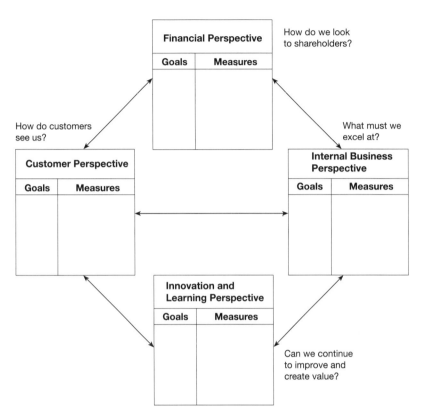

Source: Robert S. Kaplan and David P. Norton, "The Balanced Scorecard," *Harvard Business Review* (January–February 1992): 72.

Figure 4-1 indicates the linkages between the four perspectives. The advantage of the balanced scorecard over traditional measures is that three of the four perspectives (customer, innovation, and internal) are more than results—they are levers that managers can use to improve future results. The disadvantage is that scorecard measures are not public, which makes comparisons between competing enterprises impossible. Nor do the scorecards aid our analysis of year-over-year trends in specific areas of enterprise activity, such as inventory turnover and solvency. Used together, however, the balanced scorecard and traditional ratio analysis can help managers understand *and* improve their operations.

Implementing a Balanced Scorecard Program

Companies that decide to implement a balanced scorecard program often progress through a specific series of steps, which we've summarized below:[2]

1. **Clarify the vision and strategy.** The executive committee clarifies the company's vision and strategy—how the company plans to achieve that vision—with input from HR and other executives. Specifically, committee members create a corporate-level scorecard showing how they expect improvements in innovation and learning, internal business processes, and customer service all to interconnect to produce the desired financial results and other aspects of the company's vision. This top-level scorecard serves as a kind of strategy map depicting executives' hypotheses about how the company creates unique value.

   As a simple example, an organization might decide that better retention of quality personnel and a performance-based pay system would enable the firm to enter new markets more successfully, offer more affordable and higher-quality products and services to customers, and thereby boost revenues and reduce operating costs, maximizing shareholder value.

2. **Communicate the vision and strategy.** Executives communicate the vision and strategy to middle managers, using their input to make any necessary modifications to the corporate scorecard. Together, steps 1 and 2 can take as long as four months, as executives and managers discuss and refine the cause-and-effect assumptions that underlie the corporate scorecard.

3. **Develop business-unit scorecards.** Using the corporate-level scorecard as a template, each business unit develops a strategy

that supports the company-level strategy reflected on the corporate strategy. For example, if the corporate scorecard calls for improving employee retention, the HR department would develop strategies related to that goal. Unit managers also determine the metrics required to measure performance on their unit's goals. To illustrate, HR might set a goal of reducing employee turnover by 5 percent by year end. In this case, the accompanying metrics could be "number of employee departures by year end" and "number of new hires by year end."

In this way, each unit creates its own scorecard, which cascades down from the corporate scorecard. And each unit scorecard shows the same four perspectives depicted on the corporate scorecard: learning and growth, internal operations or processes, customer, and financial. At the same time, executives launch any cross-business change programs that they believe will support the corporate strategy.

4. **Eliminate nonstrategic investments.** Managers identify and eliminate any active programs and initiatives that don't contribute to the corporate strategy.

5. **Review business-unit scorecards.** Executives review the scorecards of the individual business units and provide input into the units' strategy.

6. **Refine the vision.** Executives update the corporate scorecard based on their review of the business-unit scorecards and the identification of any cross-business issues not initially acknowledged in the corporate strategy. This refining process can take place as long as a year after the development of the initial corporate scorecard.

7. **Cascade the scorecard further.** Once the management teams feel comfortable with the scorecard methodology, they let it cascade down to the remaining levels of the organization—to departments, groups, and teams, depending on how the company's hierarchy is structured.

8. **Establish managerial performance objectives.** Top managers link their individual objectives and incentive compensation to their scorecards.

9. **Update long-range plans and budget.** Managers establish five-year goals for each metric on their scorecards, then identify and fund the investments required to meet those goals.

10. **Link employee objectives to the scorecard.** Managers ask all employees to identify individual goals that support their team, department, or division scorecard. The company ties everyone's compensation to the scorecard.

11. **Conduct periodic strategy reviews.** Executives and managers meet monthly and quarterly to discuss the latest performance and, if necessary, refine their assumptions of the cause-and-effect connections between their scorecard elements. Every year, these business leaders meet again to review the overall corporate strategy and make any necessary updates.

As you might imagine, implementing a balanced scorecard program takes time (often several years) and is an iterative process. Executives and managers proceed one step at a time—observing what happens and revising their earlier assumptions based on their observations. The process can also be more difficult than the preceding steps suggest. Participants may encounter numerous obstacles as the implementation unfolds. For example, people may not agree on what constitutes the best strategy for achieving the company's vision. Or they may disagree about how to measure performance on each objective in their scorecard.

And as with any major change initiative, champions of the program will likely meet with at least some resistance. Successful implementation of a scorecard program hinges on constant and clear communication of strategy throughout the organization, the inclusion of input from people at all levels of the organization, and other principles of effective change management. (To learn more about overcoming resistance and implementing major change, see *The Essentials of Managing Change and Transition,* a volume in the Business Literacy for HR Professionals series.)

Many companies also use software to automate their score-cards. Automation enables managers to update and communicate actual versus target performance on the various metrics quickly and easily. At the heart of most of these software systems is an intranet linked to a data warehouse. Numerous organizations use other communication vehicles as well, such as company newsletter articles on the scorecard methodology and the firm's or various units' scorecard performance.

Creating an HR Scorecard

In companies using the balanced scorecard, most (if not all) major functions, units, and departments develop scorecards depicting hypotheses about how their specific actions and decisions can support the overall corporate strategy.[3] The HR scorecard plays a particularly crucial role in this process, for several reasons. First, in today's business arena, competitive advantage stems less from tangible assets (such as manufacturing plants and equipment) and more from individual organizations' internal resources and capabilities—especially the ability to develop and retain a capable, committed workforce. Because these intangible assets are difficult to quantify, rivals can't easily imitate them. Thus the HR scorecard documents a particularly powerful strategic asset.

Second, the HR scorecard lays out HR professionals' thinking about how their function can help other units implement their own strategies. For example, suppose a company's R&D unit has identified timeliness of marketable new product innovations as a key performance driver in its scorecard. This performance driver in turn supports corporate-level strategic objectives, such as entering new markets or increasing market share. And let's say you're an HR manager at this company, and you want to develop an HR scorecard. Your first step would be to understand exactly how the R&D and other units create value for the firm and enable the company to implement its overall competitive strategy. You'd then generate ideas for enabling each unit's success. For instance, you might suggest a reward system that encourages marketable innovations, a sourcing function that provides technological expertise, and incentives to encourage key R&D talent to stay with the company.

Third, the HR scorecard shows how the components within a company's HR system—that is, the firm's many different human resource policies and practices—align with one another to enable HR to support other units' strategies as well as the corporate strategy.

This alignment among HR policies and practices, top management, and company functions and units creates a powerful network of cause-and-effect connections. This network enables all managers and employees to better understand and carry out the firm's mission. Equally important, the HR scorecard empowers HR professionals to demonstrate precisely how HR contributes to the company's financial success—in concrete terms that executives and managers understand and value. For example, HR managers at Sears developed a scorecard that enabled them to cite hard evidence that a 5-point improvement in employee attitudes would drive a 1.3-point improvement in customer satisfaction—which in turn would fuel a 0.5 percent increase in revenue growth. In short, the HR scorecard enables HR professionals to manage human resources as a strategic asset.

The HR scorecard offers other benefits as well: It helps you defend investments by outlining in concrete terms the potential long-term contribution to your firm's bottom line. It also measures leading indicators—decisions and activities that will affect financial performance in the future—rather than merely measuring the outcomes of actions taken in the past. And it encourages flexibility and change by focusing on the firm's strategy implementation—which constantly demands change. By helping you focus on the big picture, the HR scorecard enables you to shift direction when needed. People view the measures on the scorecard as means to an end—not ends in themselves.

In light of all these benefits of the HR scorecard, you may well be eager to develop one for your own company—if you haven't done so already.

Steps for Creating an HR Scorecard

How to begin creating your HR scorecard? For the sake of simplicity, let's build on the R&D example cited earlier. In building your HR scorecard, you would apply the following process to *each* unit in your company.[4]

1. Find out what the R&D unit's key performance drivers are—for example, revenue growth and productivity improvement.

2. Figure out the role that HR plays in those drivers—that is, the deliverables required to support the drivers. To illustrate, by reducing recruiting cycle time, HR supports stable, high-talent staffing—which in turn supports reliable delivery schedules and thus revenue growth.

3. Identify the elements that must come together to generate the deliverables you've defined—such as regular performance appraisals, validated competency models, and retention policies that build experience in the R&D unit.

4. Select metrics for assessing progress toward providing the identified deliverables. Define target performance on each metric. For instance, you might aim to reduce recruiting cycle time from eighteen to fourteen days by a specific date. (See "Tips for Selecting Metrics" for more advice on this.)

5. Design icons or other visual cues indicating assessment of performance on each metric—for example, a red circle for "unsatisfactory," a yellow circle for "cause for concern," and a green circle for "satisfactory." These cues should make it easy for managers to spot actual performance that fell significantly below the metric's target performance (such as a twenty-day recruiting cycle time versus the intended fourteen days). These visual icons should also enable people to identify when actual performance meets or exceeds the targeted performance.

Tips for Selecting Metrics

In building an HR scorecard, you may be tempted to choose too many metrics or the wrong metrics—measures that may seem relevant but actually have little connection to the chain of cause-and-effect connections by which your firm creates value and implements its strategy. Here are some tips for avoiding these common pitfalls:

• Focus on those HR elements that make a definable and significant contribution to a particular HR deliverable. These will differ for each organization.

• Divide your metrics into two categories: (1) core metrics, which make no direct contribution to your firm's strategy implementation (e.g., benefit costs as a percentage of payroll, or workers compensation cost per employee), and (2) strategic metrics (e.g., cost per hire or cost per trainee hour), which directly measure how well you're providing the HR deliverables you've identified.

• Select metrics that enable you to describe the actual impact of the related deliverable on firm performance. For example, "HR deliverable A increased X by 20 percent, which reduced Y by 10 percent, which in turn increased shareholder value by 3 percent."

SOURCE: Brian E. Becker, Mark A. Huselid, and Dave Ulrich, *The HR Scorecard: Linking People, Strategy, and Performance* (Boston: Harvard Business School Press, 2001), 64–72.

Selecting metrics for your HR scorecard can be something of an art. If you're wondering how to choose metrics from the many different possibilities, see "Tips for Selecting Metrics" for guidance.

Summing Up

Financial statements represent the past and are strictly limited to financial measurements. As a manager, you need leading indicators

The HR Scorecard in Action

At GTE (now part of Verizon), the HR department designed an HR scorecard even though the overall company had not adopted the methodology. As part of a top-leadership planning process, GTE's HR managers identified the new behaviors and capabilities required to drive business results over the next five to ten years. They then identified five thrusts for a new HR strategy: talent, leadership, customer service and support, organizational integration, and HR capability.

These five thrusts were depicted as the foundation of the HR scorecard. Each thrust directly drove strategic objectives in the operations, customer, and financial components of the scorecard. For example, the HR scorecard showed the hypothesis that strong leadership (in the innovation and growth perspective of the scorecard) would lead to optimal service delivery through streamlined processes (in the operations or processes perspective), which would enable GTE to become a low-cost provider (in the customer perspective). Becoming a low-cost provider would in turn minimize HR costs, thereby contributing to shareholder value (both thrusts fit in the financial perspective).

Next the HR managers asked GTE's business leaders which aspect of each thrust kept them awake at night. The leaders' responses—which included concerns such as "Do we have the talent we need to succeed in the future?" and "Are we managing the cost of turnover?"—led to the selection of metrics in the HR scorecard. For instance, metrics related to the leadership objective included offer acceptance rate and executive retention rate.

GTE's HR scorecard has generated impressive results. For one thing, it has enabled the company's HR professionals to react more quickly to changing markets and technologies, as well as anticipate workforce issues rather than merely reacting to them. It has also saved costs associated with hiring, retention,

Continued

and grievance filing. Finally, it proved invaluable during GTE and Bell Atlantic's merger into Verizon. Soon after the merger, GTE's HR scorecard provided a way in which Verizon's HR leadership team could focus on common objectives and the future of the newly combined business. A shared sense of HR strategy and focus emerged—which enabled the new entity to move forward with more efficiency and less pain than what most merged companies experience.

SOURCE: Brian E. Becker, Mark A. Huselid, and Dave Ulrich, *The HR Scorecard: Linking People, Strategy, and Performance* (Boston: Harvard Business School Press, 2001), 44, 72–74, 198–199, and Valerie E. Pike, "Balanced Scorecard Basics on Implementation," SHRM White Paper, December 2000.

and nonfinancial measurements to understand and guide your business. This chapter has provided an introduction to the balanced scorecard, which many companies have adopted to complement their financial measures.

The chapter also introduced the notion of the HR scorecard as a particularly powerful strategic asset, and outlined steps for building this specialized scorecard.

To learn more about the balanced scorecard, as well as the HR scorecard, see the For Further Reading section at the end of this book.

Leveraging Chapter Insights: Critical Questions

- Does your company use the balanced scorecard methodology? If so, has the company created a scorecard for the entire organization? For several units? For a specific unit?

- Has your HR department developed a scorecard? If so, what hypotheses does the HR scorecard communicate about how the human resource function can support the company's overall strategy as well as specific units' strategies?

- If your company has not adopted a corporate-level scorecard, how might you still measure and demonstrate HR's contribution to your firm's financial success—in terms that other executives understand and value? How might you demonstrate HR's contribution to other units' strategic efforts?

CHAPTER FIVE

Important Accounting Concepts

The Rules That Shape Financial Statements

Key Topics Covered in This Chapter

- *Generally accepted accounting principles*
- *Cash versus accrual accounting*
- *Accounting for inventories*
- *Depreciation methods*
- *Accounting for leases*
- *Historical cost and its implications*
- *Cost accounting and its uses*

CHAPTERS 2 and 3 explained the financial statements and ratios you can use to assess your company's performance and financial soundness and identify ways in which the HR department might improve the bottom line. Mastery of these statements and ratios will help you at many points in your career as an HR professional. Chapter 5 further deepens your financial savvy by explaining additional important accounting concepts that shape financial statements.

Generally Accepted Accounting Principles

The values represented in financial statements are drawn from the business's accounting system. That system is designed to record, classify, and report the business's many monetary transactions in ways that conform with *generally accepted accounting principles,* or GAAP.

In the United States, GAAP is a body of conventions, rules, and procedures sanctioned by the Financial Accounting Standards Board—an independent, self-regulating body. All entities must follow GAAP in accounting for transactions and in representing their results in financial statements. This conformity to uniform standards gives shareholders, investors, lenders, customers, and regulators some assurance that the financial statements they see are accurate and fair representations of underlying business activities. As a check against manipulation, the financial statements of every corporation whose stock is publicly traded in the United States must be audited by an independent certified public accountant. This auditor examines the company's accounting records and then renders an opinion as to the fairness and consistency of the company's financial statements and its conformity to GAAP.

An audit is designed to provide "reasonable" assurance that the financial statements fairly represent a company's financial transactions. It is not, however, an absolute assurance, because the auditor examines evidence on a test basis using statistical sampling. The auditor does not examine every transaction and its corresponding amount. Some portions of a company's annual report—for example, the chairperson's letter to shareholders, management's discussion and analysis of results, and information about stock prices—are not audited at all.

Cash Versus Accrual Accounting

Businesses can use either *cash-basis accounting* or *accrual accounting.* But once they make the choice, they must adhere to it consistently.

Cash-basis accounting records transactions when cash has traded hands. Many small businesses use this method because it's simple and gives the business owner some flexibility in managing taxable income.

In contrast to cash-basis accounting, accrual accounting records transactions as they are made—whether or not cash has actually changed hands. Most companies of any size use accrual accounting. This system provides a better matching between revenues and their associated cost, which helps companies understand the true causes and effects of various business activities. Accordingly, revenues are recognized during the period in which the sales efforts occur, and expenses are recognized in the same period as their associated revenues.

Another interesting effect of accrual accounting is the treatment of so-called prepaid expenses. Some companies purchase multiyear leases and insurance policies with a single payment. These represent prepaid expenses. When initially made, they are recorded on the balance sheet as, for example, prepaid insurance.

Cash-Basis Accounting at Parker & Smith

When Parker & Smith's founder, Ann Cuneo, first launched the company as a small business, she used cash-basis accounting. Her first year was very lucrative going into the fourth quarter, and she was concerned about all the income tax she would have to pay if she made enough money to push her into a higher tax bracket. But she knew that she had two ways of reducing her taxable income for that particular year: (1) defer the cash receipt of income from her customers until the *next* tax year, and (2) increase her tax-deductible cash expenses in the current tax year.

So, as December rolled around, Ann decided to delay the billing of two customers until late in the month. That way, she would receive the income in mid-January of the next tax year. She also thought about all the business-related items she planned on purchasing over the upcoming months: stamps, a new computer, office supplies, reference materials, and so forth. And she made those purchases before December 31. These went onto her books as cash expenses in that year—further reducing her taxable income.

Each year's portion of that payment is charged off as an expense as it is used. For example, if Parker & Smith purchased a two-year property insurance policy for $6,000 in 2005, then only $3,000 would be charged off as an expense on its year 2005 income statement. Moreover, the advanced payment for 2006 would be carried as a prepaid asset on its balance sheet.

Accounting for Inventory

Inventory describes anything that goes into a company's production process: the supplies, raw materials, components, and so forth, that

Accrual Accounting at Parker & Smith

At Parker & Smith, the revenue for a customer order is booked as each order is shipped—even if the customer doesn't pay immediately. Similarly, if the company receives two thousand desk drawer knobs from a contracted supply company, those drawer knobs are not all expensed at once. Rather, they are expensed on a per-unit basis: If it takes four drawer knobs to make one computer desk, then the knobs are expensed four at a time as each desk is shipped out.

the firm uses in its operations. The term also includes work in process—goods in various stages of production—as well as finished goods waiting to be sold or shipped, or both.

Inventories constitute a significant current asset for many firms. Accounting for them has two important aspects. First, a company must determine the cost of inventory that it has purchased or manufactured. That cost is then held in the company's inventory accounts until the product is sold. Once the product has been shipped or delivered to a customer, the cost becomes an expense that is reported on the income statement as part of the cost of goods sold.

To understand the process of inventory accounting, imagine costs flowing into the inventory account and then being removed from that same account and charged to the cost of goods sold in the income statement. Just as products are physically moved into a warehouse and then physically removed as they are delivered to customers, the cost of inventory is moved into an account and later removed from it. It is important to recognize, however, that these flows need not be parallel—that is, the flow of *costs* into, and out of, the inventory account need not be in the same order as the flow of *goods* into, and out of, the warehouse. As we'll see later, we might decide to first use the inventory items most recently received because they will give us a more realistic estimate of our costs.

Inventory Cost Flows

At first glance, you may see no need to make an assumption about how costs flow through the inventory account. The cost of each item placed in the physical inventory can be entered into the account, and then, as the item is physically taken from inventory, the cost can be removed from the account. In this way, the costs accumulated in the account can perfectly match the items physically held, and the costs of goods sold can equal the sum of the cost of each item actually delivered to a customer. Such an inventory cost system can be called a specific identification system.[1]

Specifically identifying each item in inventory is relatively easy if each item is unique, such as an art object or a piece of custom-made furniture, or if each item has an identification number, such as an automobile. However, specific identification is not practical when inventory items are not individually identifiable. This is the case with bushels of wheat, caseloads of memory chips, and loads of drawer knobs like the ones used in Parker & Smith's computer desks. For these kinds of inventories, accountants commonly assume a cost flow that is not necessarily related to the actual physical flow of goods.

The accounting problem with these all-the-same inventory items gets complicated if the company has paid different prices for them. For example, suppose Parker & Smith has 5,000 drawer knobs in its parts inventory. Owing to inflation and other factors, the company paid $0.10 per knob for the first 1,500 knobs; $0.12 for the next 2,000; and the bargain price of $0.08 for the remaining 1,500. So when its assembly crews pull 200 knobs from inventory, which cost should be reflected in the cost of goods sold? The knobs are identical in every sense except their order of purchase and their cost to Parker & Smith.

Three common assumptions are used in accounting for inventory cost: *average cost, first-in, first-out* (FIFO), and *last-in, first-out* (LIFO). A company can choose any of these three assumptions and use them consistently for each classification of inventory—regardless of how the goods physically move into and out of inventory.

AVERAGE COST Using the average-cost method requires you to calculate the average cost of items in the beginning inventory plus the purchases made during the accounting period (such as one month) to determine the cost of goods sold and the cost of inventory on hand at the end of the period. The average cost is assumed to be a representative cost of all the items available for sale during the accounting period. Rather than wait until the end of an accounting period to calculate the average cost, some companies use a predetermined unit cost of all transactions that take place during the accounting period. This is a standard-cost system and is a variation of the average-cost method. Any difference between the actual average unit cost and the predetermined standard cost during a period is usually added to or subtracted from the cost of goods sold for that period.

FIRST-IN, FIRST-OUT (FIFO) If the first-in, first-out, or FIFO, assumption is used, then the oldest costs in the inventory account are the first to be transferred to the cost of goods sold when merchandise is sold. Using this assumption means that the costs retained in the inventory account will always be those most recently incurred for the purchase or manufacture of inventory. For this reason, the FIFO assumption produces an inventory account balance that usually comes the closest of the three methods to approximating the replacement cost of the inventory.

LAST-IN, FIRST-OUT (LIFO) The last-in, first-out, or LIFO, assumption is the opposite of FIFO. The cost of goods sold is measured using the cost of the *most recent* additions to inventory, and the inventory account always retains the most distant items purchased or manufactured. This assumed inventory consumption pattern may be quite different from the actual physical flow of goods, and the pattern usually is different when the LIFO method is used. If older costs are retained in the inventory account for some period because the inventory is never depleted, and if prices change substantially in the same period, the LIFO inventory balance will

It's the Law

For most accounting methods, U.S. tax law has no requirement that the same method be employed in financial reports issued to shareholders and in financial reports on which taxes are based. However, LIFO is an exception. A company that chooses to use the LIFO method in its tax returns must also use LIFO in its reports to shareholders. For this reason, there is a downside associated with paying lower taxes: Management must then report to shareholders lower earnings than might be the case if an alternative inventory assumption were used.

likely bear little relation to the current value of the same amount of inventory recently purchased.

Use of the LIFO assumption is not permitted in some countries. It is, however, permitted in the United States and is quite popular there. One important reason for this popularity is that LIFO provides a better measure of the current costs of inventory. When those costs are matched against current sales revenues, both investors and managers get a sharper sense of what's going on in the business. Another reason for LIFO's popularity is that inflation generally makes the most currently acquired inventory more expensive. This increased cost reduces the reported profitability of sales, which, in turn, reduces the tax liability. But there is a downside to LIFO, as explained in "It's the Law."

To get a better idea of how the three common assumptions— average cost, LIFO, and FIFO—affect the cost of goods sold, consider this example. Parker & Smith maintained an inventory of brass fixtures for use in several executive desk assemblies. In 2005, owing to rising materials costs, the price the company paid to suppliers for these fixtures increased significantly. A record of purchases in 2005 showed the following:

February 1	50 at $6.00	$300
April 1	50 at $7.50	$375

May 1	50 at $8.50	$425
July 1	50 at $9.00	$450
October 1	50 at $10.50	$525
Total		$2,075

Price had been stable before 2005. On January 1, 2005, there were twenty-nine fixtures on hand, each of which had cost $5.00. At the end of the year, there were fifty-four on hand.

If inventories are valued periodically, the value of inventory in terms of historical prices and the cost of fixtures sold depends on the inventory flow assumption adopted (table 5-1). Notice that in the calculation of LIFO, average cost, and FIFO, we calculate the cost of fixtures sold by starting with the cost of the fixtures available for use ($2,220 in each case). We reduce that figure by the cost of the fifty-four units available at year's end under each assumption. In the LIFO calculation, for example, the cost of the remaining fifty-four is assumed to be the cost of the first (and lowest-cost) fixtures purchased.

TABLE 5-1

Parker & Smith Value of Inventory, 2005

	INVENTORY-FLOW ASSUMPTION		
	FIFO Method	Average-Cost Method	LIFO Method
Fixtures, Jan. 1, 2005 (29 at $5.00)	$145	$145	$145
Purchases, 2005	$2,075	$2,075	$2,075
Available for use, 2005	$2,220	$2,220	$2,220
Fixtures on hand, Dec. 31, 2005	$561[a]	$430[b]	$295[c]
Cost of fixtures sold, 2005	$1,659	$1,790	$1,925

Source: Adapted from William J. Bruns Jr., "Accounting for Current Assets," Case 193-048 (Boston: Harvard Business School Publishing, 1996)

[a]FIFO method: The total cost of 50 fixtures at $10.50 (or $525) plus 4 fixtures at $9.00 ($36).

[b]Average-cost method: The total cost of 54 fixtures at the average cost of $7.96, calculated by taking the total cost of fixtures purchased and dividing by the total number of fixtures used in production.

[c]LIFO method: The total cost of 29 fixtures at $5.00 ($145) plus 25 fixtures at $6.00 ($150).

For managers, the important thing to remember is that the inventory-flow assumption has an impact on the cost of goods sold, the reported net income, and the inventory value that will be shown among the current assets on the balance sheet. What's more, if the costs of inventory have risen and the LIFO method is utilized, then dipping into old inventory costs by reducing the size of the inventory on hand (called a LIFO liquidation) will give a burst of net income, which may not be sustainable in future periods.

We can sum up our discussion of inventory accounting quite simply. Inventory accounting consists of two steps: First, you must measure the cost of items added to inventory. Second, you must decide which method you will use to account for the cost of these items as they are sold or delivered to customers.

Depreciation

Expenditures for property and capital equipment represent a commitment of resources to assets ordinarily used over several periods. The accounting concept of matching revenues with their related expenses requires that the cost of such investments be matched with the revenues obtained from using them. For buildings and equipment, the amount of expense matched with revenues is called *depreciation*. Depreciation is an expense that effectively reduces the balance-sheet value of an asset over its presumed useful life. For example, if Parker & Smith were to purchase for $50,000 (delivered and installed) a new piece of metal-bending machinery that had an anticipated useful life of twenty years, then the company could expense a portion of that $50,000 against revenues in each of the following twenty years. This would reduce the company's taxable income, dollar for dollar. At the same time, Parker & Smith's accountants would reduce the balance-sheet value of the machinery at the same rate until the value was zero.[2]

Financial experts refer to depreciation as a noncash expense—a term that is worth remembering. Even though depreciation is listed as an expense on the income statement, no money flows out of the company's pockets—unlike the situation with expenses such as salaries, supplies, utilities, and postage. Depreciation is simply a handy way of recognizing that certain assets wear out or gradually lose their productive value and must be replaced.

If the asset is a natural resource, such as forest land or mineral deposits, similar expenses would be called depletion. If the asset is intangible (e.g., a patent), its original cost would be amortized over the periods when benefits are obtained or, in some cases, over an arbitrary period.

Understanding this simple explanation of depreciation is bound to help you gain a deeper sense of your firm's financial performance. Knowledge of other, more detailed aspects of depreciation will help you even more. Let's look at some of these aspects.

The Cost of Fixed Assets

The cost of a fixed asset (and the amount at which it will be initially carried in reports) consists of the total amount of expenditures necessary to ready the asset for its intended use. This means that in addition to the price of acquiring legal title to an asset, you must add the costs of delivery, installation, employee training, and the modification of facilities necessary to use the asset as planned.

Estimating Depreciation

At the beginning of an asset's life, an estimate of the asset's salvage value is made. The salvage value is the expected selling price of the asset less any removal costs at the end of its useful life to the organization. The difference between the cost and the salvage value is called the depreciable cost. Companies match this depreciable cost to revenues earned in the accounting periods over which the asset will be used. Here's an example, using a laboratory furnace that Parker & Smith acquired to develop new alloys for the metal fixtures on its priciest executive desks.

Price of furnace	$13,000
Less discount for paying cash	$500
Price paid	$12,500

Freight charges	$500
Installation	$2,000
Training expenses	$1,000
Total cost	$16,000
Less salvage value	$6,000
Depreciable cost	$10,000

Once you've determined the depreciable cost, all that remains is to select a method for allocating that cost to periods when the asset will be used to generate revenues. In allocating the depreciable cost, any one of several methods is acceptable. Although these methods may appear arbitrary, they meet two criteria. First, the amount of depreciation charged is not subject to manipulation by management in such a way that the company's income for any period can be capriciously distorted. Second, the amounts charged bear some resemblance to the decline in value of the asset measured on a historical cost basis.

Let's look at two methods of depreciation in common use with occasional variations in each: straight-line depreciation and declining-balance depreciation. Each method has its advantages.

Straight-Line Depreciation

Under the straight-line method of estimating depreciation, an equal portion of the depreciable cost is charged each year according to some measure of the length of an asset's life. Under this method, as under any method of depreciation commonly used, the amount charged to expense is usually accumulated and shown on the balance sheet as a deduction from the historical cost of the asset. This accumulated depreciation is called a contra asset. It is always associated with the asset to which it is related, and its balance offsets part of the original cost that has already been matched against revenues. Table 5-2 shows how we might use the straight-line method to estimate depreciation for Parker & Smith's new furnace. The method employs an estimated useful life of five years and, alternatively, the furnace's anticipated lifetime metal-melting capacity and the company's production outlook (use base).

TABLE 5-2

Straight-Line Depreciation for Laboratory Furnace (with Five-Year Estimated Life)

Year	Expected Melt (in Pounds)	Time Base ($10,000/5 years = $2,000/year)	Use Base ($10,000/250,000 lbs = $0.04/lb × Expected Melt)
1	40,000	$2,000	$1,600
2	45,000	2,000	1,800
3	50,000	2,000	2,000
4	55,000	2,000	2,200
5	60,000	2,000	2,400
Total	250,000	$10,000	$10,000

Source: William J. Bruns Jr., "Accounting for Property, Plant, Equipment and Other Assets," Case 9-193-046 (Boston: Harvard Business School, 1996).

Declining-Balance Depreciation

In an attempt to reflect that an asset is often most productive in the early years of its use, accountants often employ methods that charge a larger proportion of the total depreciation expense in the early years of life than in later periods. One common method for accomplishing this is to charge to each period a fixed percentage of the original cost of the asset less any previously accumulated depreciation. (Note the difference from straight-line depreciation, in which the depreciation rate is applied to the entire depreciable cost of the asset each period.) Commonly, this figure will be 150 or 200 percent of the depreciation rate used under the straight-line method. Because the declining-balance method will never completely amortize the original cost of an asset, accountants typically do not deduct the salvage value of the asset from the original cost before applying the depreciation percentage.

Table 5-3 shows how Parker & Smith's accountants would use the declining-balance method to calculate the depreciation of its laboratory furnace. Again, this example adhered to a five-year depreciation period. However, since the $6,000 salvage value is not

TABLE 5-3

Declining-Balance Depreciation for Laboratory Furnace

Year	Book Value at Beginning of Year	Depreciation Expense (40% of Book Value)	Book Value at End of Year
1	$16,000	$6,400	$9,600
2	9,600	3,840	5,760
3	5,760	2,304	3,456
4	3,456	1,382	2,074
5	2,074	830	1,244
Total		$14,756	

Source: William J. Bruns Jr., "Accounting for Property, Plant, Equipment and Other Assets,"
Case 9-193-046 (Boston: Harvard Business School, 1996).

excluded in this method, the depreciable cost of the furnace (book value at year 1) is $16,000.

One very nice advantage of this declining-balance method is the much larger depreciation expenses allowed in the early years. This means that Parker & Smith can make much larger reductions in its taxable income in the earlier years. And as you may already know, a dollar of taxes that you can defer until later is a dollar you can use to invest in money-making operations today.

Final Comments About Depreciation

The importance of depreciation lies in its relationship to the proper determination of income. But which method is best? Ideally, the best method should provide the most accurate estimation of real profit possible. In practice, however, other criteria often dominate: simplicity of application, tax and other legal requirements, or the desire on the part of management to show earnings more favorable or less favorable than those with another method. Estimates of depreciation expense, therefore, must be used and interpreted with great care.

Another aspect of depreciation accounting deserves mention. We have dealt with the depreciation of individual assets because this was the easiest way to illustrate different methods of depreciation. In practice, however, a large firm may have many assets of a certain type—personal computers, for example. Rather than keep track of each asset, accountants find it more feasible to depreciate them as a group.

Accounting for Leases

You probably know about leasing a new automobile. The ads are enticing. "Drive away in a new MegaGuzzler SUV for only $299 per month!" Then the fine print tells you about the four-year term of the lease and the $2,500 or so you must pay up front to get that low monthly lease rate.

Car leases are convenient when you don't want to take out a loan. And sometimes, you don't even have to make a down payment (though your monthly payments will be higher). At the end of the multiyear lease term, you can return the car and walk away. For some people, this is a good alternative to owning a car.

Companies like leases for some of the same reasons. Leasing, in fact, is an extremely popular approach to acquiring assets, and everything from computers to railroad cars to skyscrapers can be leased today. Organizations that lease assets rather than purchase them may do so for various reasons. Through leasing, a company can enjoy the use of certain resources without paying for them until it can obtain receipts from customers. This practice frees the firm from having to borrow and thus deplete liquid assets. Likewise, companies that find themselves short on cash and long on fixed assets often sell their assets. Then, with the next stroke of the pen, the companies lease them back from the buyer—an arrangement known as a *sale and leaseback*. More than a few grandiose corporate headquarters buildings have gone though this transaction, usually when the selling corporation has fallen on hard times.

Leasing agreements fall into two main classes. An *operating lease* is the most familiar. The personal automobile lease usually falls into this class. In this lease, the term covers only a portion of the asset's anticipated useful life. The lessor (the asset's owner) must renew the lease one or more times to recoup the cost of the asset and make a profit.

A *financial lease,* in contrast, typically covers the entire useful life of the asset and continues until the lessee has made all the scheduled payments. Also, the lessee typically must pay the taxes, insurance, and maintenance costs related to the asset. This is very much like purchasing the asset and making monthly payments until the asset is completely paid for. Since the lease agreement requires the outflow of cash in the future, it has the essential characteristics of a liability.

In 1976, the Financial Accounting Standards Board began requiring corporations to capitalize their leases on the balance sheet (that is, show them as assets) when those leases were, in reality, purchase and loan agreements under another name. Operating leases, however, need only be shown in the footnotes of corporate financial statements.

For example, consider a company that, needing cash for other investments, has sold its sole building and leased it back in a financial lease. Table 5-4 shows what XYZ Corp.'s balance sheets would look like before and after it leased an office building. For simplicity, we assume that the company sold the building at its balance-

TABLE 5-4

XYZ Corp.'s Assets and Liabilities Before and After Leasing Its Building

	Before Leasing	After Leasing
Assets		
Cash	$0	$50,000
Building	$50,000	$0
Capitalized lease	_____	$50,000
Total assets	$50,000	$100,000
Liabilities		
Liabilities	$0	$50,000
Owners' equity	$50,000	$50,000
Total liabilities and owners' equity	$50,000	$100,000

sheet value. Prior to the sale-and-leaseback arrangement, the company had only one asset—its building—and no liabilities.

The sale converts the building asset into another asset: cash, which the company can use to finance potential money-making activities. But since this is a financial lease, GAAP requires the company to capitalize the lease and show it as a liability on its balance sheet. Notice that owners' equity remains the same despite the accounting sleight of hand.

Historic Cost and Its Implications

For the many balance-sheet assets discussed in chapter 2—cash, inventories, property, and equipment—GAAP has a strict rule: They must be recorded at their historic cost. Thus, the land and building that your employer acquired in 1966 for its headquarters in midtown Manhattan at a cost of $300,000 must be represented today at that figure less depreciation. No matter that the property is now worth $10 gazillion—it goes on the books at its acquisition cost.

Real property isn't the only category of assets whose real value may be different than its balance-sheet value. Inventory follows the same rule. Thus, if the publisher of the well-known text *Human Resource Management* (currently in its tenth edition), by John Jackson and Robert Mathis, were to come out with a new edition, the market value of the inventory of the previous edition would drop like a stone, since just about everyone would want the new edition. The listed balance-sheet value of the previous edition's inventory, however, would remain the same—at its historic cost, until an evaluation is made that the true value is lower. (Some companies include a category called inventory value reserve in their financial reporting, to reflect the lost value that some percentage of inventory will likely incur.)

The historic-cost principle obviously results in a disparity between real and accounting-statement values. So why do accountants adhere to it? The reason is that they have found no better alternative. Obviously, companies cannot be trusted to write the values up or down on their own. And it would be hugely expensive and impractical to have all corporate assets valued by an army of independent appraisers every year. So we stick with the system we have. Your best defense against misinterpreting balance-sheet values is your knowledge that they are recorded at their historic cost.

Cost Accounting

Cost accounting is a branch of accounting that enables managers to track the cost of the many things that go directly or indirectly into the production of each unit of goods and services a company sells. Managers can use this information for several purposes:

- To develop reasonable selling prices for the goods and services they produce

- To identify costs that are getting out of control

- To target particular costs for gradual reduction

- To determine which products and services are profitable and which are not

Some costs are *direct,* and others are *indirect.* Cost accountants are interested in both, and managers should take an interest as well. For Parker & Smith, for example, screws, glue, steel, lumber, purchased fixtures, and labor are all direct costs of producing the company's products. Indirect costs, often called *overhead, allocations,* or *burden,* are costs that cannot be attributed to the production of any particular unit of output—for instance, the rent on the production facility, utilities costs, the salaries and benefits of executives and administrative personnel, property taxes, and the cost of the annual company picnic. In most cases, these overhead costs are allocated to units of production according to some formula.

To illustrate, Parker & Smith's cost accountants keep track of every little thing that goes into the cost of producing the Model 1 conference tables, a key product line. The bookkeepers account for the costs of machine hours, labor hours, materials, per-unit ship-ping—even the commissions paid to the company's independent sales reps. These direct costs amount to $26 per table. In the par-lance of accounting, we say that any amount the company gets for a Model 1 conference table above that figure represents its *contribution margin,* or its contribution to overhead and profits. More specif-ically, the contribution margin per unit is defined as follows:

Contribution Margin = Net Revenue – Direct Costs

For example, if the Model 1 sold for $100 per unit, then each unit sold would contribute $74 ($100 minus $26 in direct costs) to overhead and profits.

Now let's look at the total direct and indirect costs of produc-ing the Model 1:

Oak lumber	$1.55
Purchased metal fixtures	$2.50
Glue	$0.05
Machine time	$0.60
Labor (0.75 hours at $20 per hour)	$15.00
Shipping (average)	$3.30
Commission	$3.00
Total direct cost	$26.00
Overhead charge	$17.55
Total direct and indirect cost	$43.55

Note that Parker & Smith's cost accountants have tacked on $17.55 in overhead for each Model 1. Assuming that the company's cost information is complete and accurate, this means that each sale of a Model 1 contributes $56.45 to profits ($100 minus $26 direct cost, minus $17.55 in overhead charges).

Process Versus Job-Order Costing

Accountants generally use one of two very different costing sys-tems, depending on the nature of the business: process costing, or job-order costing. Process costing is a suitable costing system for a company that mass-produces thousands of identical items, such as screws, memory chips, or light bulbs. This cost system focuses on the costs of the several steps of the process—for example, blending, extruding, cutting, and packaging. The raw materials and the cost of each step are calculated and then divided by the number of units churned out.

Job-order costing is more appropriate for custom manufacturing. For example, a builder of made-to-order machine tools or a lunar lander would use this approach. Job-order costing identifies all costs relevant to the particular job, direct and indirect.

Using Cost Information

Managers use cost information to understand and control the variables that determine profitability. For instance, most manufacturing companies determine a standard cost for each direct-cost item, such as labor cost per unit, machine hours per unit, and lumber cost per unit. The accounting department then produces a monthly statement that indicates the actual cost for each. Managers can then easily see the variances between standard and actual and can investigate the causes if those variances are getting out of hand. They can also identify the major contributors to cost and work to rein them in.

Parker & Smith's managers, for example, can see that labor is a major contributor to the cost of producing Model 1 conference tables. This information should spur them to reexamine production itself to see if they can alter the process to produce the same number of units with fewer labor hours. Alternatively, management could investigate any production equipment that might substitute for labor and at a lower per-unit cost.

As an HR professional, you can also make good use of cost information specific to your responsibilities. For example, suppose upper managers at your company have challenged everyone in the firm to find ways to better control costs. In this case, you might carefully assess what your department is spending on training, HR consulting services, employee investment plans, starting salaries for particular jobs, and other expenses. You could analyze the industry standards for these expenses and assess whether your group is spending more than, the same as, or less than those standards. You could then analyze any variances to identify and address the causes behind any spending that is higher than the industry standard. Also consider asking which HR activities are prime candidates for outsourcing, with an eye toward streamlining your department's expenses.

You might do additional cost comparisons as well. For example, compare the per-capital outlay for human resource activities and programs at your company with the same figure for competing companies or other firms in your same industry. Or calculate the ratio of HR staff members to total employees at the company to gain insight into whether your HR department is over- or understaffed. Decide whether HR department staff salaries are higher than the average earnings in the rest of the organization—and whether that's typical in your industry. The sidebar "Trends in HR Department Costs" shows some interesting information about trends in HR department costs.

Overhead, or Indirect Costs

Overhead, or indirect costs, can represent the weak point in many cost accounting systems. Traditionally, accountants used simple formulas to allocate indirect costs. For instance, many accounting departments allocated the total of indirect costs among products according to the number of labor hours attributed to each product. This was a reasonable approach as long as labor was the biggest cost of production. Other approaches divided up indirect costs in proportion to the revenues realized from each product. This, too, often made sense, as long as the products weren't too different.

Today, however, the cost of labor varies considerably across industries. In knowledge- and serviced-based industries, which depend heavily on human beings, labor constitutes the primary cost factor. In industries that center on manufacturing, labor may be decreasing as a cost factor—as companies automate more and more of their production processes. Most factories, for example, are

Trends in HR Department Costs

A 2003 benchmarking study revealed some intriguing trends in HR department costs:

- In 2003, HR department budgets represented a median of 0.9 percent of organizations' total projected expenditures for that year. This figure is a slight increase over the 0.8 percent of 2002 but is still significantly lower than the percentages from as recently as the mid-1990s. (For example, the figure was 1.1 percent in 1994–1996.)

- Compared with the 1990s, more companies in 2003 obtained outside assistance with HR programs and activities. Employee assistance and counseling, along with the administration of pension and retirement plans, seemed to be the most likely services to be outsourced.

- The ratio of HR staffing relative to total employment increased slightly in 2003 over the preceding year—rising from 0.9 HR staff per 100 employees to 1.0. This ratio change may reflect the need for HR employees to remain on staff to address the ramifications of job eliminations and layoffs.

- The ratio of HR staffing to total employment varies across industries. For example, the ratio is lower in the health-care industry, government institutions, and educational establishments.

- Sixty-six percent of HR executives said that their actual HR expenditures during 2002 were either "about the same" as the department's budget for that year or "somewhat lower" or "much lower" than the budget.

SOURCE: "HR Department Benchmarks and Analysis 2003," BNA and SHRM, executive summary.

capable of producing dozens or hundreds of different kinds of products, with little indirect labor in the form of human beings running machines. As a result, the old allocation formulas no longer produce good approximations of indirect costs.

In fact, those outdated formulas can easily lead manufacturing managers to step up production of money-losing products and drop their most profitable product lines. To understand how this mismatch of real and apparent profitability occurs, consider what would happen to a company that traditionally relied on labor hours as the formula for allocating overhead. In the days when labor was a major cost of production in manufacturing industries, this practice would put a major proportion of total overhead on the backs of company products that used lots of labor—which made sense. However, as some lines of products modernized and eliminated labor through automation, their share of the overhead burden would shrink. And the profitability of these products would appear to grow. But overhead costs would not go away; they would simply be shifted elsewhere.

Thus, other product lines—particularly those that used high inputs of labor—would have to absorb the lion's share of company-wide overhead. This arrangement would make these product lines appear relatively unprofitable. To see how this could happen, consider two products, both of which net the same revenue per unit ($14.00) and have the same direct cost of manufacture, shipping, and distribution ($5.00). Product A has the same contribution margin as does product B. Product A enjoys market leadership and growing demand. But because its manufacture involves more labor hours, the company's cost formula has allocated a much higher overhead charge to it—so much so that product A is shown to produce a $1.00 loss per unit sale. Product B, in comparison, is a weak performer in a declining market. Yet because of its low labor content, it receives a much lower overhead allocation, which makes it appear very profitable. Seeing these numbers, management could easily make an entirely wrongheaded decision: Phase out production of product A, and increase production of product B. Decisions like these can sink even the best companies!

	Product A	Product B
Total direct cost	$5.00	$5.00
Overhead charge	$10.00	$4.00
Total direct/indirect	$15.00	$9.00
Net revenue/unit	$14.00	$14.00
Contribution to profits	$(1.00)	$5.00

H. Thomas Johnson and Robert Kaplan proposed an alternative way of figuring costs.[3] That alternative came to be known as *activity-based costing,* or ABC. With ABC, managers carefully quantify the links between performing particular activities and the demands those activities make on the organization's resources. While traditional cost-accounting systems allocate indirect and support costs to products through such measures as direct labor hours, machine hours, or materials cost, ABC recognizes that different products, customers, brands, and distribution channels make very different demands on a company's resources. Accordingly, ABC starts by creating a hierarchy of activities and then assigns costs according to the activity involved. It counts the actual activities that go into making a specific product (or into delivering a specific service) and attempts to figure the costs of those activities. Rather than allocate the total cost of a machine across a range of products according to a formula, for example, ABC-trained accountants study how much machine time (including setup, etc.) each product actually requires, then allocate costs accordingly. ABC also focuses on cost drivers that can guide allocations.

The cost of the HR department, for instance, might be allocated among other departments in various ways. Perhaps the most common are the direct method and the step-down.[4] With the direct method—the simplest and most straightforward approach—the HR department might directly allocate costs to other units based on head count. For instance, suppose the HR department's costs total $50,000 and the company wants to allocate these costs among two operating units: order processing and warehouse. The order processing department has 20 employees, and the warehouse has 15. In this case, you would allocate HR costs according to these equations:

Order processing: [20 / (20 + 15)] × $50,000 = $28,571
Warehouse: [15 / (20 + 15)] × $50,000 = $21,428

With the step-down method of cost allocation, things become a bit more complicated. Companies allocate the costs of service departments to other units differently—depending on which service departments have the highest costs and which serve the largest number of users. If your HR department serves more units than other service departments do and incurs the highest costs, your company would use a corresponding ratio to allocate more of HR's costs among user units than costs associated with other service departments that serve fewer units.

ABC has spread rapidly, though not as rapidly as its proponents had hoped. One reason for the hesitation is that it involves a trade-off: For the sake of more accuracy, a company must spend more time and resources counting and measuring the activities that drive costs. A company must expect a clear benefit from embracing the idea—and even if there is such a benefit, will it be large enough to justify reprogramming the necessary systems?

Summing Up

There's a lot more to accounting than what we've discussed in these pages, but the following topics covered here will help you make sense of many important accounting issues that affect your performance as a manager:

- Generally accepted accounting principles, or GAAP
- Accrual versus cash accounting
- Accounting for inventories
- Accounting for depreciation
- Accounting for leases
- The principle of historic cost
- Cost accounting

Of these accounting issues, cost accounting is one that any manager not directly involved in finance is most likely to encounter on a regular basis. Cost accounting can help you understand which of your operations are economically contributing to profits and which are not. An understanding of cost accounting can also help you avoid arbitrary assignments of overhead that make valid profitability assessment impossible. For further information on cost accounting and the other topics covered in this chapter, please refer to the sources listed under the For Further Reading section at the end of this book.

Leveraging Chapter Insights: Critical Questions

- What fixed assets owned by your company does it depreciate?

- Does your firm engage in any sale-and-leaseback arrangements? If so, what are they? And how has the organization used the cash yielded by such arrangements? If you're not sure, how might you learn more about this?

- Based on your analysis of the costs of various HR programs and services, which costs (if any) would you identify as getting out of control? How might you gradually reduce such costs?

- Which HR programs and services are the most profitable? The least?

- How does your firm allocate HR costs among units? What do you think of the method your firm uses for this allocation? What changes, if any, would you recommend?

CHAPTER SIX

Taxes

Important Details You Should Know

Key Topics Covered in This Chapter

- *Taxes for different legal forms of business*
- *Progressive tax rates*
- *Marginal rate*
- *Tax credits versus tax deductions*
- *Tax loss carrybacks and carryforwards*

INCOME TAXES in the United States are a big, complex subject. Congress has made them that way. When federal income taxes were first instituted in 1913 under the provisions of the Sixteenth Amendment to the U.S. Constitution, the tax return consisted of only one page, and the entire tax code filled less than fourteen pages. Today, at more than twenty thousand pages, the U.S. tax code is the product of years of incremental additions, tinkering, and special exceptions for certain companies and industries. And Congress hasn't finished yet. Every year, hundreds of pages are added to the code, prompting one critic to complain that the system is like an old, leaky tire with thousands of patches.

The code is so arcane that all sizable businesses and many private citizens rely on tax professionals to steer them clear of the code's many shoals. Even tax professionals cannot fathom the entire code. Instead they specialize in one or two of its aspects: estate taxes, qualified retirement plans, real estate taxes, corporate taxes for extraction industries, and so forth.

As bad as this may seem, there is a silver lining for the HR manager who lacks a finance background: Your company assigns its tax issues to specialists, leaving you off the hook for mastering this complex aspect of finance. Nevertheless, it pays to understand some basic tax concepts, because taxes creep into most companies' financial decisions. This advice is doubly true for business owners. So if you own an HR consulting firm, for example, you can benefit hugely from understanding more about taxes.

Since business taxes are too big a subject to tackle in a single chapter—let alone in a single book—this chapter will confine itself to just a few things you ought to understand. We'll start with how the different legal forms of business are taxed in the United States. Then we'll move on to two related subjects: progressive tax rates and the concept of marginal rate. These topics set up the next section, in which we'll explore the differences between tax deductions and tax credits. We'll end with the subject of tax loss carryback and carryforward.

Taxes and the Legal Form of the Business

One of the key issues that every entrepreneur must address at the onset of a new venture is the legal form the enterprise should adopt. This decision is driven chiefly by the objectives of the entrepreneur and the firm's investors. But taxation and legal liabilities also play a part. The choice becomes even more difficult, thanks to the trade-offs built into the law. To get the most favorable tax treatment, a business must often give up some protection from liability, some flexibility, or both.[1]

Sole Proprietorships

The *sole proprietorship* is the oldest, simplest, and most common form of business entity. It is a business owned by a single individual. For example, if you're an HR consultant who runs a one-person "shop," you might structure your business as a sole proprietorship. In a sole proprietorship, the owner and the business are one and the same for tax and legal liability purposes. The proprietorship is not taxed as a separate entity. Instead, the owner reports all income and deductible expenses for the business on Schedule C of his or her personal income tax return.

Note that the earnings of the business are taxed at the individual level, whether or not they are actually distributed in cash. There is no vehicle for sheltering income.

For liability purposes, the individual and the business are also one and the same. Thus, legal claimants can pursue the personal property of the proprietor, not simply the assets that are utilized in the business.

C Corporations

The C corporation is synonymous with the common notion of a corporation. When a business incorporates, it becomes a C corporation unless it makes a special election to become an S corporation (which we'll learn about later in this chapter).

C corporations in the United States are hugely outnumbered by sole proprietorships, yet they account for almost 90 percent of all U.S. sales. This economic dominance by corporations stems from the adoption of the corporate form by most of the nation's largest enterprises. The corporate form is appealing for several reasons. First, in contrast to the sole proprietorship, the C corporation's owners are personally protected from liability. Consider the case of the massive oil spill of the oil tanker *Exxon Valdez*. Even if the damages against Exxon had bankrupted the company, the courts could not have pursued the individual shareholders for further damages. An individual owner's liability is limited to the extent of his or her investment in the firm. This corporate shell, or veil, can be pierced only in the event of fraud.

In exchange for limited liability, the C corporation is considered a tax-paying entity. Because dividends paid out to shareholders are not deductible from corporate income, the earnings of a corporation are taxed twice.

The C corporation does, however, enjoy certain tax benefits that other forms of businesses do not share, or do not share to the same extent. The tax law affords favorable tax treatment for many fringe benefits provided by the corporation to its employees and owner-employees. For example, the corporation can deduct from its taxable income the death benefits it pays to the beneficiaries of deceased employees (up to a certain limit). It can set up 401(k) and other retirement plans with fairly generous tax-exempt annual

Double Jeopardy of C Corporations

Suppose our fictional company Parker & Smith earned $647,500 before taxes and paid a little more than 46 percent of this ($300,000) in state and federal corporate income taxes, which left it with $347,500 in profit after tax. If the company paid $10,000 of that in the form of a dividend to its founder and CEO, Ann Cuneo, Cuneo would be required to add that amount to her personal income, which might be taxed at about the same rate (state and federal). Thus, the same income is taxed twice. (Note: There is a minor exception to this double-taxation issue in the case of corporations that receive dividend income from other corporations.)

contribution limits. It can also deduct its expense for employee health-care premiums.

Partnerships

A *partnership* is a business entity with two or more owners. It is treated like a proprietorship for tax and liability purposes. Earnings are distributed according to the partnership agreement and are treated as personal income for tax purposes. Thus, like the sole proprietorship, the partnership is simply a conduit for generating income for its partners. For example, if you run a small HR services company, you might have set up the business with one or more partners.

Partnerships have a unique liability situation. Each partner is jointly and severally liable. Thus, a damaged party may pursue a single partner or any number of partners for any amount—the claim may not be proportional to the invested capital or the distribution of earnings.

A partnership involves complexities not faced by the sole proprietorship. The partners must resolve, and should set down in writing, their agreement on a number of issues:

- The amount and nature of their respective capital contributions (e.g., one partner might contribute cash, another a patent, and a third property and cash)

- The allocation of the business's profits and losses

- Salaries and drawings against profits

- Management responsibilities

- The consequences of withdrawal, retirement, disability, or the death of a partner

- The means of dissolution and liquidation of the partnership

Limited Partnerships

Limited partnerships are a hybrid form of organization having both limited and general partners. The general partner (and there may be more than one) assumes management responsibility and unlimited liability for the business and must have at least a 1 percent interest in profits and losses. The limited partner (or partners) has no voice in management and is legally liable only for the amount of his or her capital contribution plus any other debt obligations specifically accepted.

In a limited partnership, the general partner may be a corporation (i.e., a corporate general partner). When a corporation is the sole general partner, the corporation must have sufficient assets to cover the unlimited liability that it must assume. For this reason, the corporate general partner must have a net worth of at least $250,000, or 10 percent of the total capitalization of the partnership, whichever is less.

Note that in a limited partnership, profits and losses may be allocated differently among the partners. That is, even if profits are allocated 20 percent to the general partner and 80 percent to the limited partners, then the limited partners may get 99 percent of the losses. Losses, however, are deductible only up to the amount of capital at risk. The distribution of profit is subject to all sorts of creative structuring, such as those observed in certain venture capital and real estate partnerships. In some of those arrangements, the limited partners get 99 percent of the profits until they have gotten back an amount equal to their entire capital contributions, at which point the general partner gets 30 percent and the limited partners get only 70 percent.

S Corporations and Limited-Liability Companies

The S corporation is another creature of the tax law. It is a closely held corporation whose tax status is the same as the partnership's, but its participants enjoy the liability protections granted to corporate shareholders. In other words, it is a conduit for passing profits and losses directly to the personal income tax returns of its shareholders, whose legal liabilities are limited to the amount of their capital contributions. In exchange for these favorable treatments, the law places a number of restrictions on the types of corporations that can elect S status. To qualify for S corporation status, an organization must meet the following requirements:

- Have only one class of stock, although differences in voting rights are allowed

- Be a domestic corporation, owned wholly by U.S. citizens, and derive no more than 80 percent of its revenues from non-U.S. sources

- Have seventy-five or fewer stockholders (husbands and wives count as one stockholder)

- Derive no more than 25 percent of revenues from passive sources, such as interest, dividends, rents, and royalties

- Have only individuals, estates, and certain trusts as shareholders (i.e., no corporations or partnerships)

The last provision leaves out venture capitalists as potential shareholders, since most venture-capitalist firms are partnerships.

The limited-liability company (LLC) is a relatively new type of entity designed to afford the same benefits as does the S corporation.

The LLC is similar to an S corporation in that it enjoys the tax advantages of a partnership and the liability protections of a corporation. Although state laws differ somewhat, an LLC is like an S corporation, but with none of the restrictions on the number or type of shareholders. The LLC is similar to a partnership in that the LLC's operating agreement (the equivalent of a partnership agreement) may distribute profits and losses in a variety of ways, not necessarily in proportion to capital contributions. Law firms are often organized as LLCs.

Table 6-1 summarizes the various legal forms of businesses in the United States and their corresponding numbers.

Which Form Makes Sense?

As you have no doubt gathered, tax implications are an important factor in the choice of a business entity. Indeed, the incentives of the tax code give rise to certain tactics that can be risky. For instance, the aforementioned double taxation of a corporation's distributed earnings provides an incentive for owner-employees to pay all the profits to themselves as compensation. Unlike dividends, compensation is deductible as an expense to the corporation and is thus not taxed twice. However, the Internal Revenue Service (IRS) has certain rules on what is considered reasonable compensation; these rules are designed to discourage just such behavior.

TABLE 6-1

Legal Forms of Businesses in the United States

	Number of Firms (Thousands)	Annual Receipts ($ Millions)
All Types	19,286	14,072
C Corporations	2,033	10,747
S Corporations	1,564	1,938
Partnerships	1,090	665
Individual Proprietorships	14,599	722

Source: U.S. Bureau of the Census, "Survey of Women-Owned Business," and unpublished data.

Note too that the tax on individuals in so-called flow-through entities such as partnerships and LLCs is on the share of income *earned,* not on the actual cash *distributed.* The income of the partnership is taxed at the personal level of the partners, whether or not any cash is actually distributed.

If the venture is projected to sustain large losses in the early years, then there may be some benefit to passing those losses through to investors, assuming that the investors are in a position to use them to offset other income and thus reduce their taxes. This would favor the partnership or LLC. Similarly, if the business intends to generate substantial cash flow and return it to investors as the primary means of creating value for investors, then a partnership or LLC is still attractive. However, if the business will require cash investment over the long term, and value is intended to be harvested through a sale or public offering, then a C corporation is probably the most attractive option.

Of course, a business may move through many forms in its lifetime. A sole proprietorship may become a partnership and finally a C corporation. A limited partnership may become an LLC and then a C corporation. Each transition, however, will require considerable legal work and administrative burden for the management and owners of the firm. The advantages of the right form of organization at each particular stage certainly may warrant these burdens. On the other hand, high-potential ventures on the fast track do not want to lose time and focus by jumping through these legal hoops, especially when different modes of external financing must be addressed. Consequently, if you are an entrepreneur, consider the likely evolution of your business before selecting a particular form of organization, and consult with a qualified tax attorney or accountant before making this important choice.

Progressive Tax Rates

Tax rates for corporate and personal income are progressive. This means that the first bundle of taxable income is taxed at a low rate,

TABLE 6-2

U.S. Federal Taxes Levied on Corporations, 2003

| | IF TAXABLE INCOME IS | | |
Over	But Not Over	Tax Is	Of the Amount Over
$0	$50,000	15%	$0
$50,000	$75,000	$7,500 + 25%	$50,000
$75,000	$100,000	$13,750 + 34%	$75,000
$100,000	$335,000	$22,250 + 39%	$100,000
$335,000	$10,000,000	$113,900 + 34%	$335,000
$10,000,000	$15,000,000	$3,400,000 + 35%	$10,000,000
$15,000,000	$18,333,333	$5,150,000 + 38%	$15,000,000
$18,333,333		35%	$0

whereas succeeding bundles are taxed at progressively higher rates. A cynic might say that a progressive tax rate is one that becomes progressively more painful. The U.S. federal taxes levied on corporations are outlined in table 6-2. These figures have been in effect since 1992.

As you can see, a corporation that reports taxable income of $50,000 or less pays at the 15 percent rate. But once this income passes $50,000, the rate jumps to 25 percent, and still higher as taxable income increases. The highest rate is on taxable incomes in the $100,001 through $334,999 range, which are tapped at a rate of 39 percent.

Oddly, the 2003 schedule of rates dips once a corporation hits the $335,000 mark and rises slightly at the $10 million mark, then continues to rise until taxable income hits $18.3 million, at which point the rate drops back again. One can only speculate about the reason for these bobbing rates. Volume discounts from the IRS? Effective corporate lobbyists? Personal income tax rates are likewise progressive, but climb steadily upward, from 15 percent to 39.1 percent.

What constitutes taxable income for the corporation? The tax code defines taxable corporate income as the entity's total income for the tax period. Total income generally means gross sales receipts, interest income, dividend income, rents received, and royalties *less* all legal deductions. Deductions include the compensation paid to employees, repairs and maintenance to corporate-owned property, rent paid, interest payments to creditors, depreciation, and advertising outlays. The corporation can also deduct its contributions to employee pension and profit-sharing plans, and what it spends on employee benefits. Dividend payments to shareholders are *not* deductible from taxable income.

Within certain limits, U.S. corporations can also deduct foreign income tax paid or accrued, or apply it as a credit against U.S. taxes due. The treatment of profits generated overseas is a major issue for U.S. corporations. The corporations often attempt to keep those profits overseas and not repatriate them for the benefit of the U.S. tax authority. This practice, however, keeps the immediate benefits of offshore profits out of the hands of U.S. shareholders.

Marginal Tax Rate

Progressive tax rates underpin the concept of *marginal tax rate,* which you can use to determine the tax benefit of a deductible expense or the tax penalty on the next dollar of taxable income. The marginal tax rate is the rate of tax paid on the next or the last dollar of income. These are the dollars affected by the decisions you make today. Thus, if your corporation has $40,000 in taxable income, its marginal rate is 15 percent. If its taxable income is $20 million, its marginal rate is 35 percent. Once you know your marginal rate, you can determine the after-tax costs of various deductible business expenses and charitable contributions. Here's the formula:

After-Tax Cost = Cost × (1 − Marginal Tax Rate)

To illustrate, consider what a $1,000 corporate contribution to the Ann Cuneo Foundation, a tax-deductible organization, is really costing, assuming that the company is in the 35 percent bracket.

$$After\text{-}Tax\ Cost = \$1,000 \times (1 - 0.35)$$
$$= \$1,000 \times 0.65$$
$$= \$650$$

Thus, the corporation is giving up just $650 when it makes this contribution, since $350 is saved on its tax obligation. In effect, the tax authority is subsidizing 35 percent of the contribution.

The same method can be used in determining the after-tax benefit of an action or a decision. For instance, if you increased revenues by $1,000 this year by charging more for coffee in the corporate lunchroom, you could calculate the after-tax benefit of that move as $650.

Credits Versus Deductions

Periodically, Congress offers tax credits for certain actions and situations. These credits are designed to motivate certain behaviors, such as job creation in low-income neighborhoods or greater capital investment. Tax credits can be found in both business and individual tax environments.

Some people think of tax credits and tax deductions as the same thing. They are not. Deductions, such as a charitable deduction or an interest expense deduction, allow a corporation or an individual to reduce the level of taxable income. Those deductions become more valuable as the marginal bracket increases. A $1,000 deduction will reduce taxes by $150 for a corporation in the 15 percent bracket; the same deduction produces a $390 tax savings to an entity in the highest bracket. To an individual who makes so little that he or she pays no taxes, a deduction is worth nothing.

A *tax credit,* in contrast, provides a dollar-for-dollar tax saving. Thus, a $1,000 tax credit reduces the tax liability by $1,000—no matter what the tax bracket may be. This is why the U.S. government's use of tax credits to spur investment or the hiring of unskilled people is so appealing to business owners and other executives. Up to the limits of these programs, the government is footing the entire bill.

Tax Loss Carryback and Carryforward

Every year that your company produces taxable income, it has to send part of that income off to Washington in the form of corporate income taxes. But what about the years in which losses are incurred? Is there a way to average out years of income and losses for tax purposes?

Fortunately, the U.S. tax code's provision for tax loss carryback and carryforward makes it possible for a company to use losses produced in bad years to recoup some or all of the taxes it paid in the previous good years. A firm can even carry forward any unused losses into future years, using them to offset tax liabilities incurred then.

Specifically, the law allows an operating loss to be carried back two years, and any still-unused portions can be carried forward twenty years beyond the loss year. (Note: This is the general rule; consult a tax professional about the exceptions.) If an individual or organization chooses to carry back the loss, however, the taxpaying entity must first carry the entire loss to the earliest carryback year. If the loss is not used up in that year, the remaining loss must be carried to the next earliest carryback year, and so on. Losses not used during the two carryback years are carried forward in ascending order. There they offset any incurred taxes.

Summing Up

Though this treatment of corporate taxes is by necessity simplified, the information may nevertheless help you make sound business decisions. For example, if you are a sole proprietor or a member of a partnership, it is important to understand the tax implications of changing to a C corporation or an S corporation. Here, the important points to remember are these:

- The taxable income of sole proprietors and partnerships flows directly onto the tax obligations of their owners. There is no "business level" of income taxation. S corporations do the same.

- C corporations and their shareholders are subject to double taxation: The entity is taxed on its earnings, and its shareholders are taxed on any distribution made to them.

The chapter also dealt with the concepts of progressive and marginal tax rates. Understanding these points is critical for decision makers in all types of for-profit organizations.

As you deal with tax issues, however, always observe these caveats:

- The rules of the game change regularly. Substantive changes to the tax code occur every few years. In addition, tax court and IRS rulings appear sporadically, changing the current understanding about the rules and how they are applied in practice. For this reason, you must keep current with the latest changes.

- Always seek professional advice when taxes are an important element of your decisions.

Leveraging Chapter Insights: Critical Questions

- If you work in the HR department of a company, how is the company structured? Is it a C corporation? An S corporation? A partnership? If you're not sure, how might you learn more about this?

- Does the company you work for receive any tax credits by, for example, hiring unskilled workers? If you're not sure, how might you learn more about this?

- If you're an HR consultant running your own business, how have you structured your company? As a sole proprietorship? A partnership? A limited partnership? A limited-liability corporation? What are the pros and cons of the business structure you've chosen? Would it make sense to change to a different structure? If so, why?

CHAPTER SEVEN

Financing Operations and Growth

Funding the Different Stages of Growth

Key Topics Covered in This Chapter

- *Start-up financing*

- *Financing current operations*

- *Financing growth*

- *Proper match of assets and financing*

- *Typical financing arrangements*

HOW DOES YOUR company finance its operations and grow the business? What might these efforts imply for you and other managers in the firm? This chapter provides a broad overview of how businesses use internal and external sources to finance their operations and stimulate growth. Several sections use the financing arrangements of eBay, the online auction company, to illustrate how one company has tapped different sources of capital to fuel rapid expansion. If you work for a large organization, you probably won't participate directly in financing strategies for your corporation overall. Still, an understanding of how such strategies work may help you gain insights into financing's impact on your firm's overall financial performance. But if you've started up your own HR services or consulting company, it's essential that you know about financing if your business goals include expanding the company.

Start-Up Financing

When Ann Cuneo started a woodworking business in 1973, she was well prepared for self-employment. Her transition from supervisor at a small desk-making concern to proprietor of her own business was very direct. As a supervisor, she knew all about shaping and fitting lumber into consumer and commercial products. She also knew the materials suppliers on a first-name basis. Frequently, she was in contact with wholesale and retail distributors of her company's finished products.

Cuneo had used the last year of her employment productively. In her spare time, she designed a small line of computer furniture and used her previous experience to calculate her production costs. She also learned a great deal about the channels of distribution through which her new products would be sold. So, when she left her job and became a business owner, she was extremely well prepared.

Starting the venture, however, required more than knowledge. Cuneo also needed financial and production assets. She calculated that she would need enough cash, say, $3,000, to tide her over a three-month start-up period in which the generation of sale revenues was bound to be minimal. She'd also need an inventory of materials, such as lumber and hardware fixtures. Those items of material inventory would be transformed into finished-goods inventory over time. And she'd need money to pay for an annual property and liability insurance policy and the first three months of rent on a small workshop. As discussed in chapter 2, these items would be Cuneo's current assets, whose monetary value is as follows:

Cash	$3,000
Inventory	
Lumber	$800
Hardware	$700
Other	$500
Total inventory	$2,000
Prepaid expenses	
Insurance (1 year)	$800
Rent (3 months)	$1,500
Total prepaid expenses	$2,300
Total current assets	$7,300

Cuneo's new business, which she decided to call Parker & Smith after two beloved ancestors, needed some fixed assets as well: a wood lathe, a few power and hand tools, workbenches for the shop, and a panel truck for picking up materials and making deliveries to customers. Fortunately, Ann already owned an old panel truck and many of the required tools, and her former employer was glad to sell her two old wood lathes and several surplus workbenches.

With these, Ann was able to complete the fixed-asset section of her balance sheet:

Panel truck	$1,200
Lathes	$1,200
Other tools	$300
Shop fixtures	$300
Total fixed assets	$3,000
Total current assets (from above)	$7,300
Total current and fixed assets	$10,300

Note that the panel truck and other tools are items owned by Cuneo. Their value was calculated at these items' market value at the time she placed them in service.

Cuneo's requirement of $10,300 in assets might not seem like much, but remember that this was 1973, when a dollar was actually worth something! Fortunately, Ann and her husband, Michael, had some money available in their savings account. They already owned the truck and tools, and Michael's uncle offered to contribute the rest as a zero-interest loan of $5,000. "You can pay me back at a thousand per year," he told them. "And good luck with the business." All together, Ann and Michael now had the financing they needed to get the business rolling.

And that's how Parker & Smith was initially financed. You've already seen the asset side of the balance sheet. Here's how the other side looked in late 1973:

Current liabilities (current portion of five-year loan)	$1,000
Long-term liabilities (five-year loan from Michael's uncle)	$4,000
Total liabilities	$5,000
Owners' equity	$5,300
Total liabilities and owners' equity	$10,300

As you can see, all contributions of capital are represented on the liabilities side of the balance sheet, and the total exactly balances the various assets on the other side.

Many, if not most, small businesses are initially financed in a manner similar to the Parker & Smith case—with the owner-operator's personal savings and with contributions from friends and family members. Some individuals even resort to using their credit-card lines of credit for start-up capital, expensive as this practice is.

Trade Credit

Many small-business owners obtain thirty- to sixty-day trade credit from their suppliers as one component of their start-up (and ongoing) financing. For instance, a shoe-store owner may be able to obtain $3,000 worth of shoes from a wholesaler, with payment due in sixty days. If she knows her customers and has picked her inventory wisely, she may be able to sell all or most of the shoes during that sixty-day period and use the proceeds to pay the bill when it comes due. In effect, the supplier will have financed that portion of the store's inventory without charge—which is a better deal for the owner than using a bank line of credit or another device that involves interest charges. Trade credit, of course, is a current liability and must be reflected on the balance sheet as follows:

Current assets	
Inventory	$3,000
Current liabilities	
Accounts payable	$3,000

If the shoe merchant sells all the shoes for $5,000, then the inventory drops to zero, but cash increases by $5,000. The accounts payable amount remains until the bill is paid. There are also income taxes payable from the sale—in this case figured at $800. And to keep both sides of the ledger in balance, owners' equity increases by $1,200, as follows:

Current assets	
Cash	$5,000
Inventory	$0
Current liabilities	
Accounts payable	$3,000
Income tax payable	$800
Owners' equity	$1,200

This is how balance sheets stay balanced as transactions are made.

Commercial Banks

Bankers are justifiably nervous about making loans to start-up businesses, since the failure rate of such efforts is high. Most local bankers will extend loans to a start-up only if they feel comfortable with the situation and with the borrower's qualifications.

What makes bank lenders feel comfortable? Bankers ask three big questions before they lend aspiring borrowers money. And these lenders rarely part with their capital if they cannot obtain satisfactory answers to all three:

1. Will the borrower be able to pay me back?

2. Is the borrower's character such that he or she will pay me back?

3. If the borrower fails to repay me, are there marketable assets that I can put my hands on?

In seeking an answer to the first question, a banker will evaluate the entrepreneur and the business plan:

- Does the applicant understand the market and have a feasible plan for satisfying it?

- Does the entrepreneur have the experience or knowledge—or both—required to operate this type of business successfully?

- Is the business plan realistic, complete, and based on reasonable assumptions?

- Are the revenue and cost projections realistic and conservative?

The banker will also address the adequacy of the venture's financing, since inadequate financing is a major force behind business failures.

Lenders generally answer the second big question, "Is the borrower's character such that he or she will pay me back?" by examining the loan applicant's credit history. Whether it's a car loan, a home mortgage, or a business loan, a banker will seek evidence that the applicant pays his or her bills on schedule.

The third question, "What can I put my hands on?" is about *collateral*. Collateral is an asset pledged to the lender until such time as the loan is satisfied. In an automobile loan, the lender retains title to the vehicle and makes sure that you've made a sufficiently large down payment so that the bank can repossess the car, sell it, and fully reimburse itself from the proceeds if you fail to make timely loan payments. Business loans are similar. The lender wants to see assets that, in the case of business failure, can be sold off to satisfy the loan. Those assets might be current assets such as cash, inventory, and accounts receivable; they might also be fixed assets such as vehicles, buildings, and equipment.

Financing Growth

A startling number of small businesses fail or are bought out by new owners. Of those that remain, most stay small. The corner liquor store, the local auto dealer, the money management firm across the street from your office—even if they survive and prosper, most of these enterprises will not grow substantially larger. If profits grow, most of that growth will be channeled into the individual owners' bank accounts. These people are not aiming to build empires; they're simply trying to create and sustain good livelihoods.

But every so often, the owner attempts to build on his or her initial success. A liquor-store owner opens a store in an adjacent community. A successful auto dealer takes on a franchise for another line of vehicles and opens a showroom on the other side of town. The successful money management firm hires additional professionals in financial and estate planning to expand its services and cast its net to draw in a wider population of clients.

Some cases of business growth are legendary in their proportions. For example, the late Dave Thomas, creator of Wendy's, followed the example set by Harlan Sanders (Kentucky Fried Chicken) and Ray Kroc (McDonald's) and expanded his fast-food restaurant chain throughout North America. Michael Dell expanded his made-to-order computer business from a one-room operation to the top of the PC heap, outpacing industry giants such as Hewlett-Packard, IBM, and Compaq. And eBay, the online auction juggernaut, quickly outgrew its founder's apartment and within the space of seven years was handling billions of dollars' worth of transactions. In each of these cases, financing greased the wheels of growth. And this financing obviously didn't come from the savings accounts of the entrepreneurs, their friends, or their families.

Financing Growth at eBay

The auction giant eBay stands as perhaps the most successful company of the dot-com explosion. It grew from a home-based hobby-business to a sizable corporation in a dizzyingly short time. The company's brief history underscores the role played by different forms of financing.

The firm was started in 1995 by Pierre Omidyar, a young man with experience in software development and online commerce. Omidyar set up his business on a free Web site provided by his Internet service. His only business assets at the time were a filing cabinet, an old school desk, and a laptop computer. His hobby-business grew quickly, which forced him to buy his own server, hire someone to handle billings and the checks that came in the mail, and eventually move the operation from his apartment to a small office. Omidyar and his business partner, Jeff Skoll, soon began paying themselves annual salaries of $25,000.[1]

This early period of growth was essentially self-financed: The cash coming in the mail from transaction fees was sufficient to cover the business's expenses and investments. But a period of explosive growth was right around the corner. By the end of December 2000, this little online company grew from serving a handful of auction devotees to 22 million registered users. By then it offered more than eight thousand product categories; on any given day, the company listed more than 6 million items for sale in an auction-style format and another 8 million items in a fixed-price format. A sizable infrastructure of office space, customer support, proprietary software, information systems, and equipment was required to host a business with this volume and keep it churning. The expanding firm used internally developed systems to operate its auction service and to process transactions, including billing and collections. Those systems had to be continually improved and expanded as the pace of transactions on the site increased.

To keep the wheels of growth turning, eBay spent liberally on new site features and categories. The company incurred $4.6 million in product development expenses in 1998, $24.8 million in 1999, and $55.9 million in 2000. It spent even larger sums on marketing, brand development, and acquisitions, with an eye toward broadening its services and extending its reach to other parts of the world.

Before long, eBay had expanded its balance-sheet assets dramatically. Here are a few highlights (rounded to millions) from the company's 10-K report for the fiscal year ending December 31, 2000:

Cash and cash equivalents: $202 million

Short-term investments: $354 million

Long-term investments: $218 million

Total assets: $1,182 million

With total assets of nearly $1.2 billion, eBay was light-years away from Pierre Omidyar's apartment office.

On the other side of the ledger are the following items from eBay's same 2000 balance sheet:

Current liabilities and long-term debt: $169 million

Total stockholders' equity: $1,014 million

Current and long-term liabilities in this case are amazingly small relative to the magnitude of eBay's assets. Recall the balance-sheet equation:

Assets = Liabilities + Stockholders' Equity

Using this equation, you can see that in eBay's case, a large percentage of its assets are claimed by shareholders—in fact, 86 percent.

By digging a bit deeper, we find that eBay's remarkable growth was principally financed in two ways: first, by cash flows from operations (self-financing) and, second, by external financing. Let's examine these sources individually, since they're so important to growing companies.

eBay's Cash Flows from Operations

As described in chapter 2, a cash flow statement totals the cash flow entering and leaving the enterprise as a result of operations, investments, and financing activities. Table 7-1 shows the highlights from eBay's cash flow statement for the years 1998 through 2000.

The first row in the table—net cash provided by operating activities—shows that the company ran some portion of its opera-

TABLE 7-1

eBay's Cash Flow, 1998 Through 2000 (in Thousands of Dollars)

	2000	1999	1998
Net cash provided by operating activities	100,148	62,852	6,041
Net cash used in investing activities	(206,054)	(603,363)	(53,024)
Net cash provided by financing activities	85,978	725,027	72,159
Net increase (decrease) in cash and cash equivalents	(19,928)	184,516	25,176
Cash and cash equivalents at end of year (after accounting for beginning balance)	201,873	221,801	37,285

Source: eBay 10-K report, 2000.

tions and paid people's salaries and company taxes and other bills (operating activities) from operating cash flow. What's more, the level of positive cash flow from operations grew substantially from year to year, helping to fund growth. Thus, an important portion of eBay's asset growth was financed internally, from its successful and profitable operations. Instead of returning even a cent of that cash to shareholders in the form of dividends, eBay plowed everything back into the business. That is typical of fast-growing firms.

eBay's External Financing

Internally generated cash was sufficient to finance eBay's operations in the early days, but not nearly sufficient to fund the firm's meteoric growth. Large as they were, eBay's cash flows from operations paled in comparison to the cash outflows caused by investments during the same period. In the best of those years (2000), cash flow from operations covered slightly less than half of the investment outflow. To make up the difference, the company had to resort to external financing (depicted in the line labeled "Net cash provided by financing activities").

The organization's financial statements (too voluminous to show here) indicate that almost all of eBay's external financing took the form of stockholders' capital—that is, the company and its subsidiaries raised cash by selling shares (almost all common shares) to investors. The first of these was a $5 million private placement with Benchmark Capital, a Silicon Valley venture capital firm. In return for its cash, Benchmark received a 22 percent equity interest in eBay. The next big capital-raising event in eBay's history came with its 1998 *initial public offering* (IPO). As the name clearly states, an IPO is a corporation's first offering of its shares to the public. An IPO is a major milestone in a corporation's life cycle: It marks the company's transition from a private to a public enterprise. As we'll see in a later chapter, this new status opens up much larger opportunities to raise equity capital. The universe of potential capital contributors expands from the small and clubby circle of private investors to a much broader group of individual investors, mutual funds, and retirement funds. But going public isn't a picnic! It subjects the company to far greater regulation and scrutiny. Suddenly (in the United States), the company must file regular, periodic reports with the Securities and Exchange Commission. And the CEO and CFO must spend substantial time making presentations to institutional investors and securities analysts.

An IPO is also an opportunity for the existing investors, including the venture capitalists and shareholding employees, to cash in some or all of their shares—turning paper certificates into real money. eBay's Omidyar, for example, held over 44 million shares of his company's common stock before its IPO. In the wake of the IPO and the stock price run-up in the months that followed, Omidyar became a billionaire four times over. The value of Benchmark's shares rose to the point that it could claim a 49,000 percent return on its investment—one for the record books!

eBay's financial managers and investment bankers used the company's high stock price and public appetite for shares to float another common stock issue in 1999. This one netted the company more than $700 million, most of which was used in the company's campaign of expansion.

Other Forms of External Financing

Thus far in this chapter, we've described supplier trade credit, bank loans, and common stock issues as important forms of external financing. Today's corporations also use a few other important forms of financing, which will be described in the following paragraphs.

Commercial Paper

Large corporations with high credit ratings often use the sale of commercial paper to finance their short-term requirements. They use it as a lower-cost alternative to short-term bank borrowing. *Commercial paper* is a short-term debt security, generally reaching maturity in 2 to 270 days. Most paper is sold at a discount to its face value and is redeemable at face value on maturity. The difference between the discounted sale price and the face value represents interest to the purchaser of the paper. Investors with temporary cash surpluses are the usual purchasers of commercial paper; for them it is a reasonably safe way to obtain a return on their idle cash.

Bonds

A *bond* is also a debt security (an IOU), usually issued with a fixed interest rate and a stated maturity date. The bond issuer has a contractual obligation to make periodic interest payments and to redeem the bond at its face value on maturity. Bonds may have short-, intermediate-, or long-term maturities (e.g., from one to thirty years). Generally, bonds pay a fixed interest rate on a semiannual basis. Chapter 8 covers bonds in greater detail.

Preferred Stock

This type of equity security is similar to a bond in that it pays a stated dividend to the shareholder each year, and once the shares begin trading in the secondary market, then the share prices, like bonds, fluctuate with changes in market interest rates and the creditworthiness of the issuer. Also like bonds, preferred stock is used by some corporations as an external form of equity financing. You'll learn more about preferred stock in chapter 8.

The Matching of Assets and Financing

One of the principles of financing—whether you're using it to start a company, maintain its operations, or advance its growth—is to make a proper match between the assets and their associated forms of financing. The general principle is to finance current (i.e., short-term) assets with short-term financing, and long-term assets with long-term or permanent financing.

The use of supplier trade credit for financing inventory, as described earlier in this chapter, is an example of matching short-term assets with short-term financing. The shoe-store owner matched sixty-day financing against an asset that she believed would be sold within that period. Likewise, eBay financed its sizable infrastructure of office space, customer support, proprietary software, information systems, and equipment with capital supplied by shareholders—a permanent form of financing. We could identify countless other enterprises that follow this sensible principle. When states and municipalities build bridges, hockey stadiums, water treatment plants, and so forth, they typically finance these long-lasting projects with twenty- to thirty-year bonds—financing vehicles whose maturities roughly match the productive life of the assets.

To understand why this principle is so important, consider first what might happen if you tried to finance the purchase of your new home (a long-term asset) with an 8 percent, nonamortizing $200,000 loan that came due in just three years. Under the terms of the loan, you'd pay $16,000 in annual interest, and then be obligated to repay the $200,000 at the end of the third year. This would be feasible *if* you could negotiate another loan at the end of three years to replace the one that's due, and *if* interest rates were still affordable. But that's two big *ifs*. Money might become so tight that you could not locate a new lender when you needed one, or the lender you did find might want 10 or 12 percent. In either case, foreclosure would be likely. You couldn't operate with such a situation, and neither can a business enterprise.

The opposite mismatch situation—borrowing long to finance a short-term asset—is just as bad. Some people take out second mortgages on their homes to finance a dream vacation. Such are the temptations of home equity loans. The vacation will soon be over, but the payments will go on and on. In business, we expect that the assets we acquire with borrowed money will produce incremental revenues (or cost savings) at rates and over periods more than sufficient to pay off their financing costs. The same can be said for owners' capital.

A Life-Cycle View of Financing

Is the company you work for, or the one you've founded, still in the start-up phase? Is it a mature enterprise that has already exploited most of its growth potential? Or is it somewhere between these two extremes? It can be useful to stand back and observe the theoretical life cycle of business inception, growth, and maturity. Doing so helps you understand how and when different forms of financing—and different financing institutions—come into play. We've already observed some of the various phases of business growth in our descriptions of our fictional firm Parker & Smith, as well as our analyses of eBay, a strong, real-life, Internet-based business. On the following pages, we consider a more general case, divided arbitrarily into four phases: Start-up, Growth 1, Growth 2, and Maturity (figure 7-1).

FIGURE 7-1

A Life-Cycle View of Financing

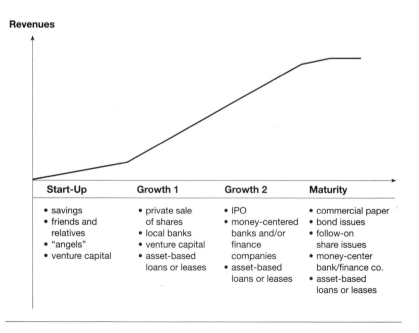

Start-Up	Growth 1	Growth 2	Maturity

• savings
• friends and
  relatives
• "angels"
• venture capital
	• private sale
	  of shares
	• local banks
	• venture capital
	• asset-based
	  loans or leases
		• IPO
		• money-centered
		  banks and/or
		  finance
		  companies
		• asset-based
		  loans or leases
			• commercial paper
			• bond issues
			• follow-on
			  share issues
			• money-center
			  bank/finance co.
			• asset-based
			  loans or leases

Start-Up

Parker & Smith is a fairly typical entrepreneurial business start-up. The founder-manager in this phase must scratch around for the capital needed to acquire assets and to finance operations. This capital generally comes from personal savings, loans or equity from friends and relatives, and, in some instances, local "angels"—businesspeople who recognize an opportunity and want to participate as either lenders or minority owners. A local bank may also extend some funds if there is adequate collateral. Although many companies in this phase are incorporated, their shares are usually held by only a handful of individuals, and those shares have no real market.

Growth 1

During the Growth 1 phase, the business expands its sales and develops a base of reliable customers. As a result, more capital is typically required. Some capital, as we've seen in eBay's case, is generated through reinvested profits from operations. But more is needed if growth is strong. By having proven its credibility as a business operation, the enterprise can generally tap external capital more easily than it could previously.

Debt capital in this phase often comes from local banks, whereas equity capital is gathered through the private sale of shares to local investors. The business is still too small to become a public company. As a result, it cannot tap broader equity markets. If the company is in a hot growth industry, or if it is close to producing a breakthrough with some proprietary, game-changing product, it many gain the attention of a venture capitalist.

Growth 2

Most companies never get beyond the first phase of growth. But those that do have access to a broader spectrum of financing opportunities—in particular, public stock and bond markets. In a sense this second phase of growth is experienced by companies that have

About Venture Capitalists

A venture capitalist (VC) or a VC firm is a high-risk investor seeking an equity position in a start-up or an early-growth company with high potential. In return for capital, the VC typically takes a significant percentage of ownership of the business and a position on its board. VCs are much engaged in the strategic management of their fledgling companies and are often instrumental in connecting them with suppliers and potential business allies. In many cases, venture capitalists recruit the technical and managerial personnel these entrepreneurial companies need to succeed.

VCs are not content with the 15 to 20 percent annual returns that would thrill most common stock investors. Knowing that they are bound to strike out on many of their deals, they seek a huge return on every venture. Generally, VCs seek out small firms with the potential to return ten times their risk capital within five years. Most aim to harvest their investments during the IPO or follow-on issues of company share, and move on to the next opportunity.

In the lore of American venture capitalism, "General" Georges Doriot, a Harvard Business School professor, is fondly remembered. Doriot organized the first VC fund, American Research & Development (ARD), in the late 1940s to benefit from the many small, high-tech companies being incubated in the research laboratories of Harvard and Massachusetts Institute of Technology (MIT). His biggest score was with Digital Equipment Corporation (DEC), a company founded by Kenneth Olsen, a young, MIT-trained engineer. Sensing an opportunity, Doriot invested $70,000 in DEC in 1957. By 1971, when Doriot cashed in, that investment had grown to $355 million.

proven their revenue-generating abilities to traditional financing sources. The prospect of further growth is a powerful lure to equity investors, who hope to buy shares while the shares are still cheap and unrecognized—and hang on for a profitable ride.

Local banks are also important sources of external financing at this stage. The business now has a confidence-inspiring record of producing revenues and paying its bills. And it has assets that it can pledge as collateral. The company may also have grown so much that it has outgrown the lending capacity of its local bank, in which case it can move upstream to a large money-center bank.

The major moment in the Growth 2 phase is the IPO, which we described in the preceding eBay example. IPOs are managed by one or more investment banking firms selected by the issuing company. The investment bankers help the issuing company through the strict regulatory requirements of issuing shares to the public. More important, the investment bank and its syndicate of broker-dealers (stockbrokers) provide direct access to millions of potential investors: individual investors, mutual funds, pension funds, and private money managers. Chapter 8 offers more information on investment bankers.

Distributing shares through an IPO is expensive, involving substantial fees paid to accountants and lawyers and a big cut to the investment bank and its syndicate. But a successful IPO is the financial equivalent of a blood transfusion. Suddenly, the company's coffers are flush with cash that it can use to pay off loans, buy back preferred stocks it might have issued and now regrets, and finance its next round of growth.

Maturity

Trees do not grow to the skies. Nor do growth companies continue growing forever. Eventually, growth tapers off for one or more reasons:

- Success and profitability draw competitors into the market.

- Demand for the product or service is largely satisfied (market saturation).

- Technology changes.

- The company loses ambition, agility, or innovation as it grows larger and older.

Whatever the cause, few companies sustain high growth rates for more than a decade. This does not mean that growth necessarily stops and that continued financing is not needed. Even saturated markets for mature products such as automobiles continue to expand incrementally as the population increases and as people in undeveloped countries become more affluent and demand them. And for a $1 billion enterprise, even a 3 percent growth in revenues may require additional financing. Then, too, mature companies are often involved in mergers, acquisitions, restructuring, or other activities, all of which have important financing implications.

Assuming that the mature company is creditworthy, it has many options for additional external financing. For short-term needs, it can issue commercial paper, tap its bank lines of credit, or negotiate a term loan with a bank or other financial institutions, such as insurance companies and pension funds. The mature company can use its existing assets and cash flow as collateral to lower the cost of loans. Alternatively, the company can obtain significant funds through the sale-and-leaseback arrangements described in chapter 5.

The healthy, mature company also enjoys access to public capital markets for debt (bonds) and equity capital (shares). Here, timing is all-important. The company naturally wants to sell its bonds when interest rates are low and sell its shares when its share price is high.

Summing Up

This chapter has described how operations and growth are typically financed at different phases in the life cycle of business enterprises. In the start-up phase, companies generally depend on the following sources for financing:

- Personal savings and lines of credit

- Loans from friends and relatives

- Thirty- to sixty-day trade credit from suppliers

- Loans from commercial banks

- Venture capitalists (usually reserved for high-profile start-ups)

Companies that are experiencing growth face the challenge of finding the financing to support it. Growing companies generally rely on some combination of internally generated funds and external financing from the sale of equity (shares) or the sale of debt (commercial paper, bonds, or preferred stock). We have not discussed the roles played by the money and capital markets, which form the focus of chapter 8.

Leveraging Chapter Insights: Critical Questions

- How has the company you work for or the one you've founded financed its growth? What financing strategies might your firm use in the future?

- What growth stage is your company currently in? How does your company plan to move on to the next stage, if it has not yet reached maturity?

- Is your company publicly owned? If not, does it plan to issue an IPO? If it has already gone public, when did it do so, and what was the outcome?

CHAPTER EIGHT

Money and Capital Markets

Another Option for Funding Growth

Key Topics Covered in This Chapter

- *Money markets*

- *Capital markets—both primary and secondary*

- *Common and preferred stocks*

- *Bonds*

CHAPTER 7 described how business assets are financed through a combination of internally generated cash flow, short-term liabilities and debt, long-term debt, retained earnings, and the capital of owners. This chapter focuses on the markets through which growing companies obtain nonbank debt financing and equity capital—specifically, the money and capital markets. In the course of this discussion, you'll learn how securities are issued in collaboration with investment bankers. You'll also learn the basics of the capital market securities—stocks and various forms of debt—that many companies use to raise funds. Again, if you work for a large company, you probably won't be involved in your firm's capital investment activities. But if you've started an HR consulting or services firm, you may well benefit from understanding these resources for funding the growth of your business.

Money and capital markets (collectively, financial markets) were once local or national in scope. Today they span the globe, linking users and suppliers of capital with the speed of electronic trading. Those links channel capital to what appear to be its highest uses. Thus, a Chicago-area manufacturer with plans for a new factory but insufficient funds may be linked through the capital markets with a German investor who wants to obtain a higher return on idle capital. Likewise, a mutual-fund portfolio manager in Boston can channel some of her cash through the same capital market to a promising enterprise in Taiwan.

Access to money and capital markets is to contemporary economies what access to food and water is to a living organism— a source of vitality, regeneration, and growth. This role was demonstrated in the decline and eventual collapse of the economy of the Soviet bloc in the waning years of the twentieth century. Western economies and their trading partners in the Far East benefited immensely from open and efficient financial markets. Thanks to those markets, cash and long-term capital were shifted away from stagnating enterprises and industries toward others with better technologies, superior management, and brighter futures. The Soviet bloc, meanwhile, had no such mechanism for moving its own cash and capital and stood outside the network of Western finance. In its stead, Soviet-bloc economies depended on cronyism and the dubious judgment of politicians and state bureaucrats to allocate capital. The result? These economies used scarce capital to prop up failing industries—and eventually collapsed.

Money Markets

When corporations need short-term financing to get through seasonal business cycles or for other purposes, they often turn to the *money market*. Marcia Stigum and Frank Fabozzi have developed a good definition of the money market: "a market in which large borrowers raise short-term money by selling various debt instruments; that is, it is a 'new issues' market for short-term securities. The money market is also a secondary market in which such securities, once issued, are actively traded."[1]

Money markets, then, are the institutions and trading channels through which short-term debt instruments are originated and distributed. In the United States, those instruments include the following:

- **Certificates of deposit:** time deposits with a specified maturity and interest rate, issued by banks and marketable through a secondary market of brokers

- **Commercial paper:** unsecured IOUs sold at discounts to face value

- **U.S. Treasury bills (T-bills):** negotiable debt securities with maturities of one year or less; sold at discounts to face value

- **Discounted notes:** notes issued by the Federal Home Loan Bank and other government agencies

These financial instruments have two things in common: They are highly liquid (i.e., they can be easily sold to other investors for cash), and they represent very low risk credit to investors. A corporation like our fictional Parker & Smith, which may have more cash than it needs for a month or more, can safely invest in these instruments with the expectation that it will get its money back *plus* receive a decent amount of interest. If Parker & Smith determines that it cannot hold these instruments until their maturity, then the company's treasurer can sell them in the secondary market. On the other side of the same transaction, some other entity (the U.S. Treasury, another government agency, or a public corporation) is using the money market to sell its short-term IOUs with the goal of obtaining capital.

Where is the money market located? In truth, the money market is nowhere in particular. It is a worldwide network of dealers—mostly money-center banks located in major Western financial centers—that buy and sell for their own accounts. The global span of the market has the effect of establishing fairly uniform worldwide rates for short-term debt. Thus, a corporation that wants to sell its commercial paper for the lowest possible interest rate can sometimes bypass high local rates and sell its paper where rates for the same maturity and risk factors are lower. The place may be on the other side of the country or the other side of the globe. Any corporation or individual can invest in money-market instruments. But the reverse is not the case. Only the largest, most creditworthy corporations can sell their paper through the money market. Entities such as Parker & Smith are too small to be issuers.

Capital Markets

The term *capital markets* describes the markets in which long-term debt instruments (bonds) and equity securities (shares of stock)—including private placements—are issued and traded. Like the money market, capital markets include primary and secondary components. The primary market consists of securities dealers and financial institutions that issue newly minted securities to the investing public. The secondary market includes both these primary market dealers plus a network of over-the-counter dealers (e.g., NASDAQ) and organized securities exchanges such as the New York Stock Exchange and Tokyo Stock Exchange. The secondary market provides opportunities for the buying and selling of securities after their initial issuance.

The Primary Market: eBay Revisited

To understand how capital markets work, let's return to our earlier discussion of eBay, the online auction company, which first began operations in the apartment of its founder in 1995. The company was incorporated as eBay Inc. in California in May 1996. Up to this point, its growth was essentially self-financed through internal cash flows. A year later, it sold a 22 percent ownership stake to the venture capital firm Benchmark Capital in return for $5 million.

Thus far, eBay's financing had been entirely private—and outside the realm of the main capital markets. Even a subsequent sale of a series of preferred shares was privately placed to a set of well-heeled private investors.

As described in chapter 7, eBay first tapped the public capital markets for financing in September 1998 with the initial public offering of common stock. How this IPO was accomplished is both typical and instructive in the ways of the primary market for corporate shares. Like other corporations eager to tap the deep pools of equity capital, eBay enlisted the aid of an investment banking firm—in this case, Goldman Sachs.

An investment bank is not like the more familiar commercial bank. This investment institution is not in the business of taking deposits from savers and making loans. Instead, it acts as an agent and a deal maker for very substantial business entities seeking capital. In return for a tidy fee and a piece of the action, the investment bank has several roles:

- **Helping the issuing corporation get its regulatory act together:** Specifically, the investment bank helps the corporation get through the stringent regulatory hurdles that go hand in hand with issuing securities. These hurdles include the development of a prospectus—called a red herring. In its preliminary form, the prospectus must provide full disclosure about the company, its business, and its finances to potential investors.

- **Pricing the securities being offered:** When shares are being offered to the public for the first time, no one knows for certain how they should be priced. Because the shares haven't been traded back and forth by willing buyers and sellers, there is no certainty as to a market-clearing price. The capital-seeking corporation would naturally want its shares priced as high as the market will bear—doing so will maximize the cash that goes into its coffers. But investors expect a new issue to be priced at a per-share amount that represents something of a bargain compared to seasoned securities. Having expertise in this difficult pricing area, the investment bank must mediate between these disparate objectives.

- **Arranging for the distribution of shares:** The issuing corporation may have the shares, but the investment bank has access to potential purchasers for them. By putting together a syndicate of distributing broker-dealers, the investment bank assures that it can "move the merchandise" into the portfolios of pension funds, mutual funds, and individual investors. In most cases, the investment bank takes the shares off the hands of the issuing corporation at a given price, marks them up to some predetermined profitable level, and uses its own distribution channels and those of its syndicate partners to sell them to the investing public. In this sense, the investment bank underwrites the risk of selling millions of shares.

That, in a nutshell, describes the role of an investment bank in an IPO. In eBay's case, Goldman Sachs was the lead underwriter of a group of investment banks that included Bancamerica Robinson Stephens and BT Alex Brown—all major players.

In the period leading up to eBay's IPO, its CEO and CFO conducted a ten-day, twenty-one-city road show, a series of presentations to the investment community. A road show is standard procedure with equity issues; it is designed to explain the issuing company's business and generate interest in the offering.

The investment climate at that time was decidedly mixed. The Dow Jones Industrial Average was trending downward, and the NASDAQ composite index was meandering beneath the 2,000 mark. The great high-tech/dot-com boom that would send the NASDAQ composite into the 5,000 area was still over the horizon. Nevertheless, believing that the time was right, eBay and its investment bankers went forward with the offering on September 24, 1998. According to the company's 10-K, slightly more than 4 million shares were sold, netting the fledgling company more than $66 million. These funds went into the war chest that eBay management would use to finance its growth in the years ahead.

The Secondary Market

Once they are issued through a primary distribution, the shares of publicly owned corporations begin trading in what is called the secondary market. The secondary market comprises stock and bond exchanges such as the New York Stock Exchange and networks of over-the-counter securities dealers that buy and sell for their own accounts. NASDAQ is an example of such a network.

In terms of corporate finance, the issuing company receives no proceeds from transactions that take place in the secondary market. Even though there may be plenty of furious buying and selling, and even though a company's share price may skyrocket once it begins trading, none of its changing value accrues to the company. It is all exchanged between buying and selling shareholders.

This is not to say that corporations are indifferent to their share prices in the secondary trading markets. Corporate management is in fact eager to see that its share prices are high and rising. On one level, their interest is personal. Most executives and board members and many rank-and-file employees are owners of their companies' shares or hold options to purchase them; their personal fortunes rise and fall with trading prices.

At the corporate policy level, there are also substantial financing opportunities bound up with a healthy stock price. First, many corporations finance their growth-oriented acquisitions with some combination of cash and a block of their shares. For example, a corporation may purchase another company with $100 million in cash and a half-million shares of its own common shares. Thus, the higher the share price, the greater the purchasing company's buying power. Second, growing companies periodically find it necessary to return to the market for more equity capital. That is, they raise additional capital by issuing more shares to the public. eBay's recent history provides examples of both motivations.

eBay's IPO was priced at what now appears to be a bargain-basement price—roughly $8 (as adjusted for subsequent splits). Once those shares began trading over the counter, enthusiastic bidding pushed that price up dramatically. The dot-com frenzy that followed, and eBay's unique position as the only major online venture actually making a profit, did the rest. Within six months, the company's share price had multiplied roughly fifteenfold.

Fast-expanding eBay employed its high share price as a form of currency and used it to fund a spate of acquisitions. In May 1999, for example, the company made three significant acquisitions, each aimed at increasing the breadth of its core business. One was Butterfield & Butterfield, an established live auction house, which eBay acquired for approximately 1.3 million shares of eBay common stock. Kruse, Inc., a specialist in classic car auctions, was another. It too was acquired entirely with eBay common stock. So was Billpoint, a small company that had developed a billing and payment solution that permitted individuals and small merchants to accept credit cards as payment for Internet-based sales transactions. Not a penny of cash was used in these deals.

Eager to continue with its expansion, in 1999 eBay's management capitalized again on its high share price—this time in another offering of 5 million new shares. The 1999 event added more than $713 million in additional equity capital to the balance sheet. Thus, although none of the trading proceeds of secondary-market activity accrue to their listed companies, a strong stock price facilitates other forms of financing, as the eBay example illustrates.

Capital Market Securities

Now that you understand how the capital markets work, let's consider the basic types of securities that corporations issue to the investing public to raise capital for operations and expansion. Three that you should know are *common stock, preferred stock,* and *bonds.*

About Dividends

A *dividend* is a distribution of after-tax corporate earnings to shareholders. Dividends are declared by the corporation's board of directors. The board is under no contractual obligation to common shareholders to declare a dividend. Typically, the directors will choose to retain all or most after-tax earnings in the business if those funds are needed for profitable growth. Financial theorists maintain that corporate earnings should be distributed when and if the corporation's investment returns are less promising than those that individual shareholders could obtain on their own. This idea is complicated by the requirement that shareholders pay a second tax on earnings distributed as dividends.

Dividends are generally paid in cash and on a quarterly basis, but may also take the form of additional shares. Thus, an owner of one thousand shares may receive an additional ten shares in lieu of a cash dividend. In one instance, a prominent whisky producer issued its dividend in kind, sending bottles of its product to shareholders!

Common Stock

Common stock is the class you generally think of whenever stocks are discussed. Each share of common stock represents a fractional ownership interest in the corporation that issued it. Here are the notable features of common stock:

- **Voting rights:** Owners typically are entitled to vote on the selection of board members and on other matters. Some classes of common stock, however, have either no voting rights or limited voting rights.

- **Dividends:** A share of stock entitles its holders to receive dividends on a pro rata basis. Thus, if you owned 5 percent of the outstanding shares of a corporation, you'd be entitled to receive 5 percent of all dividends declared by its board of directors.

- **Residual ownership:** Common shareholders stand at the very end of the line in terms of distributions in cases of liquidation. Their interests are subordinate to the creditors and bondholders to whom the corporation is contractually bound to repay. The claims of unsecured and secured creditors, bondholders, and preferred shareholders must be settled first.

Preferred Stock

Preferred stock is a form of stock that, not unlike a bond, pays a specified dividend. Further, preferred shareholders stand in line ahead of common shareholders with respect to any payment of dividends and any distribution of assets in liquidation. This means, among other things, that the corporation cannot distribute a penny of dividends to common shareholders until it has satisfied its dividend obligation to preferred shareholders.

Despite their superior position relative to common shares, preferred stocks have several drawbacks. They generally carry limited or no voting rights. And with the exception of convertible preferreds and rare "participating preferred" shares, preferred shareholders do not benefit from the expanding fortunes of the business. Also, unlike common shares, most preferred shares are callable by the issuer—that is, the issuing corporation may redeem them at a particular price if it is to the issuer's advantage.

Preferred stock is unappealing to many capital-seeking U.S. corporate financial managers. The reason has to do with the U.S. tax code, which allows the corporation to deduct the interest it pays on debt but not on the dividends it pays to shareholders. Because of this, dividends (to both preferred and common share-holders) are paid out of after-tax earnings. Faced with this situa-tion, most CFOs would rather raise capital by selling bonds—whose interest they can deduct—than by issuing preferred shares, whose dividend outlays are nondeductible.

Bonds

A bond is a capital market debt security. The traditional bond has these features:

- A face value, usually $1,000 or multiples thereof

- A maturity date on which the issuer must repay (i.e., redeem) the bond at its face value; newly issued bonds have maturities from one to thirty years

- An annual fixed interest rate (e.g., 5 percent of the face value), usually payable at six-month intervals, either via coupons or through direct payment to the bondholder

In addition to this traditional form, financial engineering has produced dozens of variations of the bond, each designed to serve the financing needs of particular issuers and to appeal to one or more types of investor. Here are a few notable variations:

- **Zero-coupon bond:** This type of bond has a stated face value and maturity, but has no stated interest rate and makes no periodic payments. Instead, it is issued at a discount to face value, which is paid at maturity. The implied interest is the difference between the issue price and the value at maturity.

For example, if a zero-coupon bond is issued for $700 with a face value of $1,000 and five-year maturity, then the compound annual rate of return to the investor works out to 7.4 percent.

- **Convertible bond:** This type of bond is generally issued with an interest rate that is less than the market rate for "straight" bonds. The issuer can get away with this because the convertible bond contains a provision whereby the holder can convert the bond into a specified number of common shares at a specified price. Thus, the bondholder receives interest on his or her capital *and* has an opportunity to benefit from the issuer's future good fortunes. Generally, this type of bond is issued with a conversion price that is higher than the company's current stock price.

  From a corporate financing perspective, convertibles can be attractive. They bring in long-term capital at less-than-market interest rates (the payment of which is also tax-deductible). And if the company's stock price should rise significantly, then the bondholders will convert to common stock, eliminating the corporation's obligation to make interest payments and to redeem the face value of the bonds. Creditors are converted into shareholders without cost or bother. Typically, the higher stock price is a consequence of corporate growth.

- **Floating- and adjustable-rate notes:** During periods of volatile interest rates, fixed-rate interest bonds are difficult to issue. Even when their stated rates are high, investors worry that rates will go still higher, which would depress the market value of these bonds. CFOs are not keen on issuing bonds with high interest rates in any case, since doing so ties the company into high, long-term interest expenses. One solution is the floating- or adjustable-rate note, whose interest rate is pegged to a stipulated rate index and adjusted at prescribed intervals. For example, an adjustable-rate note might be issued with an interest rate of 6 percent, with a contractual arrangement that the rate will be readjusted on the first business day of each year to the current average yield on ten-year U.S. Treasury bonds plus 0.5 percent. Floating-rate notes assure investors that they will receive the current market rate of interest and that their securities will hold their value in the secondary market. What's more, these bonds assure corporate financial managers that they will incur no greater interest expense than what the interest rate climate demands.

Like equity securities, bonds have primary and secondary markets. They are issued into the primary (new-issue) market with the aid of investment banks and their distribution syndicates of broker-dealers. Pricing a bond issue, however, is less challenging than pricing an IPO of shares, since bond pricing is largely a function of three factors: (1) the creditworthiness of the issuer, (2) the prevailing market interest rate for bonds with the same credit rating and maturities, and (3) the anticipated liquidity of the bond in the secondary market.

Creditworthiness, or default risk, deserves special attention here. Debt obligations of the U.S. government are considered risk-free as to repayment, since it is believed that the government would never default on its own obligations. Corporate issuers of debt are another matter. They can—and sometimes do—default on their obligations to debt holders. In measuring creditworthiness, investors rely on the ratings assigned to different issues by a handful of commercial rating companies: Moody's, Standard & Poor's, Duff & Phelps, and Fitch Investors Service. Moody's, for example, rates debt securities with the following classification: Aaa, Aa, A, Baa, Ba, B, Caa, Ca, C. Those rated Aaa represent the highest quality, whereas the C rating is attached to debt securities with little probability of any investment value. Naturally, an issuer with a B rating will have to price new-issue bonds at a higher interest rate than will a firm with an A rating, even though the maturity and other terms of the bond are identical. Investors insist on a greater return for a greater amount of risk.

Once a new issue of bonds is issued through a primary distribution, they may begin trading in the secondary market. There, the prices are bound to fluctuate as market interest rates change, the credit ratings of particular issuers change, and as individual bonds move closer to maturity.

Summing Up

This chapter has described the money and capital markets to which corporations turn for funding:

- The money market is the financing source to which corporations turn when they need short-term debt funding. In the United States, the debt instruments originated and distributed via the money market are certificates of deposit, corporate commercial paper, U.S. T-bills, and the discounted notes of the Federal Home Loan Bank and other government agencies.

- The capital markets are those in which long-term debt (bonds) and equity securities (shares of stock) are issued and traded.

As described in the chapter, the money and capital markets are a playing field in which four very different sets of participants meet:

- Business entities—the users of capital—come to the money market to obtain short-term financing and competitive rates; they come to the capital markets for intermediate and long-term capital.

- Investment bankers act as their coaches and agents in seeking these funds.

- Institutional and individual investors approach these markets with their own goals: They seek returns on their capital commensurate with the known risks.

- Government regulators—notably, the Securities and Exchange Commission in the United States—act as referees, doing what they can to assure an even playing field characterized by full and complete disclosure.

The effective interaction of these four sets of players assures a free flow of capital to it highest uses.

Leveraging Chapter Insights: Critical Questions

- Does the company you work for or the one you've founded use the money market or capital markets to raise funding? If so, which financing sources (certificates of deposits, T-bills, stocks, or bonds) does your company use? If you're not sure, how can you find out more about this?

- In what ways might your company have links to suppliers of capital around the globe?

- If your company issues bonds, what types of bonds are they— zero coupon, convertible, floating, or adjustable rate? And what is your company's bond rating? Where would you find that information if you needed to know more?

CHAPTER NINE

Budgeting

*Forecasting Your Company's
Financial Future*

Key Topics Covered in This Chapter

- *Essential functions of budgeting*

- *Types of budgets and their purposes*

- *Creating an operating budget*

- *Creating a cash budget*

- *Applying sensitivity analysis to budgets*

- *Developing an HR department budget*

"**G**OOD GRIEF, it's budgeting time again" is a common refrain among HR and other managers. Budgeting can cause stress and conflict and can eat up lots of hours. But good budgets are worth the time and trouble. They serve as action plans that help you guide your department toward its strategic goals in ways that support your company's overall objectives. And for large and small businesses alike, a good budget can mean the difference between financial success and insolvency—or the business's inability to expand to its full potential. If you work for a large corporation, you probably must prepare yearly or more frequent budgets for your HR department. Equally important, you can help managers of other departments budget their human resources costs based on their unit's strategic goals. If you own and run an HR consulting or services firm, you're probably intimately involved in preparing a master, or company-level, budget for your business.

The budgeting process forces business owners to estimate how many of each product or service they will produce and sell, the cost of those items, the pace at which receivables will be collected, general expenses, and taxes. These figures give owners a forecast of the months or year ahead. A good budget thus helps you assess whether your business (or department, if you work for a large company) will have adequate financial resources to stay the course. In this chapter, you'll learn about the many kinds of budgets that serve very different purposes and kinds of businesses. You'll also discover guidelines for developing an HR department budget.

What Is Budgeting?

Before you go on a trip, you fill your bag with the clothes, food, and money you'll need. Budgeting is conceptually similar—planning your "trip" and ensuring that you'll have sufficient resources to arrive at your "destination" (your strategic goals). An organization plans its journey toward its strategic objectives in a similar fashion, and it prepares for the journey with an action plan called a budget. A budget can accomplish various tasks:

- Cover a short time span. For example, a start-up company develops a budget to ensure that it will have enough cash to cover operating expenses for the next month or two.

- Take a long-term perspective. For instance, a pharmaceutical firm builds a multiyear budget for developing a new product.

- Focus on the required resources for a specific project. To illustrate, if a firm has decided to launch a new Web page focusing on HR policies, then its budget will plot the costs for the project.

- Account for income as well as expenditures. For example, a retailer creates a profit plan based on an expected increase in sales.

So we know what a budget can do, but what is a *budget,* exactly? It is the translation of strategic plans into measurable quantities that express the expected resources required and anticipated returns over a certain period. A budget thus can function as an action plan. It may also present an organization's estimated future financial statements. Finally, a budget is an adaptable tool for management to use to achieve its strategic goals.

Budget Functions

Budgets perform four basic functions, each of which plays a critical part in a company's ability to achieve its strategic objectives. These functions are planning, coordinating and communicating, monitoring progress, and evaluating performance. Let's examine each of these more closely.

Planning

Planning ensures that the organization will have the resources available to achieve its goals. Planning consists of three steps:

1. **Choosing goals:** The goals could be as comprehensive as the strategic mission of the organization. For example, as a manager at an Internet service provider (ISP), you might define your goal as "being the most efficient provider of Internet services for our valued customers." Or, as the owner of an HR consulting firm, your goal could be specific and very focused: to increase revenues by 10 percent during the next quarter.

2. **Reviewing options and predicting results:** Once you've determined your goals, the next step is to look at the options available for attaining those goals and predict each option's most likely outcomes. For example, if your goal as a manager at an ISP is to become the most efficient provider of Internet services, then you could opt to maintain state-of-the-art equipment at all times, train the most skilled repair teams in the field, or concentrate on providing the most timely customer service. Or, as the owner of an HR consulting firm seeking a 10 percent increase in revenues, you could consider raising fees, expanding your marketing program, or reducing business-development costs. Thus, planning includes predicting the costs and benefits of each option.

3. **Deciding on options:** After analyzing the potential costs and benefits of each option, decide how to attain your desired goals. Choosing which options to implement establishes the direction your unit or company will take. The budget reflects those decisions. As a manager at an ISP, for example, you may decide to focus on maintaining state-of-the-art equipment to provide the most efficient service for your customers. Or, as

manager of an HR consulting company, you could decide that raising fees would most effectively bring in the specified increase in revenues.

Coordinating and Communicating

Coordination is the act of gathering the pieces together—the individual unit budgets or division budgets—and balancing and combining them to achieve the master budget that expresses the organization's overall financial objectives and strategic goals. In many companies, this is quite a feat!

A master budget compiles the individual budgets from the functional areas of human resources, R&D, design, production, marketing, distribution, and customer service into one unit budget. Then the budgets from individual divisions, product lines, and subsidiaries are coordinated and integrated into a larger, cohesive result. Much like a composer who weaves the music from many different instruments together to create a symphony, the master budget brings all the pieces together to achieve the organization's overall strategic plan and company mission. We'll consider the master budget in more detail later in this chapter.

To achieve this end, communication is essential. Upper management needs to communicate the company's strategic objectives to all levels of the organization, and the individual planners need to communicate their particular needs, assumptions, expectations, and goals to those evaluating the departmental and functional budget pieces.

Additionally, the different groups within the company must always listen to one another. If one division is striving to achieve certain sales goals, then HR needs that information to determine appropriate staffing. In addition, production must have that same information to prepare for increased production capacity. If the company is introducing a new product, then the marketing department must be informed early in the planning process. The department will have to include in its budget the marketing efforts for the new product.

Monitoring Progress

Once the plan has been set in motion, the budget becomes a tool that managers can use to periodically monitor progress. They assess progress by comparing the actual results of their decisions and actions with the budgeted results. This feedback, or monitoring and evaluation of progress, in turn allows for timely corrective action. If, on the one hand, the interim evaluation shows that the organization is right on target, with actual results matching the budget's expected results, then there's no need to adjust the action plan. However, if actual results differ from expected results, then you take corrective action. For example, suppose your company's goal is to increase revenues 10 percent by boosting the number of consulting engagements. But in the next six months, you find that the number of engagements is actually dropping because of an overall economic downturn. In this case, you might take corrective action by trying new marketing approaches.

The difference between the actual results and the results expected by the budget is called a *variance*. A variance can be favorable (the actual results are better than expected) or unfavorable (actual results are worse than expected).

For example, after the first six months of the new year, you evaluate how your HR consulting company's engagements are proceeding (table 9-1). Overall, the number of new consulting

TABLE 9-1

Performance Report for June

	NUMBER OF CONSULTING ENGAGEMENTS		
	Actual Results	Budgeted Number	Variance
Executive searches	25	20	+5; favorable
Reference checks	15	20	−5; unfavorable
Outplacement services	5	15	−10; unfavorable
Total	45	55	−10; unfavorable

Source: HMM Budgeting.

engagements is lower than expected, but you observe that there is a favorable variance for executive-search services. The biggest concern you have is the higher, unfavorable variance for the outplacement services. This is where you would concentrate your corrective action, perhaps by developing new marketing approaches specifically aimed at increasing this aspect of your business. Thus, variance analysis can help you identify a problem early in the budget cycle and take the appropriate action.

Types of Budgets

The notion of the traditional budget has come under increasing criticism from those who believe that it no longer serves the needs of modern organizations. Critics complain that budgets are timed incorrectly (too long or too short); rely on inappropriate measures; and are either too simplistic (or too complex), too rigid in a changing business environment, or too unchallenging (that is, the bar is deliberately set so that managers can hit their targets and collect their bonuses). Many of the budgets described in this chapter were developed to address some of these issues. But first, let's consider different types of budgets.

Short-Term Versus Long-Term Budgets

Most budgets cover a one-year time span. But the period covered by a budget may vary according to the purpose of the budget, particularly as your company defines value creation. If an organization is concerned about the profitability of a product over its expected five-year life, then a five-year budget may be appropriate. If, on the other hand, a company is living hand-to-mouth, as some start-ups do, then a month-by-month budget that focuses on immediate cash flow might be more useful.

The length of the budget period may also depend on the type of business. A pharmaceutical company, for instance, is a relatively stable business with a long-term planning horizon; here you'd expect to see a longer-term budget period. But a dot-com start-up in the volatile Internet universe would likely stipulate a much shorter time frame for its budgeting process.

Fixed Versus Rolling Budgets

A *fixed budget* covers a specific time frame—usually one fiscal year. At the end of the year, managers prepare a new budget for the following year. You might review a fixed budget at regular intervals—perhaps quarterly—so that you can make adjustments and corrections if needed, but the basic budget remains the same throughout the period.

In an effort to address the problems of timeliness and rigidity in a fixed budget, some firms—particularly those in rapid-change industries—have adopted a *rolling budget*. A rolling budget is a plan that is continually updated so that the time frame remains stable while the actual period covered by the budget changes. For example, as each month passes, the one-year rolling budget is extended by one month, so that there is always a one-year budget in place. The advantage of a rolling budget is that managers have to rethink the process and make changes each month or each period. The payoff? A more accurate, up-to-date budget incorporating the most current information.

But rolling budgets carry a disadvantage as well. Specifically, the planning process can become quite time-consuming. Moreover, if a company reviews its budget on a regular basis (say, every quarter for a one-year budget), analyzes significant variances, and takes whatever corrective action is necessary, then the fixed budget isn't as rigid as it seems.

Incremental Versus Zero-Based Budgeting

Incremental budgeting extrapolates from historical figures. Managers look at the previous period's budgeted and actual results as well as expectations for the future in determining the budget for the next period. For example, an HR department's budget would be based on the actual costs from the previous period but with increases for

the planned installation of new technology. The advantage of incremental budgeting is that history, experience, and future expectations are included in the development of the budget.

A disadvantage often cited by critics of the incremental budget
is that managers may simply use the past period's figures as a base
and increase them by a set percentage for the following budget
cycle rather than taking the time to evaluate the realities of the
current and future marketplace. Managers can also develop a use-
it-or-lose-it point of view: They feel they must use all the budgeted
expenditures by the end of the period so that the following period's
budget will not be reduced by the amount that would have been
saved.

Zero-based budgeting describes a method that begins each new
budgeting cycle from a zero base, or from the ground up, as though
the budget were being prepared for the first time. Each budget
cycle starts with a critical review of every assumption and proposed expenditure. The advantage of zero-based budgeting is that
it requires managers to perform a much more in-depth analysis of
each line item—considering objectives, exploring alternatives, and
justifying their requests. The disadvantage of zero-based budgeting is that although it is more analytic and thorough, the development of the budget can be extremely time-consuming, so much so
that the process may even interfere with actuating that budget.
Planning needs to precede, but never overwhelm, action.

Kaizen Budgeting

Kaizen is a Japanese term that stands for continuous improvement.
Kaizen budgeting attempts to incorporate continuous improvement
into the budgeting process. Cost reduction is built into the budget
on an incremental basis so that managers continually try to reduce
these costs over time. If the budgeted cost reductions are not
achieved, then extra attention is given to that operating area. For
example, a manufacturing plant may budget a continuous reduction in the cost of components, as shown below, putting pressure on
suppliers to find further cost reductions.

January–February $100.00
February–March $99.50
March–April $99.00

This type of incremental budgeting is difficult to maintain because the rate of budgeted cost reduction declines over time, making it more difficult to achieve improvements after the "easy" changes have been achieved.

The Master Budget

The *master budget* is the heart and soul of a company's financial planning and strategizing effort. It brings all the pieces together, incorporating the operating budget and the financial budget of an organization into one comprehensive picture. In other words, the master budget summarizes all the individual financial projections within an organization for a given period.

In a typical for-profit organization, the *operating budget* consists of the budgets from functional areas—such as human resources, R&D, design, production, marketing, distribution, and customer service—and provides the budgeted income statement. The *financial budget* includes the capital budget, the cash budget, the budgeted balance sheet, and the budgeted cash flows. The master budget must integrate both the operating budget and the financial budget through an iterative process during which information flows back and forth from each element of the master budget (figure 9-1).

Master budgeting goes hand-in-hand with strategic planning at the highest level. Using the organization's strategic goals as its foundation, the budget-building process is both chronological and iterative, moving back and forth, testing assumptions and options.

Before preparing a master budget, senior managers must ask three important questions:

1. Do the tactical plans under consideration support the company's larger and longer-term strategic goals?

FIGURE 9-1

Master Budget Flowchart

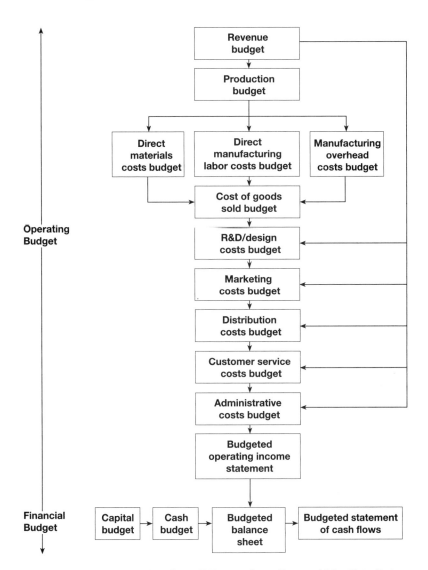

Source: HMM Budgeting. Adapted from Charles T. Horngren, George Foster, and Srikant Datar, *Cost Accounting* (New York: Prentice-Hall, 2000).

Tips for Developing Budget Assumptions

- **Use historical data as a starting point.** Even when times are changing quickly, information about past performance can establish a base from which to begin.

- **Trust your own experience.** Make educated guesses where necessary about what is likely to happen in the future.

- **Listen to your intuition.** Even though you can't verify those gut feelings, you can take them into account.

- **Conduct due diligence.** Seek out the information you need. This may involve doing research, reading trade journals, collecting industry statistics, and searching for information on the Internet.

- **Talk with and listen to knowledgeable people.** Discuss your ideas with team members, colleagues, mentors. Seek out industry participants, suppliers, concerned community leaders, and experts in the field. Engage in discussions with competitors.

- **Learn when to take risks and when to be conservative.** In a volatile market, conservative assumptions will be the safest.

- **Test your assumptions.** If possible, try out your assumptions in small experiments before you accept them.

2. Does the organization have, or have access to, the required resources—that is, the cash—to fund the activities throughout the immediate budget period?

3. Will the organization create enough value to attract adequate future resources—profit, loans, investors, etc.—to achieve its longer-term goals?

Developing Assumptions

The first step in developing a budget is establishing a set of assumptions about the future. The assumptions that managers make will be directly affected by the answers to questions such as these:

- What are sales and marketing's expectations for unit sales and revenues from new and existing products?

- Are supplier prices anticipated to rise or fall?

- What will be the cost of the company's health-care plan for the coming year?

- If the unemployment rate is expected to decline, will the company need to raise salaries to ensure an adequate work force in a tight labor market?

- What will competitors do to gain market share?

Base your assumptions on the sources that have the best information. For example, top management has a clear view of the strategic goals, and the finance group has records of past financial performance and future economic trends. The sales representatives can provide the best information about sales prospects. Likewise, the purchasing department has the latest information about suppliers and price trends. The HR group has information on shifts in the labor market—such as a leveling off of college graduates in specific fields, ethnic diversity in workforces, demographic trends (including the aging of workforces), and increases or decreases in the number of unemployed people—and can form assumptions about these shifts' impact on labor costs. Developing assumptions is a companywide endeavor in which communication and coordination play a key role.

Preparing the Operating Budget

An *operating budget* is nothing more than an agreed-upon pact between top management and other members of the management

Labor Market Trends

A recent study revealed several labor market trends important for HR professionals to consider while developing budget assumptions. Here are some examples:

- HR professionals will need to tailor workplace policies—such as flextime, sabbaticals, and cultural and technological training—to fit the needs of an increasingly diverse workforce.

- Geopolitical tensions mean that HR departments will need to orchestrate workplace security measures—such as employee screening and monitoring, as well as disaster planning.

- HR professionals will need training in a host of new HR technology products—such as intranets, self-service HR vehicles, Internet recruiting, and cyber-security.

- The labor pool from which companies can draw will span countries and continents—suggesting the need to balance differentiated pay scales and benefits levels and restructure recruiting practices.

- Certain costs—such as health-care benefits—are spiraling, and employees are demanding more coverage.

- More and more baby boomers express interest in working at least part-time during their retirement years.

- The U.S. foreign-born population is rising, and its members tend to live concentrated in cities.

- Women are making their presence felt across many traditionally male-dominated jobs.

- More employees are waiting longer to start families—which can increase the demand for costly fertility treatments and result in more women leaving the workforce after giving birth.

SOURCE: Dave Patel, "SHRM Workplace Forecast: A Strategic Outlook, 2002–2003," SHRM Research, July 2002.

team. It is a target, not a forecast. It specifies revenues and costs for the coming period in a statement that resembles the income statement first described in chapter 2. The essential difference is that we are building the statement from expected versus actual quantities. In a nutshell, the operating budget is structured as follows:

Revenues – (Cost of Goods Sold + Sales,
General, and Administrative Costs) = Operating Income

We have divided the operating budget process into five simple steps.

STEP 1: CALCULATE YOUR EXPECTED REVENUES As the first step in preparing an operating budget, managers must apply some assumptions to forecast revenue growth (or decline). For our hypothetical for-profit company, Parker & Smith, the managers of the Executive Furnishings Division translate their assumptions about revenue growth based on past performance and future expectations of sales for their products during the fiscal year (table 9-2).

If they take an incremental-budgeting approach, the managers will use the prior year's actual sales of $1,228,100 as the base for developing their projections for the next year. If, on the other hand, they follow the zero-based budgeting method, they will make their sales projections for each model from the ground up, using economic forecasts, predicted consumer behavior, and other information. These will take into account recent experience with customer behavior, economic forecasts, and other information.

Establishing projected revenue figures can create internal tensions. If managers are evaluated and rewarded on their achieving budgeted revenue targets, then they may be tempted to develop conservative revenue targets that will be easy to reach. This budgetary slack, or padding, provides a hedge for managers, making it more likely that actual revenues will be higher than budgeted revenues. With such results, the managers appear very effective.

Production constraints (the availability of qualified people for service firms, and production capacity for manufacturers) may also affect the revenue budget. If, for example, managers expect sales

TABLE 9-2

Executive Furnishings Division, Parker & Smith, Year 1 Budget

	Prior Year's Actual	Year 1 Budget	Rate of Change
Sales by model			
Mission executive desk	$201,000	$205,000	2.0%
Mahogany conference table	$358,000	$381,000	6.4%
HealthyBack chair	$515,500	$556,000	7.9%
Cherry bookcase	$72,400	$60,250	(16.8%)
Steel credenza	$81,200	$80,000	(1.5%)
Total sales	$1,228,100	$1,282,250	4.4%
Cost of goods sold			
Direct labor	$92,325	$96,500	4.5%
Factory overhead	$6,755	$7,200	6.6%
Direct materials	$211,000	$220,284	4.4%
Total cost of goods sold	$310,080	$323,984	4.5%
Marketing and administrative costs			
Sales salaries	$320,000	$331,200	3.5%
Advertising expenses	$145,000	$151,000	4.1%
Miscellaneous selling expenses	$4,200	$3,900	(7.1%)
Administrative expenses	$92,000	$94,500	2.7%
Total SG&A	$561,200	$580,600	3.5%
Operating income	$356,820	$377,666	5.8%

Source: HMM Budgeting.

demand to exceed the company's ability to manufacture and distribute, then they might adjust the revenue budget to match the production constraints rather than the actual demands of the market. Otherwise, the budget must add funds for building the capacity needed to meet demand.

STEP 2: CALCULATE THE EXPECTED COST OF GOODS SOLD Once the revenue budget has been established, managers can then develop the budget for the cost of goods sold. The total number of units to be produced will form the basis for determining the direct costs, including labor and materials. In the same way, Parker & Smith's Executive Furnishings Division calculates the indirect factory costs or overhead as part of the cost of goods sold budget. Remember here that sales are budgeted to rise 4.4 percent, to $1,282,250.

STEP 3: CALCULATE THE OTHER EXPECTED COSTS Other nonproduction costs include costs generated by human resources, R&D, product design, marketing, distribution, customer service, and administration. In our Executive Furnishings Division example, with the division's classic furnishing designs, only various sales-related and administrative expenses make up the other-costs budget.

STEP 4: CALCULATE THE EXPECTED OPERATING INCOME Finally, you can calculate the budgeted income statement. The difference between expected sales and expected costs results in the expected operating income. The managers of the Executive Furnishings Division provide their expected income statement to Parker & Smith's top management so that top management, in turn, can determine how the division's budget fits with the company's master budget and overall strategic goals.

STEP 5: DEVELOP ALTERNATIVE SCENARIOS Testing different scenarios is the "what if?" iterative process of budgeting. How will a change in one area affect the expected outcome? What if we increase advertising? How much would this change increase sales? What if the Executive Furnishings employees decide to go on strike? How can we incorporate that risk into the budget?

For example, Parker & Smith's management may decide to shift its strategic emphasis from increasing profits to developing a new product line in the Executive Furnishings Division. The division's managers would then develop another set of budget figures indicating R&D costs that would reduce the current budgeted operating income. Alternatively, these managers could decide to accept from a new group of suppliers some bids that would in turn

Calculating Labor Costs

When unit managers prepare their operating budgets, they must calculate the direct and indirect (or overhead) labor costs they expect to incur over the budgeted period, as well as plan the required head count for their area.

Direct labor costs are those a company expects to incur in order to produce a product or deliver a service. Here's an example of how you might calculate these costs:

Total Hours Paid = (52 Weeks per Year × 40 Hours per Week) × 8 Employees = 16,640

Average Labor Rate = $400,000 (Total Salaries) + $160,000 (Fringe Benefits and Taxes) / 16,640 (Total Hours Paid) = $33.65 per Hour

Direct Labor Costs per Unit for Product or Service A = Estimated Number of Labor Hours per Product or Service Unit × Average Labor Rate

Note: You can calculate total departmental spending on labor by employee—totaling each full-time and temporary employee's salary, payroll taxes, vacation and sick pay, commissions, bonuses, fringe benefits, and overtime. You can also calculate by position—estimating payroll expenses by using average salary and the number of employees required for each budgeted position.

Indirect labor costs (or overhead) are all the costs required to run a particular operation except for direct labor and direct materials—for example, accounting, information systems, and other support departments. Indirect labor costs are derived from a manager's head-count plan. To estimate a required head count, compare the total labor hours required to meet your budgeted product or service volume levels with the total labor hours available in your department. Here's an example of how to calculate available labor per nonexempt employee:

Total Hours in One Year (52 Weeks × 40 Hours per Week) = 2,080

Holidays = 10 Days × 8 Hours per Day = 80

Vacation Days = 10 Days × 8 Hours per Day = 80

Sick Leave = 4 Days × 8 Hours per Day = 32

Mandated Breaks = 236 Days × 0.5 Hours per Day = 118

Total Available Labor Hours per Year = 1,770

If the total available labor hours per year is less than the total labor hours required to meet your goals, take steps to address the labor shortage. Once you've planned your department's head count, allocate indirect labor costs using the overhead rate established by your company. Some companies use a single overhead rate; others, multiple departmental rates to reflect more and less labor-intensive processes. Here's an example of how to calculate a single overhead rate based on labor:

Total Factory Overhead Costs = $121,200

Total Labor Hours = 30,300

Budgeted Overhead Rate per Labor Hour = $121,300/30,300 = $4.00

Overhead Costs Assigned to Product A = 0.16 Labor Hour per Unit at $4.00 per Labor Hour = $0.64

SOURCE: Lianabel Oliver, *The Cost Management Toolbox* (New York: AMACOM, 2000), 77–83, 94–95, appendix C.

reduce materials expenditures and increase the budgeted operating income.

Creating Financial Budgets

Once the managers of operations have developed their operating budgets, or expected income statements, financial managers then plan for the capital required to support those operating budgets. You can't anticipate a 10 percent increase in sales, for example, without creating a parallel plan for the extra working capital and other inputs that will be required if the anticipated increase is realized. To plan for the requirements, managers need to develop three other budgets:

1. A cash budget that includes estimated cash from operations as well as other sources of cash (accounts payable, borrowing, or equity). The cash budget predicts and plans for the level and timing of cash inflow and outflow.

2. An operating asset investment plan that ensures that adequate capital will be available for operating assets such as inventory and accounts receivable.

3. A capital investment plan that budgets for proposed investments in long-term productive assets such as property, plant, and equipment expenditures and extended R&D programs.

These financial plans support the company's strategic objectives, planning for both the near-term (cash budget) and the long-term (capital investment plan) financial needs. The plans are expressed in forecasted (or pro forma) balance sheet and cash flow statements to form a complete picture of the organization's expected financial position during the budget period.

The *cash budget* is particularly important for the firm's financial managers, because it indicates shortages or surpluses of cash in each period (usually months). No business can afford a shortfall of cash, as the company would be unable to pay bills as they come due. Table 9-3 shows one company's simplified cash budget for a five-

TABLE 9-3

A Simplified Cash Budget (In Thousands of Dollars)

	Dec.	Jan.	Feb.	March	April	May
Cash inflows						
Sales revenues		1,100	875	600	500	600
Other revenues		250	225	200	200	0
Interest income		___	34	34	34	___
Total inflows		1,350	1,134	834	734	600
Cash outflows						
Purchases		400	380	320	300	350
Salaries		200	200	200	200	200
Hourly wages		170	165	150	195	220
Health-care payments		20	20	20	20	20
Retirement contributions		25	23	25	23	25
Interest payments		15	15	15	15	15
Taxes		305	295	270	260	240
Utilities		20	18	15	20	25
Total cash outflows		1,155	1,116	1,015	1,033	1,095
Cash surplus or deficit		195	18	(181)	(299)	(495)
Beginning balance		220	415	433	252	(47)
Ending balance	220	415	433	252	(47)	(542)

month period (January through May). Notice that it identifies all cash inflows and outflows for each month. The ending cash balance of a given month becomes the beginning balance for the next month. Thus, December's $220 ending balance becomes January's beginning cash balance. By adding the monthly surplus (or deficit) and the beginning cash balance, the budget finds the ending balance for the month. A glance across the bottom line indicates when the enterprise will encounter a cash shortfall, as happens here in April. (The cash shortfall becomes larger in May.) Companies whose businesses are heavily seasonal—agricultural producers, garment makers, ski manufacturers, and so forth—routinely experience wide swings in ending cash balances.

During months of surplus, financial managers store company cash in interest-bearing money market instruments such as short-term bank certificates of deposit (CDs), commercial paper, and U.S. Treasury bills. As surpluses disappear, managers convert those instruments back into cash and draw on lines of credit and short-term bank loans to eliminate any cash deficits. As shown in table 9-3, managers must begin drawing on past surpluses in March. The surpluses have evaporated by April, forcing the company to seek outside sources of cash. Seasonal and cyclical businesses use periods of heavy cash inflows to pay off their lines of credit and to build money market positions in anticipation of the next cash-consuming cycle.

Here are the steps to follow in building your own cash budget:

1. **Add receipts.** Determine the expected receipts—collections from customers and other sources—that will flow into the cash account each period. Cash collections may vary during the budget period. For example, many retail stores expect to receive most of their receipts during holiday seasons.

2. **Deduct disbursements.** Based on expected activity, calculate how much cash will be required to cover disbursements—cash payouts—during the period. Disbursements could include payment for materials, payroll, taxes due, and so on. Some of these expenditures may be evenly distributed throughout the budget period, but some, such as payroll and materials costs, may fluctuate as part of the production process.

3. **Calculate the cash surplus or deficiency.** To calculate the cash surplus or deficiency for a period, subtract the disbursements from the sum of the beginning cash balance and the receipts expected during that period.

4. **Add the beginning cash balance.** The beginning cash balance is the ending balance from the previous period. By adding them together, you have a new ending balance.

5. **Determine financing needed.** The ending balance will be positive or negative. A positive balance indicates that you have

more than enough cash to cover operations during that period. A negative balance indicates that the company must develop a plan for financing the shortfall from other sources, such as a bank loan. Repayment of any such loan must be reflected among the cash outflows of subsequent budget periods.

The Human Side of Budgeting

To some degree, preparing a budget is a matter of crunching numbers, a process that more and more companies are leaving to financial modeling software, computers, and technology. But behind those numbers are real people like you—individuals who make assumptions, who think about future situations, and who understand the idiosyncrasies of managers, customers, and competitors. Ideally, everyone involved in the budget process has the same goal in mind—achieving the organization's strategic objectives.

What some may see as a straightforward, even mechanical, process, however, is in reality complicated by genuine disagreements about assumptions of future trends and events, by conflicting functional needs, and by individual agendas that overshadow the larger corporate good. For this reason, the budget process can be defined as a series of negotiations between disparate interests. Top management wants the highest possible economic value in terms of profit. Middle management may have contrary needs, such as new equipment or new personnel. This human element is what can make the budget process so engaging and, at times, so frustrating.

Top-Down Versus Participatory Budgeting

Top-down budgeting describes the process whereby upper management sets budget goals—revenue, profit, and so on—and imposes these goals on the rest of the organization. Thus, for example, the CEO of Parker & Smith gives division manager Claude Jones the goal of attaining an operating profit—or earnings before interest and taxes—of $400,000 for the upcoming fiscal year. It's then up to Claude to shape his operating budget with $400,000 as the operating profit target.

Top-down budgeting has many advantages. Since senior management has a clearer concept of the organization's strategic objectives, top-down budgeting assures the following benefits for senior management:

- Budget goals that reflect management's larger strategic objectives

- Better coordination of the budget requirements for all the elements of the organization

- The discouragement of padding managers' unit budgets

- High goals that challenge managers to stretch

Yet top-down budgeting has two main disadvantages. First, upper management may be out of touch with the realities of the individual divisions' costs, processes, or markets. As a result, the goals the executives set may be inappropriate or unattainable. Second, middle managers may feel left out of the decision-making process and, consciously or unconsciously, may not fully participate in achieving the budgeted goals.

With participatory budgeting, the people responsible for achieving the budget goals are included in goal setting. Jones, for instance, would develop the budget for his own division, with the active participation of the heads of purchasing, HR, production, marketing, and administration. Once his team had completed the budget, Jones would send it to Parker & Smith's senior management. After review and possible feedback to Jones, executives would incorporate this unit's budget, along with all the other budgets, into the master budget.

One advantage of participatory budgeting is that the people closest to the line activities—people who presumably have the best information—make the budget decisions. Also, the participants in this type of budget process are more likely to make the extra effort

Tips for Negotiating Your Team's Budget

Effective budgeting requires a certain organizational savvy. Here are some tips for dealing with organizational issues surrounding the budgeting process:

- Understand your organization's budgeting process. What guidelines do you need to follow? What is the timing of the budget process? How is the budget used in the organization?

- Communicate often with the controller or finance person in your department or company. Ask questions about points you don't understand. Get that person's advice about the assumptions your team is making.

- Know what real concerns are driving the people making the decisions about your budget. Then be sure to address those concerns.

- Get buy-in from the decision makers. Spend time educating the finance person or decision maker about your area of the business. This will lay the groundwork for implementing changes later.

- Understand each line item in the budget you're working on. If you don't know what something means or where a number comes from, try to find out. Walk the floor. Talk to people on the line.

- Have an ongoing discussion with your team throughout the budget period. The more you plan, the more you will be able to respond to unplanned contingencies.

Avoid unpleasant surprises. As the numbers become available, compare actual figures to the budgeted amounts. If there is a significant or an unexpected variance, find out why. And be sure to notify the finance person who needs to know.

to achieve the budgeted goals. Nevertheless, participatory budgeting has disadvantages as well. First, the people closest to the line
activities may not see the larger strategic picture. Second, if performance evaluations are tied to budget achievement, then managers
will have an incentive to pad their budgets by either underestimating revenues or overestimating costs.

Iterative budgeting attempts to combine the best of both top-
down and participatory budgeting. In the initial step, senior management provides the unit heads with a clear understanding of the
organization's strategic goals. The unit heads then work with their
teams to develop operating budgets that incorporate both their
own tactical goals and the organization's larger strategic goals.
After the unit heads send their budget proposals to upper management, upper management reviews the individual budgets and may
ask for adjustments. And the negotiating process continues back
and forth until a final master budget is achieved.

The key to success in any budgeting process is communication.
Senior management has to communicate strategic goals in a way
that makes sense to unit heads. In turn, the unit heads communicate their resource needs and concerns when presenting budget
proposals to management. All participants in the budget process
have an obligation to listen to one another's various and sometimes
conflicting positions.

Slack, Padding, and Sandbagging

Budgetary slack or padding occurs when managers believe they are
going to be evaluated on their performance relative to the budget.
To ensure that they will achieve their budgeted figures and be
rewarded, they budget revenues conservatively. This budgetary
slack provides managers with a hedge against unexpected problems, reducing the risk that groups will not make their numbers.
Other managers assume that no matter how carefully they budget,
they'll be asked to cut the figures even further. Thus they pad their
budget by exaggerating anticipated costs, to ensure that they have
enough money to operate effectively after the cuts. Slack and padding

make the budget game easier to win. Both tactics are moves in an old game that people from the top to the bottom learn to play.

Sandbagging is related to padding, but the misrepresentation can be something other than presenting lower-than-expected sales figures or higher costs. Sandbagging occurs when a manager conceals the true intent of a budgetary proposal. For example, Jones wants to aggressively expand the high-end line of executive furnishings offered by Parker & Smith's Executive Furnishings Division—but senior management has discouraged major investments in this project. So he may propose a minor investment in adding one new product in this budget cycle, knowing that he will aim for a much more ambitious plan if he receives approval for this more modest expansion. This budgetary game is a form of sandbagging called the foot-in-the-door ploy.

What-If Scenarios and Sensitivity Analysis

Budgets are only as good as the assumptions that inform them. But assumptions are often wrong. We assume that customer A will purchase ten thousand units from us next year—and we have the sales agreement to back it up. But if customer A experiences a major business collapse, then that sales agreement isn't worth much. We assume that our energy bills will increase at roughly the current rate of inflation. But guess what? A cold winter and huge demand for energy may push prices through the roof.

Managers use sensitivity analysis to test their assumptions and generate alternative options. This analysis can greatly enhance the value of budgets as instruments for planning, feedback, and course correction. A sensitivity analysis applies a what-if situation to the budget model to see the effect of the potential change on the original data. For example, what if the cost of materials rises 5 percent, or what if sales rise 10 percent? Calculations for sensitivity analyses can be complicated when an analyst is dealing with a master budget that has "rolled up" multiple divisional or functional budgets, or a combination of both. Software packages for financial planning are available and commonly used to perform these calculations, giving

TABLE 9-4

Parker & Smith, Executive Furnishings Division, Sensitivity Analysis

What-If Scenarios	Units Sold	Direct Materials Cost	Operating Income
Budget model	21,400	$214,000	$383,950
Increase unit sales 10%	23,540	$235,000	$422,730
Decrease unit sales 5%	20,330	$203,300	$360,900
Decrease materials cost 5%	21,400	$203,300	$398,700

Source: HMM Budgeting.

managers a powerful tool to estimate the costs and benefits of various options and possibilities.

For example, if the Executive Furnishings Division wanted to test its assumptions with what-if scenarios, it could determine the effect of some likely alternative scenarios (table 9-4). Given the results of these analyses, Claude Jones may decide to direct his efforts toward lowering materials costs to achieve the best bottom-line result. You'll learn more about sensitivity analysis in chapter 12.

Developing an HR Department Budget

HR professionals who are unit managers must prepare a yearly department budget just as other unit managers do. You probably also participate in high-level budget planning for your company and help other departments with personnel budgeting. Indeed, in some organizations, the HR department supplies all the "people" figures, including training costs, for each department.

But to sharpen the focus in this section, let's think specifically about how to develop a budget for your HR department. Where do you begin? The following process can prove helpful:[1]

1. **Determine your department's short-term goals and plans.**
   Based on your company's strategic direction for the upcoming

HR Budget Trends

Recent reports on surveys of HR professionals contain interesting responses to questions about trends related to HR budgets. Consider these examples:

- Of the respondents, 75 percent said that all HR costs are part of their company's annual budget. This is especially true in the utilities industry, though less true in the transportation industry.

- Some 57 percent said that the CEO or president of their organization has final approval of the HR budget. This is particularly common in the construction and mining/oil and gas industries and less common among government respondents.

- As organization size increases, so does the likelihood that all HR costs will be part of the annual budget—or that HR will have a separate budget. And in larger companies, the chief HR officer, rather than the CEO or president, is more likely to have final HR budget approval.

- HR department budgets for 2003 represented a median of 0.9 percent of organizations' total projected expenditures for that year—up slightly from 0.8 percent in 2002 but significantly under levels recorded during the mid-1990s (for example, 1.1 percent in 1994–1996).

SOURCES: Jessica Collison and Cassandra Frangos, "Aligning HR with Organization Strategy Survey," SHRM/Balanced Scorecard Collaborative, November 2002, and "HR Department Benchmarks and Analysis 2003," Executive Summary, BNA/SHRM.

year or so, define the goals that HR needs to achieve in the next fiscal year to support that direction. For example, if your company has set out to leverage new technology advances, perhaps the HR department will define a goal of launching a Web-based HR self-service option for employees. Next lay out the tactical plans for achieving the goals you've defined.

Specify what your department will do in the coming year, who will do it, and when.

2. **Formulate a head-count plan.** Define the current and future staffing, by job classification, needed to achieve your department's goals. Provide written justification for any new positions.

3. **Estimate departmental spending.** Gauge the following types of expenses that you expect your department to incur over the coming year:

   • **Recurring expenses:** those that come up on a regular, predictable basis, such as payroll-related expenses or utilities. You can often estimate these from historical data.

   • **Nonrecurring expenses:** those that come up infrequently, such as the implementation of a new computer system.

   • **Discretionary costs:** those that arise at the HR manager's discretion, such as training, travel, and supplies.

   • **Committed costs:** those resulting from contractual obligations, for example, purchase agreements.

   In considering departmental spending, pay particular attention to major expense categories:

   • **Labor costs:** These derive from your head-count plan and include salaries and expected pay raises, payroll taxes, vacation and sick pay, commissions, bonuses, fringe benefits, overtime, and temporary employees.

   • **Depreciation expenses:** These come from spreading the cost of a capital asset (property, plant, or equipment) over the number of periods the asset is expected to benefit the company. In many companies, the finance manager provides the budgeted depreciation figure to department managers.

   • **Other expenses:** These may include travel, training, supplies, maintenance, subcontractor fees, and so forth. You can estimate such costs in several ways—including using historical costs, obtaining vendor quotes, and obtaining comparative data from other companies in similar industries.

With any cost estimating, document the methods you've used—particularly while gauging expenses that often get top management's attention, such as travel, overtime, temporary labor, and subcontractors.

4. **Determine your department's capital budget.** Identify any long-term projects that will require major funding and generate benefits during future budgeting periods. Examples might include major investments needed in training, new technologies, or significant overhauling of a process.

5. **Clarify assumptions, risks, and opportunities.** Be ready to explain the assumptions that underlie your estimates; for example, "I am assuming that training costs will increase 3–5 percent next year." Also assess and be ready to describe what you see as the risks and opportunities facing your department in the coming year. For instance, "Changes in employment law could mean that we need to revise HR policies and overhaul our employee handbook" or "HR software developers may face stiffer competition in the coming year, which could present us with opportunities to purchase a new database for less money than we've budgeted."

The sidebar "GenCo's HR Department Budget, 2005" shows a simplified sample HR department budget for a fictional company.

GenCo's HR Department Budget, 2005

Irene Foster, GenCo's HR director, must prepare a departmental budget for the year ending December 31, 2005. From her participation in executive strategy meetings, she knows that the company wants to improve workforce performance and speed up key operations over the coming years. With those overall corporate goals in mind, Foster develops the following budget for 2005:

Continued

Short-Term Strategies and Plans

• HR research team will conduct employee-performance and morale survey during first quarter; will tabulate and interpret results during second quarter.

• HR group will step up workforce training by year end.

• HR director will work with information technology team to select and install new payroll database by end of third quarter.

Head-Count Plan

• Add one new trainer, increasing training staff from one to two.

• Reduce the number of payroll administration positions by one, decreasing payroll staff from three to two.

Departmental Spending

Labor

Salaries, wages and benefits	$231,872
Labor total	$231,872

Operating expenses

Materials and supplies	$3,210
Office supplies	$2,123
Printing and binding	$3,030
Telephone	$2,000
Postage	$1,600
Travel and training	$5,250
Equipment rental	$1,270
Contractual services	$65,000
Total	$83,483

Capital outlay

Machinery and equipment	$3,500
Total	$3,500
Total for department	$318,855

Tips for Effective HR Budgeting

If you want to use budgeting as an HR planning and team-building tool, you need to develop a game plan. Even if you recently finished this year's budget, it's not too early to start thinking about next year. In fact, doing so can make it more likely that your budget requests will be approved. Here are a few points to keep in mind:

- If you're a new manager, become familiar with your company's budgeting process.

- Spend time learning and understanding company priorities, as well as helping your team understand them.

- Make sure that any request for funds is in sync with the objectives set by senior management.

- Determine your HR department's cost per employee.

- Start gathering any information you will need for next year's budget, such as labor market changes, cost trends in health-care services, and anticipated training needs.

- Help your team members begin learning about the budget. Ask for volunteers to research line items.

- Start by drafting a preliminary budget that estimates your costs and outputs. If they're not within the parameters set by management, look for ways to make adjustments.

- If you need to reduce costs, identify the activities that add value for your internal customers and those that don't. Analyze the cost of each activity, and begin by cutting nonvalue-added costs.

- Show how your budget request will generate income for the company by raising revenues, streamlining costs, or a combination of both. In other words, your budget should be not so much a request for funds as a proposal showing how you will help the company realize its goals.

Summing Up

This chapter began by describing the four basic functions of budgeting: planning, coordinating and communicating, monitoring progress, and evaluating performance. Together, these functions help an organization move forward and keep on track. And they make the time and trouble associated with budgeting worthwhile.

Several types of budgets, and their uses, were explained:

- Short-term versus long-term

- Fixed versus rolling

- Incremental versus zero-based

- Kaizen

- Master budget

The master budget brings together operating and cash budgets and various financial projections into a comprehensive picture. The steps for constructing operating and cash budgets were detailed.

The applications of what-if scenarios and sensitivity analysis were introduced. These methodologies can help budget makers predict the effects of specific changes in any important assumptions built in to the budget.

Finally, we explored strategies for developing a budget for your HR department.

Note: If you'd like to get beyond the basics provided here, you can learn about activity-based budgeting (ABB) in appendix A. ABB is a new way of approaching the budgeting process using the activity-based costing concepts first introduced in chapter 5.

Leveraging Chapter Insights: Critical Questions

- In thinking about the next HR department budget you'll develop, what key business or industry trends will have the biggest impact on your budget?

- What kind of budget do you generally develop for your department? What are the advantages and disadvantages of the budget type you use?

- What steps might you take to learn more about your company's strategic goals and its budgeting process?

CHAPTER TEN

Practical Tools for Management Decisions

Making the Numbers Work for You

Key Topics Covered in This Chapter

- *Cost-benefit analysis*

- *Return on investment (ROI)*

- *Payback period*

- *Breakeven analysis*

- *Estimating nonquantifiable benefits and cost*

- *Tracking performance*

THE FIELD OF FINANCE and its accounting base of information provide a rich trove of practical tools that HR managers can use to assess business situations and to make decisions about how best to invest in and use their firm's human capital. These tools can help answer some of the most important questions that will ever come your way:

- What are the costs and benefits of a particular course of action?

- What is the estimated return on a potential investment?

- How long will it take for your group to recoup its investment in a particular project?

- How many units will a company have to sell at specific prices to break even on a venture?

- How can a company estimate nonquantifiable costs and benefits?

This chapter shows you how to answer these questions. It also explains how to track the performance of an investment project undertaken in the wake of these forms of analysis.

Cost-Benefit Analysis

Parker & Smith is considering two investment options: (1) buying a new piece of machinery with which to make plastic shelving for office use and (2) creating a new product line. The new machinery is a smart-technology, high-temperature plastic extruder costing $100,000. The company's executives believe that this extruder will save time and money over the long term and is safer than the machinery currently in use. The second option, launching a new line of high-end leather office furniture, will require a $250,000 investment in plant, equipment, and design. How can Parker & Smith decide which of these investment options makes the best economic sense?

The process of determining the answer is known as *cost-benefit analysis.* This form of analysis evaluates whether, over a given time frame, the benefits of the new investment or the new business opportunity will outweigh the associated costs.

Before beginning any cost-benefit analysis, it's important to understand that there's also a cost associated with the status quo— with making no changes at all. You want to weigh the relative merits of each investment against the negative consequences, if any, of not proceeding with the investment. Cost-benefit analysis of a particular investment involves the following steps:

1. Identify the costs associated with the new purchase or business opportunity.

2. Identify the benefits of additional revenues that will result from the investment.

3. Identify the cost savings to be gained.

4. Map out the timeline for expected costs and anticipated revenues.

5. Evaluate the nonquantifiable benefits and costs—and there may be several.

The first three steps are fairly straightforward. Begin by identifying all the costs associated with the venture—this year's upfront costs as well as those you anticipate in subsequent years. Then consider the possible benefits. For example, additional revenues could come from more customers or from increased purchases by existing customers. To understand the benefits of these revenues, make sure to factor in the new costs associated with them. Ultimately, this means you'll be looking at profit. With cost savings, it's a little simpler, at least in the sense that such savings represent incremental profit—they go straight to the bottom line. However, cost savings are sometimes more subtle and more difficult to recognize and quantify. These savings can arise from a variety of sources, including the following:

- **More efficient processing:** Perhaps fewer people are required to do the same work, or a process requires fewer steps, or the time spent on each step decreases.

- **More accurate processing:** Perhaps both the time required to correct errors and the number of lost customers could decrease. The "scrap" rate—that is, the rate at which a manufacturing process produces unsalable output—may also go down.

- **Expedited training:** If the new machine is easier to operate, then training people to use it may also be easier.

- **Lower worker compensation claims:** Greater safety can translate into fewer claims.

Next, map out the costs and the revenues—or cost savings— over the relevant period. When do you expect the costs to be incurred? In what increments? When do you expect to receive the benefits (additional revenues or cost savings)? In what increments? Once that's done, you're ready to begin the evaluation phase using one or more of the analytical tools subsequently covered in this chapter: accounting return on investment, payback period, and breakeven analysis.

Accounting Return on Investment

As discussed earlier, return on investment (ROI)—or, to use the more technical term, accounting return on investment—is not always the best measure of an investment's success. But because many managers still use ROI, it pays to understand how they look at this measure. Accounting ROI can take the form of cost savings, incremental profit, or value appreciation. You begin by determining the net return. To calculate the net return from an investment, subtract the total cost of the investment from the total benefits received. Then, to calculate the ROI, divide the net dollar amount of return by the total cost of investment.

Let's suppose that the new $100,000 extruder Parker & Smith is considering would realize an annual $18,000 savings for the company over the lifetime of the machine, which is estimated to be seven years. The total savings would thus be $126,000 ($18,000 × 7), making for a net return of $26,000 (i.e., $126,000 − $100,000). Applying the formula for ROI—that is, net return divided by the total cost of the investment, or $26,000 divided by $100,000 in this example—the ROI is 26 percent.

Is 26 percent a good return? In isolation, the figure has no particular meaning. Why? ROI is a way of comparing returns on money a company invests internally with returns available to it elsewhere at the *same level of risk*. The notion of equal risk is very important here, since all investors demand higher returns for higher risk. Thus, it makes no sense to compare the returns the company believes it could make from an investment in, say, the relatively safe expansion of a current product line, with an investment in, for example, a totally new product line for an untested market. The risk levels of the two potential investments are simply not equivalent. The higher-risk investment should have a higher potential return.

ROI as described in this example is flawed for another reason as well: It ignores the time value of money, a core financial concept you'll learn more about later in the book. For example, which would you rather have (assuming equal risks): an investment that gave you a 26 percent return in one year, or an investment that gave you the same return at the end of seven years? No contest there. Any rational investor would want the money sooner rather than later.

Thus, the utility of ROI as a decision-making tool is rather limited. Nevertheless, since many businesspeople use ROI, it's important to understand both the measurement and its weaknesses.

HR in Action: Analyzing Costs, Benefits, and Returns for a Team-Building Investment

So, how might you use cost-benefit and ROI analysis to evaluate the potential of HR investments? Let's consider an example. Suppose you're the HR director at a printing company that's facing stiffening competition from companies that have copied your firm's specialty printing techniques. Your company is already using state-of-the-art equipment, has streamlined its administrative processes, and has a dedicated, highly skilled workforce. The firm needs to identify other ways of boosting its profitability to stay ahead of rivals.

You suggest to the company's president that the firm explore possible HR-oriented solutions to the problem. You propose a one-day, off-site team-building session attended by the president and the company's ten department heads. Your theory? That such a workshop might help the department heads collaborate in new ways that lead to increased profitability. The president says, "If you can show me how the session will pay off, I'll consider supporting it."

You head back to your office and, over the coming week, tally the costs of the session. Here's what you come up with:

Participants' daily salary and benefits (11 participants × $600 per day)	$6,600
Consultant's fee	$4,000
Conference-room fee, meals, refreshments	$1,040
Total	$11,640

Next you consider the potential benefits of the session. If the consultant you've hired is as good as his references suggest, you anticipate seeing results from your investment in the form of increased sales from various improvements generated by the session. For example, some of the consultant's former clients explained that their team-building session led to better communication among department heads, more sharing of information, and more identification of opportunities to serve new markets that they hadn't considered before. One HR director you phoned for a reference said, "Thanks to the team-building session we held, our company has been taking in about two hundred thousand dollars per year in new orders." Two other HR directors quoted similarly impressive achievements.

Using your knowledge of these reference companies' industries and your own firm's industry, you translate the sales gains you've heard about into potential sales gains for your company after the team-building session. You estimate (conservatively) that improvements from the team-building session could lead to $1,000 in increased sales per week for the coming year. That's $52,000, you calculate—a cost-benefit ratio of 1 to 4 ($11,640 divided into $52,000). When you factor in the costs associated with processing all those new orders, you come up with an increase in profitability of $28,000 per year—a cost-benefit ratio of about 1 to 2. Not bad, you say to yourself, especially if these financial improvements are repeated year after year.

Next you compare these numbers with the sales and profitability your firm would see if you *didn't* hold the team-building session—or if you invested in a different program, such as quality circles. After weighing all the numbers, you decide that, of all your options, a one-day team-building session indeed seems to promise the most benefits for the least costs. You present your analysis to the president, and he agrees not only to support the session, but also to attend it.

SOURCE: Adapted from Michael W. Mercer, *Turning Your Human Resources Department into a Profit Center* (New York: AMACOM, 1989), 173–175.

Payback Period

Companies also want to know the *payback period:* how long it will take a particular investment to pay for itself. We already know that the plastic extruder is expected to save Parker & Smith $18,000 a year. To determine the payback period, divide the total amount of the investment by the annual savings expected. In this case,

TABLE 10-1

Parker & Smith, Cumulative Annual Savings from the Installment of a Plastic Extruder

Year	Savings	Cumulative Savings
1	$18,000	$18,000
2	$18,000	$36,000
3	$18,000	$54,000
4	$18,000	$72,000
5	$18,000	$90,000
6	$18,000	$108,000
7	$18,000	$126,000

Source: HMM Finance.

$100,000 divided by $18,000 equals 5.56. In other words, the extruder will pay for itself in 5.56 years. Table 10-1 provides a year–by–year illustration of how annual savings will accumulate.

Note that Parker & Smith will not truly begin to reap the benefits of the investment for more than five years. But what if the life-span estimates are wrong, and the extruder wears out after four years? The investment now appears to be not particularly attractive—certainly less attractive than an investment with a similar ROI and a payback period of three years.

As an analytical tool, the payback period tells you only one thing: how long it will take to recoup your investment. Although the payback period is just one of several criteria useful in comparing real alternatives, some executives still rely on it.

Breakeven Analysis

Breakeven analysis tells you how much (or how much more) you need to sell to pay for the fixed investment—in other words, at what point you will break even on your cash flow. With that information in hand, you can look at market demand and competitors' market shares to determine whether it's realistic to expect to sell that much. Breakeven analysis can also help you think through the impact of changing price and volume relationships.

More specifically, the breakeven calculation helps you determine the volume level at which the total after-tax contribution from a product line or an investment covers its total fixed costs. But before you can perform the calculation, you need to understand the components that go into it:

- **Fixed costs:** These are costs that stay mostly the same, no matter how many units of a product or service are sold— costs such as insurance, management salaries, and rent or lease payments. For example, the rent on the production facility will be the same whether the company makes ten thousand or twenty thousand units, and so will the insurance.

- **Variable costs:** Variable costs are those that change with the number of units produced and sold; examples include utilities, labor, and the costs of raw materials. The more units you make, the higher the variable costs.

- **Contribution margin:** This is the amount of money that every sold unit contributes to paying for fixed costs. As described in chapter 5, it is defined as net unit revenue minus variable (or direct) costs per unit.

With these concepts understood, we can make the calculation. We are looking for the solution to this straightforward equation:

$$\text{Breakeven Volume} = \frac{\text{Fixed Costs}}{\text{Unit Contribution Margin}}$$

And here's how we do it. First, find the unit contribution margin by subtracting the variable costs per unit from the net revenue per unit. Then divide total fixed costs, or the amount of the investment, by the unit contribution margin. The quotient is the breakeven volume, that is, the number of units that must be sold so that all fixed costs are covered.

A Breakeven Complication

Our Parker & Smith breakeven analysis represents a simple case. It assumes that costs are distinctly fixed or variable, that costs and unit contributions will not change as a function of volume (i.e., that the sale price of the item under consideration will not change at different levels of output). These assumptions may not hold in your more complicated world. Rent may be fixed up to a certain level of production, then increase by 50 percent as you rent a secondary facility to handle expanded output. Labor costs may in reality be a hybrid of fixed and variable. And as you push more and more of your product into the market, you may find it necessary to offer price discounts—which reduce the contribution per unit. You will need to adjust the breakeven calculation to accommodate these untidy realities.

To see breakeven analysis in practice, let's look again at the Parker & Smith plastic extruder example. Suppose that each set of shelving produced by the extruder sells for $75, and that the variable cost per unit is $22. Then:

$75 (Price per Unit) − $22 (Variable Cost per Unit) =
$53 (Unit Contribution Margin)

Therefore:

$$\frac{\$100,000 \text{ (Total Investment Required)}}{\$53 \text{ (Unit Contribution Margin)}} = 1,887 \text{ Units}$$

The preceding calculations indicate that Parker & Smith must sell 1,887 sets of shelving to recover its $100,000 investment.

At this point, the company must decide whether the breakeven volume is achievable: Is it realistic to expect to sell 1,887 additional sets of shelving, and if so, how quickly?

Operating Leverage

The goal of any businessperson, of course, is not to break even but to make a profit. Once a company has covered all its fixed costs with the contributions of many unit sales, every subsequent sale goes directly to the bottom line. As we observed above,

Unit Net Revenue – Unit Variable Cost = Unit Contribution to Profit

You can see at a glance that the lower the unit variable cost, the greater the contribution to profits. In the pharmaceutical business, for example, the unit cost of cranking out and packaging a bottle of a new wonder drug may be less than a dollar. Yet if the company can sell each bottle for $100, a whopping sum of $99 contributes to corporate profits once sales have gotten beyond the breakeven point! The trouble is that the pharmaceutical company may have invested $400 million up front in fixed product development costs just to get the first bottle out the door. The company will have to sell many bottles of the new medication just to break even. But once it does, the profits can be extraordinary.

The relationship between fixed and variable costs is often described in terms of *operating leverage.* Companies whose fixed costs are high relative to their variable costs are said to have high operating leverage. The pharmaceutical business, for example, generally operates with high operating leverage. So too does the software industry—the greater percentage of its costs come in the form of fixed product development outlays; the variable cost of the CDs on which programs are distributed represent only pennies.

Now consider the opposite situation: *low* operating leverage. Here fixed costs are low relative to the total cost of producing every unit of output. A consulting firm is a good example of low operating leverage. The firm has a minimal investment in equipment and fixed expenses. The bulk of its costs are the fees it pays its consultants, and these fees vary depending on the actual hours they bill to clients.

Operating leverage is a great thing once a company passes its breakeven point. If breakeven is never achieved, however, operating leverage can cause substantial losses. In other words, operating leverage is risky. This is why managers give so much thought to finding the right balance between fixed and variable costs.

Estimating Nonquantifiable Benefits and Costs

Because the numbers alone seldom tell the whole story, your cost-benefit, breakeven, and other forms of analysis must often incorporate qualitative factors as well. Examples here include the strategic fit of the new opportunity with the company's mission, the ability to take on the new opportunity without losing focus, the likelihood of success given market conditions, and perhaps the increase in customer goodwill that the new investment would bring about.

Even though such factors are not fully quantifiable, try to quantify them as much as possible. Make assumptions that can help you come up with a ballpark figure. Suppose you're trying to assess the value of improved information—more comprehensive data that is easier to understand and more widely available—that a new investment would bring. You could try to come up with a dollar figure that represents the value of employees' time saved by the new information, or the value of the increased customer retention that might be gleaned from your company's better understanding of purchase patterns. Such estimates should not necessarily be incorporated into your ROI or other quantified analysis, but they can be very persuasive nevertheless.

Weigh the quantifiable and the nonquantifiable factors. For example, if an investment opportunity is only marginally positive, you may want to give equal weight to more qualitative considerations such as strategic fit in your final decision.

Tracking Performance

Once you've decided to undertake an investment opportunity, monitor its progress—checking to ensure that ongoing results and

TABLE 10-2

Parker & Smith, Shelving Division, January 2004 Budget

	Budget Jan.	Actual Jan.	Variance
Shelving revenues	$39,000	$38,725	–$275
Cost of goods sold	$19,500	$19,200	–$300
Gross margin	$19,500	$19,525	+$25
Marketing expense	$8,500	$10,100	+$1,600
Administrative expense	$4,750	$4,320	–$430
Total operating expense	$13,250	$14,420	+$1,170
Operating profit (EBIT)	$6,250	$5,105	–$1,145

Source: HMM Finance.

earlier projections are on course. Track your projections against actual revenues and expenses. It's a good idea to do this on a monthly basis, so that you can spot potential problems early on. With that in mind, let's revisit the projections for the new shelving division at Parker & Smith. Table 10-2 shows the shelving division's state of affairs early in the first quarter.

The division is doing reasonably well on revenues and cost of goods sold. Its only really large negative variance is in the marketing expense line. Because the numbers are based on just the first month's figures, it's difficult to know whether the variance is simply a onetime, or seasonal, variation or if Parker & Smith is going to have to spend more on marketing than anticipated. If your investment is not tracking according to budget, and if it looks as if the pattern of unexpectedly high costs (or unexpectedly low revenues) is going to hold, then you may need to rethink the initiative—or even discontinue it.

Summing Up

Finance and accounting concepts can help managers make better decisions. This chapter has described several of these concepts:

- Cost-benefit analysis

- Accounting return on investment

- Payback period—a way to estimate the number of months or years required to recoup your initial investment

- Breakeven analysis, which tells you how much (or how much more) you need to sell in order to pay for the fixed costs

The chapter has also shown how you can deal with nonquantitative cost-benefit factors and track investment performance. Understanding these concepts, and their limitations, can help you do your job more effectively.

Leveraging Chapter Insights: Critical Questions

- Think of two HR investments you're considering making. What are the potential costs and benefits of each? The estimated ROI? When would each investment begin paying off? How do the investments compare with the status quo? Overall, which investment (if either) seems the most promising? Why?

- Think of a new HR program you've implemented. How has the investment in this program paid off so far, compared with the performance you expected? Based on your comparison of the program's actual performance versus expected performance, would you advise continuing the program or canceling it? Why?

CHAPTER ELEVEN

Measuring and Reporting Human Capital

A Vital Exercise

Key Topics Covered in This Chapter

- *What human capital is, why it's important, and why companies must measure it*

- *How companies measure human capital*

- *Initiating a human-capital measurement program in your firm*

- *Reporting your firm's human capital*

T HE WORDS *human capital* have cropped up increasingly in the business press and during workplace conversations in recent years. But what is human capital, exactly? And why does it constitute a crucial theme in HR professionals' financial literacy? Equally important, how do HR professionals help their firms measure and report human capital so as to get the most value from this vital resource? This chapter takes a closer look at these questions.

What Is Human Capital?

Most firms think of human capital as an important intangible asset. According to one publication, a company's human capital is "the collective sum of the attributes, life experience, knowledge, inventiveness, energy, and enthusiasm that its people choose to invest in their work."[1] Human capital can generate numerous forms of value that can in turn improve a company's financial bottom line. These forms of value include the following:[2]

- **Intellectual property:** people's ideas that result in marketable products or services that can be trademarked or patented. Intellectual property can also include work processes that customers perceive as unique to a firm

- **Customer relationships:** interactions with customers that lead to increased revenues for the firm

- **Vendor relationships:** mutually beneficial interactions that employees may develop with suppliers and that lead to new business, generate important new knowledge, or enable favorable financial deals

- **Social relationships:** the connections that occur between people within the organization and that facilitate knowledge transfer, such as mentor/protégé relationships and peer networks

- **Structures and processes:** codified knowledge embedded in documented policies and procedures and in databases and corporate files

- **Time:** the "inventory" with which employees generate ideas, solve problems, and create value for the firm

- **Company brand or reputation:** customers' and employees' perceptions of a company's values (what it stands for) and its ability to uphold those values consistently.

As the foundation of the U.S. economy has shifted from manufacturing to services and information processing, human capital has played an increasingly vital role in most American firms' ability to create value and compete. Indeed, one study revealed that up to 70 percent of a company's expenses may be related to human capital.[3] Another observer found that "the value of a firm's intangible assets may exceed that of its book (tangible) assets by two- or threefold."[4] Simply put, succeeding in the knowledge economy requires organizations to generate profitable ideas—and it's people who create ideas.

As you might imagine, human capital is generally more difficult to measure than tangible assets such as manufacturing plants or office furniture. Why? There are several reasons:[5]

- **Definitional confusion:** Unlike tangible assets, companies don't own their human capital. (Rather, employees own their human capital and decide when and where to invest it.) In fact, calling human capital an asset creates some confusion—because accountants define assets as company-owned things

Trends in Measuring Human Capital

A recent study generated several interesting statistics about companies that are measuring their human capital:

• While 77 percent of the study respondents said that they do measure human capital, only 36 percent reported that they have a consistent way of describing it. And just 25 percent said that their companies had developed a clearly articulated approach to measuring it.

• Small organizations are more likely than medium-sized or large organizations to have a consistent way of describing human capital and to link the management of human capital to their business strategy.

• The construction and mining/oil and gas industries are half as likely to have a clearly articulated approach to measuring human capital than other industries.

SOURCE: Jessica Collison and Cassandra Frangos, "Aligning HR with Organization Strategy Survey," SHRM/Balanced Scorecard Collaborative, November 2002.

that have an agreed-upon trading or exchange value. But it's difficult to determine the exchange value of a human being.

• **Dynamism:** The amount and type of human capital that employees create can change as people develop and grow professionally. These forms of value also change depending on how well or poorly matched the people are to their jobs.

• **Sentience:** The value of human assets fluctuates with employees' thoughts and feelings about themselves, the world, and their jobs. With distractions and personal problems, productivity declines; with self-esteem, focus, and mental and physical health, it rises.

Even though human capital is challenging to measure, the practice of consistently quantifying it within the company has become more and more important—for several reasons. Human capital now constitutes most organizations' primary asset, and if firms don't *measure* it, they can't *manage* it. The more carefully companies measure their human capital, the better they can analyze the cause-and-effect connections between HR-related decisions and the value that the workforce is generating for the firm. This analysis, in turn, helps organizations manage their human capital in ways that generate the *most* value. For instance, firms can use this approach to determine whether investments in HR policies such as variable compensation, work-life balance programs, and other efforts are maximizing employees' ability to improve the bottom line.

In fact, some experts maintain that "companies that dedicate themselves to counting tough-to-count intangibles, as well as financially denominated assets, apparently distinguish themselves by superior performance.... [One] survey ... revealed that 'measurement-managed companies outperform other organizations.'"[6] According to this same study, such firms excel in three ways: becoming industry leaders, reporting financial performance in the top one-third of their industry, and achieving success at implementing major cultural or operational change.

There's another reason to measure human capital: In some economies (such as that of the United States), demographic changes have set the stage for a labor scarcity. One study pointed out that as the U.S. population ages and the national birthrate declines, the labor supply will likely grow at just 6–7 percent—all during a time when the *demand* for labor will increase 9–11 percent.[7] These trends have put the forces in motion for a war over talent—signaling the need for firms to better measure and manage this increasingly precious resource.

Perhaps most important to HR professionals, measuring human capital enables HR managers to increase their strategic contributions to their company. By showing in quantifiable terms how the employees in your firm create value for the organization, you make a contribution to the company's competitive efforts and strengthen your interactions with other strategic players in the organization. When you provide this type of analysis to your CEO, and he or she then shares it with the board of directors, everyone sees how the value created by human capital contributes to shareholder value. The most measurement-savvy companies aim "to determine who is generating how much profit per dollar of company investment in salary, benefits and training—and why—to make the best use of their human capital."[8]

Measuring Human Capital: Techniques and Challenges

Given the many benefits of measuring human capital, it's clear that companies that hope to keep their competitive edge must master this emerging field. But how do firms actually go about measuring this most elusive intangible asset? Different firms handle it in various ways—but most approaches involving gathering and evaluating primarily nonfinancial data. And because the discipline is still evolving, many companies have found that it's not always clear how best to measure certain aspects of human capital.

But most managers agree that firms *can* go beyond traditional, familiar metrics, such as time to hire or recruiting costs. Table 11-1 shows examples of additional baseline metrics developed by one research organization, the Saratoga Institute. Additional organizations have created other tools and models for measuring human capital—such as the balanced scorecard, the Malcolm Baldrige Award for Quality, total quality management (TQM), and customer relationship management (CRM).

In addition to the baseline metrics shown in table 11-1, organizations can measure myriad other aspects of human capital. Here are just a few examples, with possible measurement strategies:

- **Employee engagement:** as indicated by responses to workforce surveys

- **Retention:** number of employees who remain with the company for a specified number of years

TABLE 11-1

Examples of Human Capital Metrics

Organizational Effectiveness

Revenue Factor	Revenue/Total Full-Time Equivalent (FTE)
Expense Factor	Operating Expense/Total FTE
Income Factor	(Revenue – Operating Expense)/Total FTE
Human Capital Value Added	Revenue – (Operating Expense [Compensation Cost + Benefit Cost])/Total FTE
Human Capital ROI	Revenue – (Operating Expense [Compensation Cost + Benefit Cost])/(Compensation Cost + Benefit Cost)

Compensation

Compensation Revenue Ratio	Compensation Cost/Revenue
Compensation Expense Ratio	Compensation Cost/Operating Expense
Compensation Factor	Compensation Cost/Workforce Head Count

Training and Development

Training Cost Factor	Total Training Cost/Employees Trained
Training Investment Factor	Total Training Cost/Total Head Count
Training Staff Ratio	Total FTE/Training Staff FTE
Training Cost per Hour	Total Training Cost/Total Training Hours

Source: Leslie A. Weatherly, "The Value of People: The Challenges and Opportunities of Human Capital Measurement and Reporting," *SHRM Research Quarterly* 3 (2003): 6.

- **Diversity:** number of employees from different ethnic, educational, or other backgrounds

- **Trainee learning:** trainee's test scores

- **Managerial bench strength:** number of people who can fulfill managerial responsibilities

- **Promotions over time:** number of people promoted over a specified time period

- **Teamwork:** surveys of team members' attitudes toward team-based projects; percentage of workforce working on teams

- **Creativity:** number of new ideas generated; number of mistakes made

Launching or Enhancing a Human-Capital Measurement System in Your Firm

So how do you begin measuring human capital at your firm—or fine-tune your existing system to make it more effective? Each company will want to measure different things, depending on its strategy and its own unique challenges. But experts recommend the following basic process:[9]

1. **Perform a human-capital audit.** On a scale of 1 to 5 (where 1 indicates "rarely agree" and 5 indicates "strongly agree"), rank your company on criteria such as "Our employees understand the company's mission and values," "Our managers give people opportunities to shine," "We encourage our people to take risks," "We provide appropriate training," and "We encourage professional and personal development."

2. **Consider your company's strategy.** When developing your audit criteria, you need to think about the attitudes, knowledge, and behaviors the organization's workforce needs to best support your company's strategy. For example, is employee loyalty to the firm essential? Knowledge of competitive strategy? The sense that the company supports people's professional development? Consider conducting one or more workforce surveys that shed light on the attitudes, knowledge, and behaviors most essential to your firm's success. Or do some judicious one-on-one interviews with key managers and employees to get a sense for these same things.

3. **Analyze the audit information.** Based on what you're seeing in the human-capital audit rankings, identify your firm's most pressing human-capital problems. For example, is the company suffering higher-than-average turnover? If so, what are the attendant costs?

4. **Decide what you want to measure.** Is it training and education? Pay for performance? Retention? Leadership strategies? Teamwork? Innovativeness? Which measures seem most tightly linked to the problems you identified in step 2?

5. **Break measures into components.** Decide how each measure will be quantified. For instance, you might quantify the measure "superior performance" through several criteria—such as "finishing a project ahead of schedule," "finishing within or under budget," "receiving additional business as a result of the completed project," "attracting additional talented team members," "using new methods to complete the project," and so forth. Do this for every measure you identified in step 3. As you might guess, these lists can soon become quite lengthy. The key is to choose measurement criteria that indicate what *your* firm considers most valuable.

6. **Get executive buy-in.** Present the measures and criteria you've developed to the full executive team, showing how your methodology supports the company's overarching goals and addresses its most pressing challenges. Point out how the measures you've selected tie into your corporation's core competencies; for example, "We have a particularly innovative marketing team, so I think we can really shine if we take a closer look at what drives innovation in our firm."

7. **Get others' buy-in.** Share your methodology with people who will be involved (directly or indirectly) with gathering and interpreting data on the measures you've identified. By getting their buy-in, you encourage a sense of ownership of the results of the data analysis.

8. **Communicate results.** As you begin measuring and recording results on all the measures you've identified, communicate those results on a regular basis to everyone involved. Be willing to consider suggestions for improving the process.

9. **Make necessary adjustments.** As time passes, you may find that you need to fine-tune your human-capital measurement

Human-Capital Measurement: Dos and Don'ts

- **Do** clarify the rationale behind your choice of measures—showing how they connect with corporate goals.

- **Don't** hesitate to seek help from in-house or outside experts in developing and improving your human-capital measurement system.

- **Do** go beyond measures specific to HR to include all human-capital drivers of business success.

- **Don't** underestimate the power of senior management's buy-in. Without its interest and support, you may end up wasting time and resources.

- **Do** gather only the most useful data—information that enables concrete organizational improvements.

- **Don't** get pulled into trying to measure too many different things. Excessive data can overwhelm people and sour them on the project.

- **Do** present your findings in accessible formats that employees and managers can easily understand. Avoid the temptation to use flashy reporting software just for its looks.

- **Don't** keep pushing forward with the program if you get stuck or feel unsure of your findings. Instead, step back and reconsider your goals and ways to reach them.

SOURCE: Steve Bates, "The Metrics Maze," *HR Magazine*, December 2003.

process. For example, perhaps you need less or more data than you originally anticipated. Or you need a slightly different set of measures than you thought earlier. Refine the process to make the information it generates as useful and consistent as possible.

Clearly, measuring human capital presents numerous challenges. For one thing, it's not always clear *what* you should measure in your effort to determine exactly which aspects of human capital most influence productivity and profitability in your firm. Is it creativity or innovativeness? Customer relationships? Training? Any combination of the remaining possibilities? Even if you feel confident about what to measure, *how* do you measure something so elusive as creativity? Intangible assets are difficult to quantify precisely, because they're intangible. Finally, measuring human capital takes significant time and involves the gathering and evaluation of large volumes of data. Managers must ask themselves if their companies have the resources to handle the data—and if they're able to find the data they need.

On top of these difficulties, many managers who express interest in measuring human capital discover that others don't necessarily feel equally enthusiastic about the idea. For instance, top management may question the complexity or costs involved in initiating a human-capital measurement program. And some employees may resent having to fill out new surveys or track additional data in addition to carrying out their existing job responsibilities. Other employees may also worry that a more focused attempt to examine human capital in the company may call their performance or job skills into question. Advocates of human-capital measurement may thus encounter resistance from several directions in the company.

Yet despite these challenges, many experts maintain that companies must at least attempt to determine how their investments in—and treatment of—employees affect the financial bottom line. Only by clarifying the big picture in this way can firms hope to better manage their most important resource. Though human-capital management won't likely ever yield absolutes, it sheds lights on the cause-and-effect linkages between managerial decisions and actions—and the company's financial success. Rather than seeking absolutes, managers interested in measuring human capital can look for *patterns* in the data they gather and evaluate. Even patterns can reveal valuable insights about how the company is investing in its human capital.

HR in Action: Measuring Human Capital Successfully

Financial-services company National City Corp. was suffering unusually high turnover rates and set out to develop a company-wide solution. Theorizing a link between training and retention, HR executives and others worked to develop the National City Institute, a department that provides ongoing orientation and training for new employees. To evaluate the institute's effectiveness, the firm decided to assess how much the trainees learned, how their work performance changed, and how the institute affected the business's financial performance.

The company began collecting extensive data on sales, performance, and employee behavior, soon discovering that it needed different performance measures for people in different jobs. For instance, bank tellers, debt collectors, and check-coding employees each required different types of training and had different impacts on company performance. Therefore, their work had to be measured in slightly different ways.

This human-capital measurement initiative has paid big dividends. According to Michael H. Hannibal, curriculum and measures manager for the institute, "We found some positive differences between those who took the training and those who did not," including longer stays with the company. In addition, he said, "we're beginning to demonstrate some impact on sales. We've improved branch-level performance."

SOURCE: Adapted from Steve Bates, "The Metrics Maze," *HR Magazine,* December 2003.

Reporting Human Capital

It's one thing to begin measuring and interpreting data on various aspects of your firm's human capital. It's another to decide how you'll communicate your findings and interpretations. In reporting on human capital, you'll probably have two audiences to consider: people within your organization, and individuals outside your organization.

To communicate your findings within your company, establish a routine reporting schedule in which you share your analysis of the data you've gathered with various audiences, including your executive team and relevant departments. Present your findings in accessible formats, including graphs or tables, if appropriate. Gather feedback from the meeting attendees, and invite suggestions for fine-tuning the data-gathering and interpreting process. Incorporate any recommendations that promise to improve your methodology. Some performance-management consulting firms have developed software applications for analyzing data, preparing reports, and presenting information in graphical format. If you feel comfortable using these tools, and they help you present your data and interpretations in easy-to-understand ways, then consider using them. But resist any temptation to use them simply because they offer colorful interfaces and lots of bells and whistles. Whiz-bang software, if misused, will merely obscure the thinking behind the numbers you're presenting.

You've also got several opportunities to communicate your human-capital measurement work to audiences outside your company's staff. For example, New York University professor Baruch Lev recommends that companies record "systematic information on key [human-capital] variables, such as training, incentive-based compensation, and turnover" in footnotes to the company's financial statements.[10] Such disclosure gives valuable tools to people seeking to evaluate HR practices. For instance, it enables people to examine possible correlations between increased training expenses and decreased turnover, along with other measures of productivity or profitability.

By voluntarily disclosing information about human-capital measurement in financial statements and annual reports, companies give a more complete picture of their worth to shareholders, analysts, and the public. They also "demonstrate leadership by stepping out ahead of the pack."[11]

Summing Up

In this chapter, you learned about several aspects of measuring and reporting the elusive asset known as human capital. You saw that many companies define human capital as the collective sum of the attributes, life experience, knowledge, inventiveness, energy, and enthusiasm that its people choose to invest in their work. You also read about why it's so important for organizations to measure their human capital—despite the many challenges associated with this emerging field.

In addition, you saw examples of the types of metrics that firms may identify while developing a human-capital measurement program. One section in the chapter laid out a step-by-step process and tips for initiating such an effort—starting with conducting a human-capital audit and identifying your firm's most pressing human-capital concerns.

Finally, the chapter offered recommendations for reporting human-capital data and interpretations of that data in accessible presentations to executives, managers, and employees within your organization. It also addressed the advantages of disclosing human-capital measurements and analysis in financial reports and other communications to shareholders, analysts, and the public.

Leveraging Chapter Insights: Critical Questions

- How is human capital currently defined and measured at your firm?

- What's working well about the way your organization now defines and measures its human capital? What's not working as well?

- What changes, if any, would you recommend in the way your company defines and measures human capital? Why?

- Do you think that the method your firm uses to measure its human capital has helped the organization manage that intangible asset better? Why, or why not?

- How does your company currently report human-capital data and the interpretations of that data to audiences inside and outside the organization? In what ways, if any, might current reporting methods be improved?

CHAPTER TWELVE

The Time Value of Money

Calculating the Real Value
of Your Investment

Key Topics Covered in This Chapter

- *Present and future value*

- *Net present value*

- *Internal rate of return*

- *Hurdle rate, discount rate, and the cost of capital*

- *Economic value added*

I N CHAPTER 10, we examined return on investment (ROI) and payback period analysis—two tools that HR managers can use to make program investment decisions and assess the performance of their investments. We noted, however, that these tools have one important weakness: They fail to account for the time value of money. That is, though they indicate (or estimate) inflows and outflows of cash, ROI and payback analysis fail to recognize *when* those cash flows take place. As we'll explain here, the timing of those cash flows matters and should be factored into management decisions.

This chapter introduces you to financial decision-making tools that account for time value: specifically, present and future value, net present value, and internal rate of return. You will also become acquainted with associated concepts that you're likely to encounter when management discusses serious long-term investments—hurdle rate, discount rate, and the company's cost of capital. The chapter also includes additional discussion of sensitivity analysis, a method that increases the practicality of these time-value tools.

These are all complex concepts, with formulas that many laypeople find daunting. You may know how to construct a spreadsheet that shows these concepts, but understanding how the supporting formulas are constructed might be another story entirely. What is the best way to educate yourself on this? Visit your company's chief financial officer (or equivalent executive or manager), and ask for a fully developed copy of the spreadsheet that your company uses for these calculations.

What Is Time Value?

The time value of money is a mathematically based recognition that money received today is worth more than an equal amount of money received months or years in the future. If you have any doubts about this statement, consider the following scenario:

> *Your father-in-law takes you aside and says, "The grim reaper is going to catch up with me one of these days. And as much as I'd like to take all of my money with me, I've decided to give you youngsters a bundle of it before I go—say, three hundred thousand dollars."*

Naturally, you're pleased to learn of your father-in-law's generous intention. You are also eager to learn *when* the money will be coming your way. "I'm not sure when I'll give you the money," he continues. "It might be this year, next year, or five years down the road. But that shouldn't matter, since it will be three hundred thousand in any case."

Your father-in-law got that last point dead wrong. *When* you receive the money *does* matter. Thanks to the effect of compounding interest, $300,000 put today into a bank CD or savings account with a 5 percent annual interest rate would be worth almost $383,000 five years from now—and slightly more than $483,000 if your investment compounded at a 10 percent annual rate! Let's look at how compounding works over time using the $300,000 in our example, with annual compound interest at 10 percent per year over five years (table 12-1).

TABLE 12-1

Time Value of an Investment with 10% Compounded Interest

Period	Beginning Value	Interest Earned	Ending Value
1	$300,000	+$30,000	$330,000
2	$330,000	+$33,000	$363,000
3	$363,000	+$36,300	$399,300
4	$399,300	+$39,930	$439,230
5	$439,230	+$43,923	$483,153

This example demonstrates the importance of time in the receipt of cash amounts. If your father-in-law were to give you the $300,000 today, you'd be $183,153 better off (assuming a 10 percent compounded return) than if he delayed his gift to you by five years. (Note: This analysis assumes that you reinvest the interest you earn at the same rate.)

The example also introduces a number of important terms in the language of finance. The $300,000 is a *present value* (PV), that is, an amount received today. The $483,153 is a *future value* (FV), that is, the amount to which a present value, or series of payments, will increase over a specific period at a specific compounding rate. The number of periods (*n*) in this example is five years. And the interest rate (*i*) is 10 percent. Understand these terms, and you'll probably rise a notch or two in the estimation of your company's CFO.

Generations of business students have been forced to learn how to calculate time values using tables like the one in table 12-2. This table indicates the future value of $1, given various compounding rates and compounding periods. (Such periods could be of any duration—days, months, or years.) Each cell in the table is com-

TABLE 12-2

Future Value of $1 (FVIF)

Period	8%	9%	10%	11%	12%
1	1.0800	1.0900	1.1000	1.1100	1.1200
2	1.1664	1.1881	1.2100	1.2321	1.2544
3	1.2597	1.2950	1.3310	1.3676	1.4049
4	1.3605	1.4116	1.4641	1.5181	1.5735
5	1.4693	1.5386	1.6105	1.6851	1.7623
6	1.5869	1.6771	1.7716	1.8704	1.9738
7	1.7138	1.8280	1.9487	2.0762	2.2107
8	1.8509	1.9926	2.1436	2.3045	2.4760
9	1.9990	2.1719	2.3579	2.5580	2.7731
10	2.1589	2.3674	2.5937	2.8394	3.1058
11	2.3316	2.5804	2.8531	3.1518	3.4786
12	2.5182	2.8127	3.1384	3.4985	3.8960

monly referred to as a future value interest factor, or FVIF. Tables such as these are easy to use.

The table shows that the FVIF for five periods at 10 percent is 1.6105. Considering the example of your father-in-law's $300,000 gift, you can now find the future value of $300,000 after five years at a 10 percent annual interest rate. To do so, follow this simple formula:

Present Value × FVIF = Future Value
$300,000 × 1.6105 = $483,150

This amount is the future value we found earlier using a long-handed method (with a slight difference due to rounding).

Every finance text has an appendix of tables you can use to solve time-value problems. But thanks to today's preprogrammed business calculators and electronic spreadsheets, this exercise has become even easier. Many business calculators have several keys programmed to make these solutions simple. The keyboard has keys for present value (PV), future value (FV), compounding rate (i), and number of compounding periods (n). If you know any three of these variables, the calculator will solve for the fourth. The instruction books that come with such calculators explain the sequence to follow in entering the values and obtaining the solution. Likewise, PC spreadsheet programs such as Microsoft's Excel have built-in formulas that make time-value problems easy to solve.

Present Value and Net Present Value

Future value is an easy idea to grasp, since most of us have been exposed to the principle of compound interest. Put money in an interest-bearing account, leave it alone, and it will grow to a larger amount over time. The longer you leave it alone, or the higher the compounding rate, or both, the larger the future value. The idea of the present value of a future sum is less familiar and less intuitive, but financial people and other savvy managers use it all the time. You can, too.

Present Value

Present value is the monetary value today of a future payment discounted at some annual compound interest rate. To understand the concept of present value, let's go back to our initial example—the bequest from your father-in-law. In that example, the present value of $483,153 is $300,000. This is calculated through a process of discounting, or reverse compounding, at a rate of 10 percent per year over a period of five years. In the parlance of finance, 10 percent is the *discount rate*. If your father-in-law had said, "Look, I'm planning on giving you $483,153 five years from now, but if you'd rather have the money today I'm willing to give you $300,000," he'd be giving you an equivalent value, assuming you could invest it at 10 percent annually. In short, you would be indifferent about the choice between getting $300,000 now or getting $483,153 in five years—unless you worried about your father-in-law's not making good on his promise.

As with future value, tables are available for calculating the present value of $1 received in the future. Table 12-3 indicates the present-value interest factors (PVIFs) for $1 received in the future within a range of discount rates and discounting periods.

TABLE 12-3

Present Value of $1 (PVIF)

Period	2%	4%	6%	8%	10%	12%
1	0.980	0.962	0.943	0.926	0.909	0.893
2	0.961	0.925	0.890	0.857	0.826	0.797
3	0.942	0.889	0.840	0.794	0.751	0.712
4	0.924	0.855	0.792	0.735	0.683	0.636
5	0.906	0.822	0.747	0.681	0.621	0.567
6	0.888	0.790	0.705	0.630	0.564	0.507
7	0.871	0.760	0.665	0.583	0.513	0.452
8	0.853	0.731	0.627	0.540	0.467	0.404
9	0.837	0.703	0.592	0.500	0.424	0.361
10	0.820	0.676	0.558	0.463	0.386	0.322

Note that the PVIF for five periods at 10 percent is 0.621. We can use this factor to calculate the present value of your father-in-law's $483,153 gift received five years in the future:

Future Value × PVIF = Present Value
$483,153 × 0.621 = $300,038

We're off by just a little as a result of rounding of the PVIF in the table.

The PVIF table clearly indicates how the present value of money received in the future shrinks with time. Scan any discount rate column in the PVIF table from top to bottom. The first number is the value of $1 received a year from now. In the 10 percent column, that value is $0.91. The same dollar is worth only $0.39 if you must wait ten years to get your hands on it. Strictly chump change. Notice, too, the role that the discount rate plays in shrinking future values over time. At 6 percent, $1 received ten years from now is worth $0.59. But at a discount rate of 12 percent, that same dollar is down to a mere $0.32! Thus, present value "shrinkage" has two sources: time and the discount rate. The greater the time and the higher the rate, the less your future cash flows will be worth.

Your financial calculator and PC spreadsheet can handle this same calculation. You simply enter the known values (future value, discount rate, and number of compounding periods) and solve for the unknown present value, PV.

Net Present Value

Now that you understand present value, let's move on to a typical business situation and see how time-value calculations can help your decision making. But first let's broaden the concept of present value to *net present value* (NPV), which is the present value of one or more future cash flows *less* any initial investment costs. To illustrate this concept, let's say that Parker & Smith expects a new filing-cabinet line to start generating $70,000 in annual profit (or, more specifically, net cash flows) beginning one year from now. For simplicity,

Beginning or End of the Period

In calculating net present value and other time-value problems, it's important to know whether the cash flows take place at the beginning or end of the period in question. The present value of a cash flow received in early January is worth more than the same amount received in late December of the same year. Your financial calculator and electronic spreadsheet are set up to accommodate this important difference.

we'll also say that this level of annual profit will continue for the succeeding five years (totaling $350,000). Bringing the product line on stream will require an up-front investment of $250,00. The questions for the company can thus be phrased as follows: Given this expected profit stream and the $250,000 up-front cost required to produce it, is a new line of filing cabinets the most productive way to invest that initial $250,000? Or would Parker & Smith be better off investing the money in something else?

A net-present-value calculation answers this question by recognizing that the $350,000 in profit that Parker & Smith expects to receive over five years is not worth $350,000 in current dollars. Because of the time value of money, the $350,000 is worth less than that. In other words, that future sum of $350,000 has to be discounted back into an equivalent of today's dollars. How much it is discounted depends on the rate of return Parker & Smith could reasonably expect to receive had it chosen to put the initial $250,000 investment into something other than the new filing-cabinet line (but similar in risk) for the same period. As explained earlier, this rate of return is often called the discount rate. We define the discount rate as the annual rate, expressed as a percentage, at which a future payment or series of payments is reduced to its present value. In our Parker & Smith example, let's assume a discount rate of 10 percent. But before we describe the calculation, let's lay out the situation as follows, with the values in thousands of dollars:

Year 0	−250
Year 1	+70
Year 2	+70
Year 3	+70
Year 4	+70
Year 5	+70

Here we see a negative cash flow of $250,000 in year zero, the starting point of our investment project. This is the cash outflow required to get the project off the ground. The company then experiences a positive cash flow of $70,000 *at the end* of each of the next five years.

To find the net present value of Parker & Smith's stream of cash flows, we need to find the present value of each of the $70,000 cash flows, discounted at 10 percent for the appropriate number of years. If we add together the present values of the five annual inflows and then subtract the $250,000 initially invested, we will have the NPV of the investment. We can determine the NPV for this set of cash flows using table 12-4 and its present-value interest factors.

Note: An NPV calculation determines the net present value of a series of cash flows according to the algebraic formula

$$\text{Net Present Value} = \frac{CF_0 + CF_1}{(1 + i)_1} + \frac{CF_2}{(1 + i)_2} \cdots + \frac{CF_n}{(1 + i)_n}$$

where each CF is a future cash flow, n is the number of years over which the profit stream is expected to occur, and i is the desired rate of return, or the discount rate. When you supply the values for each future cash flow, the discount rate, and the number of years, your spreadsheet or calculator will do the rest.

Calculations such as this one can be laborious, but the financial calculators and computer spreadsheets now available make them fast and accurate. But you still need to plug in the right numbers in the right sequence. The NPV function on your calculator or spreadsheet takes into consideration your initial investment, each periodic cash flow, your discount rate, and the number of years over which you will receive the cash flows.

TABLE 12-4

Net Present Value of Parker & Smith's Filing-Cabinet Cash Flow

Year	Cash Flows (in $1,000)	PVIF (at 10%)	PV (in $1,000)
0	–250		–250.00
1	+70	0.909	+63.63
2	+70	0.826	+57.82
3	+70	0.751	+52.57
4	+70	0.683	+47.81
5	+70	0.621	+43.47
Total			+15.30

If the resulting NPV is a positive number, and no other invest-ments are under consideration, then the investment should be pur-sued. In the Parker & Smith case depicted in table 12-4, the NPV for the line of filing cabinets is a positive $15,300, which suggests that venture would be an attractive investment for Parker & Smith. (Note: You'll get a slightly different number if you make the calcu-lation on a financial calculator or spreadsheet program. The reason? A rounding error. Our PVIF goes to three decimal places, whereas calculators and spreadsheets generally go to higher decimal places.) The investment's compound annual return is at least 10 percent.

But what about another investment Parker & Smith is consider-ing—the $100,000 plastic extruder described in chapter 10? Let's reanalyze that investment option through the lens of NPV. As men-tioned, the company was considering spending $100,000 to pur-chase and install a new extruder that, according to its best esti-mates, would save $18,000 each year over the seven-year lifetime of the machine. We can set up the problem as shown in table 12-5, with cash flows in thousands of dollars.

Notice something else about the NPV calculation for the extruder, as seen in table 12-5. Even with a 6 percent discount rate, the NPV is far less positive than the rosy 26 percent return on investment (ROI) we calculated in chapter 10. That ROI repre-sented 26 percent over a seven-year period but failed to account for

TABLE 12-5

Net Present Value of Parker & Smith's Plastic Extruder Cash Flow

Year	Cash Flow (in $1,000)	PVIF (at 10%)	PV (in $1,000)
0	−100		−100.00
1	+18	0.909	+16.36
2	+18	0.826	+14.87
3	+18	0.751	+13.52
4	+18	0.683	+12.29
5	+18	0.621	+11.18
6	+18	0.565	+10.17
7	+18	0.514	+9.25
Total			−12.36

the time value of money. Clearly, as a decision tool, ROI has limited value. NPV analysis provides a more precise evaluation of investment opportunities.

At a discount rate of 10 percent, and using the PVIF table in table 12-5, we determine that the NPV of the extruder project is −$12,360. As a negative NPV, the investment probably shouldn't be pursued.

Here we should emphasize the effect that the discount rate has on NPV. The greater the discount rate, the lower the present value of future cash flows. Suppose that Parker & Smith's discount rate were 6 percent instead of 10 percent. In that case, the NPV for the extruder would be slightly positive. However, the filing-cabinet venture would then be even more positive than it is now.

Complications

Of course, business situations are almost always more complex than the conveniently simple ones we've contrived in the Parker & Smith examples. Project investments are rarely made in a single lump sum at the very beginning, and cash flows are almost always irregular—some positive, others negative—over time. What's more, it is often difficult or impossible to accurately estimate what cash flows will look like far in the future, or when they will finally end. Some investments end abruptly with the sale of the product line or factory building—the net sale value of which must be entered as a terminal-value cash flow. Other investments may go on for decades and gradually fade to nothing.

With this complexity in mind, we will try to present a slightly more realistic picture of a business using NPV analysis. Let's deliberately make Parker & Smith's new filing-cabinet product line investment project slightly more complex. We'll do this in three ways and then show how you could assess the investment project through the same NVP analysis framework:

1. We'll spread the $250,000 investment over three periods instead of one. This is more typical of business practice in developing a new product line.

2. Cash flows will be made more irregular, with a loss in the first full year and growing profitability in later years.

3. We'll arbitrarily plan for Parker & Smith to sell the product line at the end of five years for $170,000, and we'll treat the sale price as a terminal value.

Table 12-6 shows the results of these assumptions. Using 10 percent as the discount rate, we calculate a NPV of about $69,800 for this series of negative and positive cash flows. If 10 percent is the interest, or "cost of capital," to Parker & Smith, we could say that this investment would (1) earn its cost of capital *and* (2) make a positive present-value contribution of $69,800.

More Complications

Our presentation makes NPV analysis seem as straightforward as the mathematics on which it rests. It *is* straightforward—but the cash flows we use are, unfortunately, merely estimates. Consider Parker & Smith's $250,000 investment. Where did that number come from? Chances are, it would be an agreed-upon estimate pro-

TABLE 12-6

Net Present Value of Parker & Smith's Cash Flow, with Complications (Values in Thousands of Dollars)

			YEAR			
	0	1	2	3	4	5
Cash investments	−150	−75	−25	0	0	0
Cash flow from operations		−15	+40	+80	+90	+100
Terminal value						+170
Net cash flow	−150	−90	+15	+80	+90	+270
Present value interest factors		0.909	0.826	0.751	0.683	0.621
Present value	−150	−81.81	+12.39	+60.08	+61.47	+167.67
Net present value	+69.80					

Note: Discount rate = 10%; interest rate (cost of capital) = 10%.

duced by people in Parker & Smith's R&D and manufacturing units. Those people have experience in designing new products and setting up the manufacturing equipment needed to crank them out. But past experience is an uncertain guide to the future. The only thing that you can say with certainty is that the cost of the investment will be more or less than $250,000!

Estimates of the net cash flows from operations are bound to be even less certain. Consider how cash flow from operations is determined. The product line manager no doubt asks the marketing department several questions:

1. How many of these new products (in units) can your people sell in each of the next five years?

2. What would be our net revenues from each sale?

3. What level of marketing budget would you need to achieve those sales at those prices?

4. What training and staffing would enable you to achieve those sales?

HR in Action: Evaluating the NPV of Retention Strategies

Joan Perkins, an HR executive at Latham Industries, knows how valuable employee retention is for her firm. She's mulling over three ways to improve retention: raising salaries, adding fringe benefits, and providing job-specific training. She knows she needs to calculate the net present value (NPV) of each of these three alternatives. So, she estimates costs and revenue for each option over five years, with revenue estimates including productivity associated with more experienced workers. She then converts the results to a single NPV measure for each option.

Table 12-7 shows what Perkins comes up with, based on certain assumptions—such as salary costs increase 4 percent in the first year and then 5 percent annually, and training costs are highest in the first year but drop to maintenance levels while increasing annually by 5 percent.

Perkins's calculations suggest that raising salaries is barely sensible on financial grounds. The NPV is positive, but not by much. Adding benefits makes no sense, because its NPV is negative. Providing new training seems very attractive—the NPV is substantially positive. Combining salary and increases and training appears particularly promising.

SOURCE: Adapted from Steve Bates, "Accounting for Time," *HR Magazine*, September 2003, 52.

The manager would likewise get a unit production and labor and materials cost estimate from the manufacturing unit. In effect, the new-product manager would have to develop a detailed "mini" income statement similar to the enterprise income statement described in chapter 2. This statement would detail the revenues and costs (i.e., materials, labor, marketing, and all other costs) associated with the new product line over the five-year span of the analysis. The sum of the revenues and costs would be the cash flow from operations.

TABLE 12-7

Using NPV to Compare Employee Retention Strategies

Retention Strategy	Current Year	+1 Year	+2 Years	+3 Years	+4 Years	NPV
Continue current policies (expected revenue)	$3,500,000	$3,657,500	$3,822,088	$3,994,081	$4,173,815	
Raise salaries						
New cost	–$96,000	–$99,840	–$104,832	–$110,074	–$115,577	
New revenue		$182,875	$152,844	$119,822	$83,476	
Net gain	–$96,000	$83,035	$48,052	$9,749	–$32,101	$6,224
Add benefits						
New cost	–$35,000	–$38,500	–$42,350	–$46,585	–$51,244	
New revenue		$54,863	$38,221	$19,970	$4,174	
Net gain	–$35,000	$16,363	–$4,129	–$26,615	–$47,070	–$79,115
Add training						
New cost	–$250,000	–$50,000	–$52,500	–$55,125	–$57,881	
New revenue		$146,300	$210,215	$219,674	$229,560	
Net gain	–$250,000	$96,300	$157,715	$164,549	$171,679	$340,243
Combine salary increases and training						
New cost	–$346,000	–$149,840	–$157,332	–$165,199	–$173,458	
New revenue		$336,490	$371,507	$346,087	$319,923	
Net gain	–$346,000	$186,650	$214,175	$180,888	$146,465	$382,178

Taken together, these annual estimated cash flows from operations would be used to determine the NPV of the project. Obviously, there are lots of assumptions here, and there is plenty of room for error—especially as people attempt to forecast sales further and further into the future. There's even a chance that sales of the new product line will cannibalize the sales of existing product lines. As a consequence, opponents of the particular investment can usually find plenty of opportunities to take potshots at the numbers, and experienced decision makers usually insist on fairly conservative sales forecasts and cost estimates.

Nevertheless, careful NPV analysis based on sound assumptions is an excellent decision-making tool—and it's certainly better than the alternatives. Its value can be improved if the NPV of an investment is presented in worst-case, most-likely-case, and best-case scenarios. This approach captures a broader range of opinions in the organization about future unit sales, various costs of production, and other assumptions.

Internal Rate of Return

The *internal rate of return* (IRR) is another tool managers can use to decide whether to commit to a particular investment opportunity, or to rank the desirability of various opportunities. The IRR is defined as the discount rate at which the NPV of an investment equals zero. Let's consider what that means in terms of our more complicated version of Parker & Smith's net cash flow projection (in thousands of dollars) for its new line of filing cabinets:

Year 0	−150
Year 1	−90
Year 2	+15
Year 3	+80
Year 4	+90
Year 5	+270

As calculated earlier, the NPV of this stream of cash flows discounted at 10 percent was a positive $69,800. That told us that these numbers, if realized, would cover Parker & Smith's cost of capital (10 percent) *and* contribute an additional present value of $69,800. But the IRR also tells us something more. It captures the discount rate *and* the additional present value contribution in a single number. To calculate it, we need to determine the discount rate that would reduce the NPV to exactly zero. The IRR is that discount rate.

We know right off the bat that the IRR for our example must be greater than 10 percent since the cash flow discounted at 10 percent produced a positive NPV. But how much more? Well, if we had a few blackboards and several hours, we could calculate the IRR

Hurdle Rate and the Cost of Capital

We've defined *hurdle rate* as the minimal rate of return that all investments for a particular enterprise must achieve. The firm's *cost of capital* is more specific: It's the weighted average cost of the organization's different sources of capital—both debt and equity.

Most people understand that the debt capital employed by corporations has a cost—namely, the interest paid on bonds and other IOUs. But few nonfinancial people think of the capital contributed by owners as having a real cost. It does. It has an *opportunity cost*—what the shareholders could earn on their capital if they invested in the next-best opportunity available to them at the same level of risk. For instance, if you had $100,000 of your money tied up in the shares of XYZ, Inc., a corporation whose share price fluctuates greatly, your opportunity cost for that capital might be 14 percent—the return you'd be able to obtain for an investment of equivalent risk. Thus, for a big, stable corporation, the shareholders' opportunity cost might be 10 percent; for a risky, high-tech company, the owners might expect an 18 percent return.

The methodology for calculating the cost of capital for an individual business or for business units is beyond the scope of this book. Put simply, however, the cost of capital is the weighted average cost of the organization's different sources of capital.

From a practical standpoint, you might equate your company's cost of capital with the hurdle rate mentioned in our discussion of NPV. The CFO can provide this number, but will likely adjust the hurdle rate upward for projects of increasing risk.

through an iterative process that used higher and higher discount rates. Eventually, we'd get to the one that produced an NPV of zero. But again, financial calculators and electronic spreadsheets come to the rescue, making IRR calculations very easy. All we need to do is enter the values for each of the cash flows and calculate the discount rate (*i*). The IRR calculation is based on the same algebraic formula as the NPV calculation. With the NPV calculation, you know the discount rate, or the desired rate of return, and are solving the equation for the NPV of the future cash flows. In contrast, with the IRR, the NPV is set at zero and the discount rate is unknown. The equation solves for the discount rate. For the Parker & Smith filing-cabinet project just described, the IRR is about 17.7 percent.

Typically, when the IRR is greater than the opportunity cost (the expected return on a comparable investment) of the capital required, the investment under consideration should be undertaken. You can use your company's *hurdle rate* as the IRR target. A company's CFO usually prescribes the hurdle rate. The hurdle rate is a minimal rate of return that all investments for a particular enterprise must achieve. The IRR of the investment under consideration must exceed the hurdle rate in order for the company to go forward with the investment.

What's a reasonable hurdle rate for a business? It varies from company to company. Typically, the hurdle rate is set well above what could be obtained from a risk-free investment, such as a U.S. Treasury bond. You can, in fact, think of the hurdle rate as this:

Hurdle Rate = Risk-Free Rate + Premium That Reflects the Enterprise's Risk

Like any investor, a business entity expects to be rewarded for the uncertainty to which it is subjected. And new product lines and other such activities are, by nature, filled with uncertainty. For this reason, executives demand that prospective projects show particularly good promise.

Some companies use different hurdle rates for different types of investments, with low-risk investments having to clear a lower hurdle than that imposed on the higher-risk type. For example, a company might require that replacement of an existing assembly line or a specialized piece of equipment use a hurdle rate of 8 percent, whereas the expansion of an existing product line would have a 12 percent hurdle rate. The development of a new product line, which is riskier still, might require a 15 percent hurdle rate.

Sensitivity Analysis

Every business forecast includes one or more assumptions. In proposing the company's new filing-cabinet line, Parker & Smith managers no doubt assumed that its dealers would pay X dollars per unit, that materials costs would be Y dollars per unit, and that the investment needed to get the operation off the ground would be Z dollars. These are just a few of many assumptions.

What would happen if one or more of these assumptions failed to hold? Sensitivity analysis helps you ask just that question—and helps you consider the ramifications of incremental changes in the assumptions that underlie a particular projection.

Parker & Smith expects its new line of filing cabinets to generate $70,000 in annual cash flow beginning a year from the initiation of the project. But what if some variable in the scenario changed? How would this shift affect the overall evaluation of the investment opportunity?

Charles Peabody, the vice president of Parker & Smith's cabinet division, is projecting $70,000 in annual cash flow for five years—as in our initial present-value example. Natasha Rubskaya, the company's CFO, is less optimistic. She believes that Peabody has drastically underestimated the marketing costs necessary to support the new line. She predicts an annual cash stream of $45,000. Then there's Theodore Small, Parker & Smith's senior vice president for new business development. Ever the optimist, he feels certain that the filing cabinets will practically sell themselves and will produce an annual profit stream of $85,000 a year.

Parker & Smith conducts a sensitivity analysis using the three profit scenarios. The NPV for Peabody's scenario is $15,355. Rubskaya's is in negative territory, at −$79,415. Small's scenario results in an NPV of $72,217.

If Rubskaya is right, the filing cabinets won't be worth the investment. If either of the other two is right, however, the investment will be worthwhile. The investment will really prove itself if Small's projections are on target. This is where judgment comes in to play. If Rubskaya is the best estimator of the three, then Parker & Smith's board of directors might prefer to take her estimate of the line's profit potential. Better still, the company should analyze its marketing costs in greater detail. Whichever route the directors take, sensitivity analysis will give the board a more nuanced view of the investment and how it would be affected by various changes in assumptions. Other contingencies, or changes in other variables, could be mapped out just as easily.

How to conduct a sensitivity analysis? Start by examining your underlying assumptions. If you're looking at breakeven analysis, reexamine your assumptions about each of these key components:

1. **Fixed costs and variable costs:** Are you certain that your estimates for these costs are on target? Get the views of others on this consideration, and try to establish a range of likely cost scenarios. Point estimates are almost always wrong.

2. **Contribution:** The unit contribution is based on the selling price less the unit variable cost. Thus, if you're looking at a new product or service, chances are that the selling price is still to be tested. Question the validity of that assumption. If your product or service will be very similar to others already on the market, then the price that people are already paying may be a reliable guide. But if your product or service is new to the world, then there may have been some guesswork involved in the determination of the selling price—even if your company conducted customer research. So again, it's a good idea to establish a range of likely selling prices for the new product or service.

You can perform the same type of sensitivity analysis on NPV calculations. In the Parker & Smith case, for instance, you'd want to look more closely at the positive cash flows forecasted in years one through five. Most people cannot accurately forecast next year's cash flows, let alone those that occur many years in the future. So Peabody's point forecast of $70,000 per year may not be reliable. Careful study may reveal a range of possible cash flows, with that range widening with each passing year, as shown here (in thousands of dollars):

Year 0   −250
Year 1   +68 to +72
Year 2   +65 to +75
Year 3   +62 to +78
Year 4   +60 to +80
Year 5   +58 to +82

Again, you're much more likely to get it right if you forecast future cash flows as *ranges* of possible outcomes. Once you've determined the ranges for your situation, calculate the NPV for the best case, the worst case, and the most likely case. This will help your senior executives make a better decision. It will also help everyone understand which assumptions make or break the investment itself. These assumptions might involve the selling price, the timing of the new product launch, or the cost of raw materials. Management can then focus its time and energy on making more accurate forecasts on those items. And once the project is in play, management will know that it must give those important points the greatest attention.

Economic Value Added

Our last tool is one that many corporations have adopted since the early 1990s. *Economic value added,* or EVA, gives shareholders and managers a better sense of business or business unit performance. Many use EVA as a metric for determining management bonuses. In many ways it's related to the NPV and IRR concepts we've just covered.

For many years, CEOs and unit managers would pat themselves on the back for producing income statement profits. "My company (unit) has produced yet another year of profitable operations," they would crow. They were big heroes. Then, in the late 1980s, financial consultants Joel Stern and Bennett Stewart blew the whistle on many of these executives. Sure, these executives had produced accounting profits, but these were not *real* economic profits. The reason for the discrepancy? A failure to recognize an important cost—the cost of the capital used in their operations.

Simply stated, EVA is net operating income after taxes *less* the cost of the capital used to obtain it:

EVA = Net Operating Profits After Taxes − (Capital Used × Cost of Capital)

By failing to account for the cost of capital, many businesses appear profitable even as they deplete shareholder wealth. But unless a business returns a profit greater than its cost of capital, it operates at a loss. A company may pay taxes and report a profit on its income statement, but it destroys shareholder value if its gains are less than its cost of capital. And lots of seemingly profitable enterprises are doing just that, reporting a profit while operating at a loss. By taking all capital costs into account, including the cost of owners' equity, EVA calculates the monetary value that a business— or one of its operating units—creates or destroys in any given accounting period.

EVA is both a tool for evaluating new projects and a metric for gauging and rewarding managerial performance. In using it as an evaluation tool, we ask, "Will this project increase economic value?" By forecasting the impact of a new project or investment on net operating income after taxes (per our formula), and subtracting the cost of capital, we can determine the investment's economic value added—or value lost. NPV does the same thing and, thanks to the discount rate, also recognizes the cost of capital. EVA is more effective, however, as a metric for measuring and rewarding management. The metric encourages managers to look at how capital is employed in their units and to ask, "Is this or that particular application of capital really returning at least its full costs?" They begin to take a hard look at assets that everyone customarily thought of as free goods: freight trains, machinery, buildings, assembly lines, and so forth. And they often discover that the company would be better off liquidating those assets and redeploying the proceeds into activities with higher returns.

Summing Up

This chapter has presented what many experts consider the most valuable financial tools available to business managers and analysts: net present value, internal rate of return, economic value added, and their various related concepts. These tools are far superior to payback and return on investment, both of which fail to recognize either the timing of cash flows or the firm's cost of capital (or hurdle rate). In brief, these tools' characteristics are as follows:

- Net present value (NPV) is the monetary value today of a future stream of positive and negative cash flows discounted at some annual compound interest rate. You can use NPV analysis for any number of decision-making purposes.

- Internal rate of return (IRR) is another tool that you can use to decide whether to commit to a particular investment opportunity, or to rank the desirability of various opportunities. IRR is the discount rate at which the NPV of an investment equals zero.

- Economic value added (EVA) is net operating income after tax less the cost of the capital used to obtain it. Many companies use EVA as a discipline to evaluate operations, investments, and business performance. Like NPV, it forces managers to take account of the cost of capital used in their decisions.

Whether you're considering launching a new initiative, purchasing a new asset, or making any other type of investment, time-value tools can greatly enhance your decision-making ability. They can even help you determine the value of assets, a subject you'll learn more about in the next chapter.

We've just skimmed the surface of this important subject in this chapter. If you wish to learn more about these topics, our advice is threefold: (1) read more about time-value concepts in any of the many corporate finance textbooks currently available; (2) learn how to use a financial calculator or financial spreadsheet programs; and (3) practice the application of these tools to business problems as you encounter them.

Leveraging Chapter Insights: Critical Questions

- Think of two or three HR initiatives or programs you're considering developing to address an issue at your company. Based on what you've learned in this chapter, which of the efforts under consideration promises to generate the most value in the long run? Why? How would you go about assessing the time value of the investments the company would need to make in these efforts? Would a combination of these efforts make the most sense?

- What steps could you take to learn more about NPP, IRR, and EVA and ways to apply these concepts to your work in HR?

CHAPTER THIRTEEN

Business Valuation Concepts

Evaluating Opportunity

Key Topics Covered in This Chapter

- *Asset-based valuation methods*
- *Earnings-based valuation methods*
- *Discounted cash flow approach to valuation*

HAVE YOU FOUNDED an HR-services start-up that you're now considering selling? Have you grown your business and started mulling over the possibility of acquiring another firm to spur further expansion? Is the corporation you work for considering buying or selling an operating division or acquiring another firm? If any of these circumstances describe your situation, the question, "What is a business's value?" outweighs most other issues, and for good reason. Why? The rate of return from a purchased division company is likely to be disappointing if the buyer paid too high a price. Likewise, underestimating the value of a division or company in a sales transaction can leave plenty of the owners' money on the table.

Valuing an ongoing business—large or small—is neither easy nor exact. The field of finance, however, has developed methods for getting close to the value. This chapter introduces you to several methods.[1]

An Uncertain Science

Before we get started, consider several cautions. We can never know the exact value of a business with certainty. This lack of certainty stems from two problems. First, alternative valuation methods consistently fail to produce the same outcome, even when meticulously calculated. Second, the product of valuation methods is only as good as the data and the estimates we bring to them, and these often prove incomplete or unreliable. For example, one method depends heavily on estimates of future cash flows. In the very best cases, those estimates will only be close. In the worst cases, they will fall far from the mark.

Here's another consideration: A company is worth different amounts to different parties. Different prospective buyers are likely to assign different values to the same set of assets. For example, suppose you're a book collector who already owns first editions of every Hemingway novel except *For Whom the Bell Tolls.* That book would probably have a lot more value to you than to another collector who owned just one or two first-edition Hemingways. The reason? For you, the acquisition would complete a set, the value of which is greater than the sum of the individual volumes considered separately. Businesses view acquisitions with a similar perspective. The acquisition of a small, high-tech company, for example, might provide an acquirer with the technology it needs to leverage its other operations. This explains, in part, why so many firms are bought for more than the market value of their existing shares.

Also keep in mind that valuation is the province of specialists. Small and closely held businesses typically turn to professional appraisers when the business's value must be established for purpose of its sale, for determining the value of its shares when an employee stock ownership trust is used, or for some other purpose. When large, public firms or their business units are the subjects of a valuation, executives generally turn to a variety of full-service accounting, investment banking, or consulting firms. Many of these vendors have departments devoted entirely to mergers and acquisitions, in which valuation issues form the central focus. Nevertheless, a well-rounded HR manager will take steps to understand the nature of different valuation methods—and their strengths and weaknesses.

Closely held businesses—that is, businesses with only a few owners—are particularly difficult to value. The sale of an operating unit of a public company presents similar challenges. In neither case do publicly traded ownership shares exist. Public markets for ownership, such as NASDAQ or the New York Stock Exchange, make value more transparent. Everyday buying and selling in these

Valuing a Possible Acquisition

The first e-mail of the day has just hit your screen, and it's marked URGENT. It is from your boss, the division general manager, and the CFO: "We'll be meeting tomorrow afternoon at 2:00 in the boardroom to discuss a possible acquisition of Parker & Smith Inc., which we believe would have a good strategic fit with our current home/office furnishings line. Please come prepared to discuss the valuation issues."

You're familiar with Parker & Smith and its founder and CEO, Ann Cuneo, whose story was featured in a recent issue of *Furniture Times*. It's likely that this same story spurred your company's interest in acquiring Parker & Smith. Given Cuneo's age and given that her company is closely held by the Cuneo family, key employees, and retired managers, you speculate that Parker & Smith is ripe for a sale. This might be a good opportunity, but you are unsure of how to approach the valuation issues at tomorrow's meeting.

markets establishes a company's per-share price. And that price, multiplied by the number of outstanding shares, often provides a basis for a fair approximation of company value at a point in time.

Asset-Based Valuations

One way to value an enterprise is to determine the value of its assets. There are four approaches to asset-based valuations: equity book value, adjusted book value, liquidation value, and replacement value.

Equity Book Value

Equity book value is the simplest valuation approach and uses the balance sheet as its primary information source. Here's the formula:

Equity Book Value = Total Assets – Total Liabilities

To test-drive this formula, consider the balance sheet of Parker & Smith introduced in chapter 2. Table 2-1 showed that the company's total assets equal $3,635,000, whereas the total liabilities are $1,750,000. The difference—the equity book value—is $1,885,000. Notice that this is the same as total owners' equity. In other words, reduce the balance sheet (or book) value of the business's assets by the amount of its debts and other financial obligations, and you have its equity value.

This equity-book-value approach is easy and quick. Many executives in a particular industry roughly calculate their company's value in the context of equity book value. For example, one owner might contend that his or her company is worth at least book value in a sale because that was the amount that he or she had invested in the business. But equity book value is not a reliable guide for businesses in many industries. Why? Assets are placed on the balance sheet at their *historical* costs, which may not express their value today. The value of balance-sheet assets may be unrealistic for other reasons as well. Consider Parker & Smith's assets:

- Accounts receivable could be suspect if many accounts are uncollectible.

- Inventory reflects historic cost, but inventory may be worthless or less valuable than its stated balance-sheet value (or "book" value) because of spoilage or obsolescence. On the other hand, some inventory may be *under*valued.

- Property, plant, and equipment after depreciation should also be closely examined—particularly land. If Parker & Smith's property was put on the books in 1985—and if it happens to be in the heart of Silicon Valley—then its real market value may be ten or twenty times the 1985 figure.

The preceding are just a few examples. For many reasons, however, book value is not always true *market* value.

Adjusted Book Value

The weaknesses of the quick-and-dirty equity-book-value approach have led some businesspeople to adopt *adjusted book value,* which attempts to restate the value of balance-sheet assets to realistic market levels. Consider the influence of adjusted book value in a leveraged buyout of a major retail store chain in the 1990s. At the time of the analysis, the store chain had an equity book value of $1.3 billion. Once its inventory and property assets were adjusted to their appraised values, however, the enterprise's value leaped to $2.2 billion—an increase of 69 percent.

When adjusting asset values, it is particularly important to determine the real value of any listed intangibles, such as goodwill and patents. In most cases, goodwill is an accounting fiction created when one company buys another at a premium to book value— that is, at a price higher than book value. The premium must be put on the balance sheet as goodwill. But to a potential buyer, the intangible asset may have no value.

Liquidation Value

Liquidation value is similar to adjusted book value. It attempts to restate balance-sheet values in terms of the net cash that would be realized if assets were disposed of in a quick sale and all liabilities of the company were paid off or otherwise settled. This approach recognizes that many assets, especially inventory and fixed assets, usually do not fetch as much as they would if the sale were made more deliberately.

Replacement Value

Some people use *replacement value* to obtain a rough estimate of value. This method simply estimates the cost of reproducing the business's assets. Of course, a buyer may not want to replicate all the assets included in the sale price of a company. In this case, the replacement value represents more than the value that the buyer would place on the company.

Pros and Cons of Asset-Based Valuations

The various asset-based valuation approaches described here generally share some strengths and weaknesses. On the up side, the
approaches are easy and inexpensive to calculate. They are also easy
to understand. On the down side, both equity book value and liquidation value fail to reflect the actual market value of assets. And all
approaches fail to recognize the intangible value of an ongoing
enterprise, which derives much of its wealth-generating power
from human knowledge, skill, and reputation.

Earnings-Based Valuations

Another approach to valuing a company is to capitalize its earnings. This involves multiplying one or another income statement
earnings figure by some multiple. Some earnings-based methods
are more sophisticated than others. There is also the question of
which earnings figure and which multiple to use.

Earnings Multiple

For a publicly traded company, the current share price multiplied
by the number of outstanding shares indicates the market value of
the company's equity. Add in the value of the company's debt, and
you have the total value of the enterprise. Think of it this way: The
total value of a company is the equity of the owners *plus* any outstanding debt. Why add in the debt? Consider your own home.
When you go to sell your house, you don't set the price at the level
of your equity in the property. Its value is the total of the outstanding debt and your equity interest. Likewise, the value of a company
is shareholders' equity plus the liabilities. This is often referred to as
the *enterprise value.*

   For a public company whose shares are priced by the market
every business day, pricing the equity is straightforward. But what
about the closely held corporation, whose share price is generally
unknown, because the firm doesn't trade in a public market? We

can reach a value estimate by using the known price-earnings multiple (often called the P/E ratio) of similar enterprises that are publicly traded. The price-earnings approach to share value begins with this formula:

Share Price = Current Earnings × Multiple

We calculate the multiple from comparable publicly traded companies as follows:

$$\text{Multiple} = \frac{\text{Share Price}}{\text{Current Earnings}}$$

Thus, if XYZ Corporation's shares are trading at $50 per share and its current earnings are $5 per share, then the multiple is 10. In stock market parlance, we'd say that XYZ is trading at ten times earnings.

We can use this ratio approach to price the equity of a nonpublic corporation if we can find one or more similar enterprises with known multiples. This is a challenge, since no two enterprises are exactly alike. The uniqueness of every business is why valuation experts recognize their work as part science and part art. To examine this method further, let's return to our example firm.

Since Parker & Smith is a closely held firm, we have no readily available benchmark for valuing its shares. But let's suppose that we succeeded in identifying a publicly traded company (or, even better, several companies) similar to Parker & Smith in most respects— in terms of industry and size. We'll call one of these firms Stockton Industries. And let's suppose that Stockton's multiple is 8. Let's also suppose that our crack researchers have discovered that another company, this one private, was recently acquired by a major office-furniture maker at roughly the same multiple: 8. This gives us confidence that our multiple of 8 is in the right ballpark. With this information, let's revisit Parker & Smith's income statement presented in chapter 2 (table 2-2) to find its net income (earnings) of $347,500.

Plugging the relevant numbers into the following formula, we estimate Parker & Smith's value:

$$\text{Earnings} \times \text{Appropriate Multiple} = \text{Equity Value}$$
$$\$347,500 \times 8 = \$2,780,000$$

Remember that this is the value of the company's equity. To find Parker & Smith's total enterprise value, we must add the total of its interest-bearing liabilities. Table 2-1 showed that the company's interest-bearing liabilities (short-term and long-term debt) for 2005 are $1,185,000. Thus, the value of the entire enterprise is as follows:

$$\text{Enterprise Value} = \text{Equity Value} + \text{Value of Interest-Bearing Debt}$$
$$\$3,965,000 = \$2,780,000 + \$1,185,000$$

The effectiveness of the multiple approach to valuation depends in part on the reliability of the earnings figure. The most recent earnings, for example, might be unnaturally depressed by a onetime write-off of obsolete inventory, or pumped up by the sale of a subsidiary company. For this reason, you need to factor out random and nonrecurring items. Likewise, you should review expenses to determine that they are normal—neither extraordinarily high nor extraordinarily low. To illustrate, inordinately low maintenance and repair charges over one period would pump up near-term earnings but result in extraordinary expenses in the future for deferred maintenance. Similarly, nonrecurring, windfall sales can also distort the earnings picture.

In small, closely held companies, pay particular attention to the salaries of the owner-managers and the members of their families. If these salaries have been unreasonably high or low, you'll need to make an adjustment of earnings. You should also assess the depreciation rates to determine their validity and, if necessary, to make appropriate adjustments to reported earnings. And while you're at it, take a hard look at the taxes that have reduced bottom-line profits. The amount of federal and state income taxes paid in the past may influence future earnings, because of carryover and carry-back provisions in the tax laws.

EBIT Multiple

The reliability of the multiple approach to valuation we have just described depends on the comparability of the firm or firms used as proxies for the company whose value we seek to estimate. In the preceding Parker & Smith example, we relied heavily on the observed earnings multiple of Stockton Industries, a publicly traded company whose business is similar to Parker & Smith's. Unfortunately, these two companies could produce equal operating results yet indicate much different bottom-line profits to their shareholders. How is this possible? The answer is twofold: how they are financed, and taxes. If a company is heavily financed with debt, its interest expenses will be large, and those expenses will reduce the total dollars available to the owners at the bottom line. Likewise, one company's tax bill might be much higher than the other's for some reason that has little to do with its future wealth-producing capabilities. And taxes reduce bottom-line earnings.

Consider the hypothetical scenario in table 13-1. Notice that the two companies produce the same earnings before interest and taxes (EBIT). But because Stockton Industries uses more debt and less equity in financing its assets, its interest expense is much higher

TABLE 13-1

Hypothetical Income Statements of Parker & Smith and Stockton Industries

	Parker & Smith	Stockton Industries
Earnings before interest and taxes (EBIT)	$757,500	$757,500
Less interest expense	$110,000	$350,000
Earnings before income tax	$647,500	$407,500
Less income tax	$300,000	$187,000
Net income	$347,500	$220,500

($350,000 versus $110,000). This expense dramatically reduces its earnings before income taxes relative to Parker & Smith. Even after each pays out an equal percentage in income taxes, Stockton ends up with substantially less net income.

This earnings variation between two otherwise comparable enterprises would produce different equity values for the two, and would have to be reconciled by the adding in of each company's liabilities. The problem can be circumvented, however, if we use EBIT instead of bottom-line earnings in our valuation process. Some practitioners go one step further and use the EBITDA multiple. EBITDA is EBIT *plus* depreciation and amortization. Depreciation and amortization are noncash charges against net income— accounting allocations that tend to create differences between otherwise similar firms. By using EBITDA in the valuation equation, we can avoid this potential distortion.

Discounted Cash Flow Method

The earnings-based methods just described have a big problem: They're based on historical performance—what happened last year. And as the oft-heard saying goes, past performance is no assurance of future results. If you made an offer to buy a local small business, chances are you'd base your offer on the company's ability to produce profits in the years *ahead*. Likewise, if your company were hatching plans to acquire Parker & Smith, you would be less interested in what the company earned in the past than in what it is likely to earn in the future under new management and as an integrated unit of your enterprise.

We can direct our earnings-based valuation toward the future by using a more sophisticated valuation method: *discounted cash flow* (DCF). The DCF valuation method is based on the same time-value-of-money concepts we covered in chapter 12. DCF determines value by calculating the present value of a business's future cash flows, including its ending value. Since those cash flows are available to both equity holders and debt holders, DCF can reflect the value of the enterprise as a whole or can be confined to the cash flows left available to shareholders.

For example, let's apply this method to your own company's valuation of Parker & Smith, using the following steps:

1. The process should begin with Parker & Smith's income statement, from which your firm's financial experts would try to identify the company's current actual cash flow. They would use EBITDA and make some adjustment for taxes and for changes in working capital. Necessary capital expenditures, which are not visible on the income statement, reduce cash and therefore must also be subtracted.

2. Your analysts would then estimate future annual cash flows— a tricky business, to be sure.

3. Next, you would estimate the terminal value. You can either continue your cash flow estimates for twenty to thirty years (a questionable endeavor), or you can arbitrarily pick a date at which you will sell the business, and then estimate what that sale would net ($4.3 million in year 4, in the analysis that follows). That net figure after taxes will fall into the final year's cash flow. Alternatively, you could use the following equation for determining the present value of a perpetual series of equal annual cash flows:

$$\text{Present Value} = \frac{\text{Cash Flow}}{\text{Discount Rate}}$$

Using the figures in the illustration, we could assume that the final year's cash flow of $600,000 will go on indefinitely (referred to as a perpetuity). This amount, divided by the discount rate of 12 percent, would give you a present value of $5 million.

4. Compute the present value of each year's cash flow using the technique described in chapter 12.

TABLE 13-2

Discounted Cash Flow Analysis of Parker & Smith (12% Discount Rate)

Year	Present Value (in $1,000)	Cash Flows (in $1,000, Rounded)
1	446.5	500
2	418.5	525
3	398.7	560
4	381.6 + 2,734.8	600 + 4,300
Total	4,380.1	

5. Total the present values to determine the value of the enterprise as a whole.

We've illustrated these steps in a hypothetical valuation of Parker & Smith, using a discount rate of 12 percent (table 13-2). Our calculated value there is $4,380,100. (Note that we've estimated that we'd sell the business to a new owner at the end of the fourth year, netting $4.4 million.)

In this illustration, we've conveniently ignored the many details that go into estimating future cash flows, determining the appropriate discount rate (in this case we've used the firm's cost of capital), and gauging the terminal value of the business. All are beyond the scope of this book—and all would be beyond your responsibility as a nonfinancial manager. Such determinations are best left to the experts. What's important for you is to gain a general understanding of the discount cash flow method and its strengths and weaknesses.

The strengths of the DCF valuation method are numerous:

- It recognizes the time value of future cash flows.

- It is future oriented, and estimates future cash flows in terms of what the new owner could achieve.

- It accounts for the buyer's cost of capital.

- It does not depend on comparisons with similar companies—which are bound to be different in various dimensions (e.g., earnings-based multiples).

- It is based on real cash flows instead of accounting values.

The DCF method has a weakness as well: It assumes (wrongly) that future cash flows, including the terminal value, can be estimated with reasonable accuracy.

Summing Up

This chapter has examined the important but difficult subject of business valuation. It described three approaches:

- **Asset based:** The first category of valuation approach is asset-based and includes equity book value, adjusted book value, liquidation value, and replacement value. In general, these methods are easy to calculate and understand, but they have notable weaknesses. Except for replacement and adjusted book methods, they fail to reflect the actual market values of assets. They also fail to recognize the intangible value of an ongoing enterprise, which derives much of its wealth-generating power from human knowledge, skill, and reputation.

- **Earnings based:** The second valuation-approach category described in this chapter is earnings-based and includes the P/E method, the EBIT, and the EBITDA methods. The earnings-based approach is generally superior to asset-based methods, but depends on the availability of comparable businesses whose P/E multiples are known.

- **Cash-flow based:** Finally, we presented the discounted cash flow method, which is based on the concepts of the time value of money. The DCF method has many advantages, the most important being its future-looking orientation. This method estimates future cash flows in terms of what a new owner could achieve. It also recognizes the buyer's cost of capital. The major weakness of the method is the difficulty inherent in producing reliable estimates of future cash flows.

In the end, these different approaches to valuation are bound to produce different outcomes. Even the same method applied by two experienced professionals can produce different results. For this reason, most appraisers use more than one method in approximating the true value of an asset or a business.

Leveraging Chapter Insights: Critical Questions

- Is the company you work for considering buying or selling a division, or acquiring another firm? If so, how is your company valuing the affected division or firm? If you're not sure, how might you learn more about this?

- Given what you've read in this chapter, which valuation approach do you think would be most appropriate for the affected division or firm? Why?

- If you've started up a company and are considering selling it or buying another firm to stimulate growth, which valuation approaches do you think would be the best to use in this case? Why?

CHAPTER FOURTEEN

Developing and Using Your Financial Know-How

Next Steps for You and Your Firm's HR Department

Key Topics Covered in This Chapter

- *How to strengthen your financial knowledge*
- *How to use financial know-how to serve as a better strategic business partner*
- *How to forge positive working relationships between HR and finance*
- *How to operate your HR department as a profit center*

ONGRATULATIONS! By working your way through the chapters in this book, you've greatly beefed up your financial know-how. What steps might you take next to best apply your new knowledge? This chapter shows you how to continue strengthening your financial literacy and leveraging it in your company. You do this by serving as a strategic business partner, creating positive working relationships between your firm's HR and finance departments, and positioning your HR department as a profit center rather than a cost center.

Enhancing Your Financial Know-How

As with any other skill, you need to keep strengthening and practicing your financial know-how to ensure that those "muscles" stay limber and toned. Here are some recommendations for continuing to deepen your financial understanding and sharpen your skills:

- **Read.** Explore additional books and articles on finance—especially those that relate the subject area to the world of HR. See the For Further Reading list at the end of this book for ideas.

- **Learn from peer managers.** As often as possible, discuss financial matters with department heads and financial experts in your firm. Take them to lunch, explaining that you want to keep strengthening your understanding of financial matters. Ask them what their most pressing financial concerns are and how they handle them. And invite them to describe how *they* maintain and deepen their financial knowledge.

- **Use a financial lens.** Practice viewing your company's operations and challenges through a financial lens. For example, with every decision you make and action you take, think through how that decision or action may ultimately affect your firm's financial performance. In particular, try to gauge a decision's or an action's impact on the company's profitability—its bottom line.

- **Attend courses.** Numerous organizations provide valuable business education programs that include financial literacy. For example, visit www.shrm.org/shrmacademy to learn more about the SHRM Academy—the Society for Human Resource Management's business essentials program. The academy offers various curriculum domains, including finance, strategy, communications, information and operations, and implementation management. Depending on how many courses you complete, you can earn a certificate of achievement, a certificate of specialization, or a certificate in business management.

In addition to helping you build solid business knowledge with the help of top-notch faculty, attending such programs can provide excellent networking opportunities.

See assessment tool 14–1 for a worksheet that can help you lay out an action plan for enhancing your financial know-how.

Serving as a Strategic Business Partner

As you saw in chapter 1, enhancing your finance literacy yields numerous benefits for you, your HR department, and your entire

Assessment Tool 14-1
Action Plan for Enhancing Your
Financial Know-How

Use this worksheet to plan strategies for strengthening your
financial literacy.

1. **Further Reading.** Which books and articles strike you as
   the most valuable for further deepening your financial
   knowledge? List them below, indicating how you'll obtain
   them and when you intend to have finished reading them.

   Book or Article

   Where/How Obtain

   When Complete Reading

2. **Peer Learning.** Which individuals inside and outside your
   firm might shed additional light on the world of finance?
   Write their names below, and indicate how and when you
   plan to interact with them. For example, will you design a
   rotating-assignment program that enables you to learn
   more about other functions' financial challenges and
   strategies? Will you take certain individuals to lunch or
   coffee? Ask to attend a meeting focusing on financial
   matters? Invite someone to facilitate a brown-bag session
   on finance basics for yourself and other managers? Stop by
   for casual conversations with particular managers?

   Name

   Networking Plan

   Target Networking Dates

3. **Practice.** What steps might you take to practice using a financial lens? For instance, will you create financial statements for your household, so as to link your new understanding to something familiar and manageable? Will you inspect and ask questions about your firm's financial statements more frequently? Write your ideas below, and indicate how and when you intend to take these steps.

Practice Strategy

How Achieve

When Achieve

4. **Educational opportunities.** What educational opportunities do you think would help you maintain and enhance your financial knowledge? List them below. Also indicate how you'll get approval and funding (if needed) to take advantage of these opportunities, and when you'll attend courses or programs.

Educational Opportunity

How Obtain Approval/Funding

When Attend

5. **Additional ideas.** In addition to further reading, peer learning, practice, and educational opportunities, what other ideas come to mind for enhancing your financial know-how? List them below, and show how and when you'll implement these ideas.

Strategy

How Implement

When Implement

company. Financial know-how enables you to practice the following worthwhile business activities:

- Demonstrate the value generated by HR investments.

- Measure the value of human capital.

- Implement an HR balanced scorecard.

- Encourage ethical financial practices and conduct.

- Prevent or reduce embezzlement and other forms of theft by employees.

- Comply with new federal regulations, such as the Sarbanes-Oxley Act of 2002.

- Help your company avoid, prepare for, or recover from bankruptcy.

Together, the benefits generated by your financial savvy can help you and other HR professionals be more knowledgeable strategic business partners in your firm. When you pair awareness of your company's strategy with a deep understanding of financial matters, you can more easily see how HR decisions and actions affect the firm's bottom line: its profitability. And by grasping those links, you can make smart choices about where and how to invest in your firm's human capital and leverage your department's resources.

As an informed strategic partner, you can also help others throughout your organization strengthen their own financial understanding. For example, you can develop training sessions and workshops in finance literacy for managers and employees. You can also initiate a rotating-assignment program that enables people (including yourself and other HR professionals) to learn more about one another's job responsibilities. Rotating assignments help open a window onto the financial ramifications of each function's decisions and actions.

Creating Positive Working Relationships Between HR and Finance

More and more companies are realizing that close cooperation between HR executives and the CFO and other finance experts can generate important strategic value for firms. Why? Each side brings unique experiences and perspectives to the question of how a company can best leverage its human capital to boost profitability. When both sides share their thinking about HR initiatives and their potential impact on the firm's financial performance, they can gain fresh insights that might not have come to light had they neglected to collaborate. Indeed, "there is no intrinsic conflict between wise stewardship of human capital and the sober, just-the-facts-please perspective of a model CFO."[1]

New pressures are also causing more organizations to see the value of HR–finance cooperation. For example, with stiffening competition and the rising importance of human capital to corporate financial performance, everyone—including HR professionals—must be true human *capitalists.* That is, managers in every function must constantly think about how best to invest in and leverage their human resources to boost productivity and profitability. And according to Rutgers University professor Mark Huselid, "greater scrutiny of corporate governance has . . . put more pressure on businesses' HR and finance functions to cooperate."[2]

Whether an HR executive is on the same level as the CFO in a company's organizational chart, reports to the CFO, or reports elsewhere, collaboration between these two professionals can pay big dividends for the entire organization. (See the sidebar "HR in Action: Collaborating with Finance at First Tennessee National Corp.") Towers Perrin's Jeff Schmidt maintains that such partnering is particularly important for projects related to governance reform and the development of methods for measuring human capital and other intangible assets.[3]

But how, exactly, might you encourage successful cooperation between HR and finance on important initiatives in your firm? Consider these guidelines:[4]

HR in Action: Collaborating with Finance at First Tennessee National Corp.

Sarah Meyerrose, executive vice president of corporate employee services for the large, Memphis-based banking organization First Tennessee National Corp., faced a daunting challenge: how to help align her firm's HR strategy behind the company's overall business strategies. Meyerrose took several steps to support this effort, including creating several "employee relationship manager" positions and assigning the managers to different bank divisions or regional offices. These managers began working closely with division financial executives and attending meetings to deepen their understanding of business strategy.

The move generated several benefits. For one thing, it gave HR managers a clear line of sight between strategic initiatives and HR decisions. As Meyerrose pointed out, "They became proactive in saying, 'If you want to [launch that business initiative], this is what we have to do' from an HR perspective to achieve the result." Thus HR managers were "networked into the business."

The HR-finance collaboration also enabled the company to address strategic challenges in an orchestrated way. For instance, when customer retention hit a plateau after rising for several years, Meyerrose's department collaborated with finance to define several HR initiatives aimed at helping First Tennessee get over the plateau, including a new variable pay plan and a leadership development program. "The more people you have proactively asking, 'How can we do things differently?' the better," Meyerrose maintained. This HR professional has also overseen the launching of surveys and studies designed to reveal connections between high performers, customer loyalty, and corporate profitability—as well as retention of valued workers.

At First Tennessee, HR and finance also work together to quantify the return on human capital investment. As one illustration, the two departments collaborated on developing a staffing model for the firm's sales forces. The company examined traffic patterns and transaction volume to determine the needed full- and part-time staff. Now, if one office loses an employee, the model helps managers figure out if another office has more than the ideal number of workers. Through such analysis, employees can be redeployed—saving the company the costly and time-consuming process of hiring.

SOURCES: Richard F. Stolz, "Human Capitalists," *Human Resource Executive,* June 16, 2003, 17–18, and Steve Bates, "Business Partners," *HR Magazine,* September 2003.

- Ensure that HR, finance, and the executive team all agree on the ultimate goal of a project.

- Select project leaders who excel at generating specific recommendations even with imperfect data.

- Establish accountability—specifying who will deliver what within which time frame.

- Rather than generating ideas for HR-finance initiatives and trying to fit them into the overall corporate-strategy picture, start by understanding the company's broad strategy—and then determine which initiatives and HR-finance partnering efforts will support that strategy.

- Rather than expecting the spontaneous sharing of ideas, take advantage of regular executive team meetings to keep your CFO in the loop at early stages of HR initiatives. That way, he or she can challenge your thinking and contribute fresh insights. Also consider taking the CFO to lunch or swapping jobs for a short time with a finance staff member, to begin seeing things from a finance perspective. Likewise, a rotation program that enables finance professionals to spend time in HR can further stimulate cross-pollination of ideas and experiences.

- In discussions with your CFO about the possible return on investment (ROI) of a proposed HR initiative, resist the urge to spend lots of time crunching numbers to prove that the project will generate a 100 percent ROI. Instead, ask what ROI is necessary to receive funding for the initiative. The CFO may want just 25 percent—in which case it wouldn't make sense to invest time analyzing how to get a 100 percent return.

- Be willing to makes leaps of faith and concessions to finance experts if necessary to encourage collaboration between the two groups. Remember that each group brings its own skills and responsibilities to the cooperation process.

Operating Your HR Department as a Profit Center

In addition to enabling you to serve as a strategic partner and collaborate with finance professionals for the benefit of your company, financial savvy can help you begin operating your HR department as a profit rather than cost center.[5] Why is a profitability orientation so crucial among HR professionals today? As with many other business-world developments, increasing competition, rising costs, globalization, investor expectations, and other trends are putting more and more pressure on companies to demonstrate that they can deliver value to customers and shareholders. And profit is what enables businesses to deliver that value. Profit making isn't the sole purpose of an organization; rather, it's like oxygen: It enables the organization to stay alive so as to fulfill its purpose—whether that purpose involves high-tech solutions to consumers' entertainment needs, the improvement of health care, educational programs for needy youngsters, or some other reason for existing. If an organization (whether for-profit or not-for-profit) spends more money than it takes in, it can't expect to survive for very long.

For these reasons, more companies now expect *everyone* to adopt a profitability orientation. Managers in functions traditionally seen as cost centers, such as HR, must now continually look for ways to improve their firm's bottom line. Managers who succeed in this effort not only help their company fulfill its purpose. They also tend to earn more; receive high levels of respect from peers, supervisors, and direct reports; keep their jobs during financial downturns, mergers, and reorganizations; and become highly sought after by executive recruiters and other firms.

So how, exactly, might you improve profitability at your firm? You can do so through applying four levers:

- Increasing revenues

- Decreasing costs

- Enabling employees to work more efficiently

- Improving productivity

As an HR professional, you have numerous opportunities to apply any combination of these levers. Table 14-1 shows just a few examples of HR initiatives that are profit-oriented and those that are not.

The more you understand and speak the language of finance, the stronger your ability to determine—and demonstrate to others on your executive team—how various HR initiatives ultimately affect your firm's bottom line.

Summing Up

In this chapter, you read about strategies for further enhancing your financial savvy, including additional reading, peer learning, practicing examining HR decisions and actions through a financial lens, and structured educational opportunities.

You also saw how continually strengthening and practicing financial know-how and skills can help you serve as a strategic partner in your firm—through efforts such as collaborating with your company's CFO and other financial experts and positioning your HR department as a profit center. The chapter provided several examples of how HR initiatives can boost a company's bottom line

TABLE 14-1

A Profit- Versus Nonprofit-Oriented Approach to HR

HR Endeavor	Profit-Oriented Initiative	Initiatives Not Oriented Toward Profit
Compensation	An incentive-pay system that rewards employees for what they produce	A wage survey that aims to affirm the company's traditional salary structure
Benefits	A sick-day and vacation-time policy that reduces absenteeism	A sick-day program that allows employees to use medical time off even if they're not ill
Training	Analysis showing that salespeople who attended a specific training program sold more than those who didn't attend	Analysis showing that a specific number of people attended a certain training program
Recruiting	A hiring method ensuring that new employees are above-average to excellent performers	A hiring method that reduces time required to recruit all new employees
Equal Employment Opportunity Regulations	Examination of the number and types of EEO complaints the company received in the past two years, and efforts that reduce the number and cost of such complaints filed against the company	An affirmative-action plan that follows the letter of the law

Source: Michael W. Mercer, *Turning Your Human Resources Department into a Profit Center* (New York: AMACOM, 1989), 8–10.

HR in Action: DelCo Boosts Profitability Through Turnover Reduction

DelCo, a large engineering firm, had a problem: A rise in turnover among branch managers was costing the company $4.5 million annually in lowered productivity, lost billings, and new hiring. Myra Banks, DelCo's HR director, set out to restore the company's sagging bottom line. Her strategy included the development of an exit-interview program that would enable her department to identify the causes behind the turnover and remove those causes—thus improving retention among these key managers.

But Banks knew that to get approval for the program, she needed to show how its potential benefits compared with its possible costs. After conducting some research, she prepared the following cost-benefit analysis. The first step was to determine the cost of the exit-interview program:

Develop exit-interview format	$500
Conduct exit interviews	$7,500 (30 interviews with former branch managers at $250 per interview)
Analyze interview data; plan follow-up actions	$4,200 (time to systematize data, plus one-day meeting with one consultant and four company executives to analyze data)
Implement action plans	$1,100,000 per year (55 branch managers at $20,000 per year in action plans, such as bonuses, developed from data analysis)
Total cost	$1,112,200

To calculate the improvement benefit of the exit-interview program, Banks subtracted the estimated cost of the turnover problem a year after the exit interviews from the cost of the problem *before* the exit interviews:

Cost of annual turnover before interviews	$4,500,000
Cost of annual turnover after interviews	$250,000 turnover costs (5 estimated at $50,000 per resignation) plus $500,000 in lost productivity and billings (5 resignations at $100,000 per resignation) = $750,000
Improvement benefit	$4,500,000 − $750,000 − $1,112,200 = $2,637,800

Clearly, Banks's exit-interview program generated valuable benefits for her company.

SOURCE: Fictionalized adaptation of Michael W. Mercer, *Turning Your Human Resources Department into a Profit Center* (New York: AMACOM, 1989), pp. 158–160.

by increasing revenues, decreasing costs, enhancing employee efficiency, and raising productivity. You also read a case study of how one HR director enhanced her firm's profitability by developing an exit-interview program to combat high turnover among branch managers.

Leveraging Chapter Insights: Critical Questions

- After reading this book, which aspects of finance do you feel you understand best? Which aspects do you feel uncertain about?

- Which aspects of finance seem most important to your ability to serve your company? Why? How will you deepen your understanding of those aspects?

- In what ways might you initiate or improve cooperation with your company's CFO and other financial experts?

- How might you better position your HR department as a profit center for your firm?

Activity-Based Budgeting

Activity-based budgeting (ABB) is a new way of approaching the budgeting process. To understand ABB, we must first understand activity-based costing (ABC), which we touched on briefly in chapter 5. You can't do ABB unless your company has an ABC system.[1]

ABC is a new way to allocate the cost of resources consumed to the cost of objects such as products, customers, and distribution channels. Under traditional cost allocation, overhead costs are allocated to products using cost drivers such as direct labor hours and machine hours. These are referred to as volume drivers, because these drivers vary proportionately with the total volume of output. The problem with traditional cost-allocation mechanisms is that they don't reflect the independent relationship between some costs and the number of units produced in a batch. ABC, on the other hand, takes into account the reality that smaller batches of a product are usually more expensive to produce than larger batches—owing to setup costs. This is true even though the per-unit labor hours or machine hours might be the same for both batches.

Under ABC, the costs of resources such as rent, utilities, depreciation, and wages are first allocated to activities and then allocated from activities to cost objects using unit-, batch-, product-, customer-, and facility-level cost drivers. ABC looks at all the activities associated with producing something. An activity can be any event, task, or unit of work with a specified purpose. For example, the Executive Furnishings Division of Parker & Smith has operating activities such as the following:

- Purchase materials

- Prepare materials

- Schedule production

- Inspect products

- Package products

These operating activities are supported by management activities such as these:

- Hire new employees

- Train employees

- Manage computer network

- Manage payroll

- Prepare tax information

- Communicate with shareholders

Hierarchy of Activities

Managers can now look at how the various operating activities fit together in a hierarchy. At the base are the unit-level activities required to produce one executive desk or to make one repair service call. For example, these activities could include staining the wood, drilling holes in the drawers for drawer pulls, and attaching metal parts to the desk. The number of unit activities performed is based on the production and sales volumes. At this level, the traditional cost-allocation methods based on labor hours, machine hours, or units produced work fairly well.

The next step up the hierarchy is the batch-level activities. These activities are performed for each batch. For example, Parker & Smith produces different models of executive desks. When it changes production from one model to another, the activities for this batch might include processing the new production orders, reconfiguring manufacturing equipment, and so forth. The resources required for these batch activities are unrelated to the number of units produced in the run or batch.

The traditional budgeting methods of allocating overhead costs based on direct labor hours or units produced don't necessarily relate to the actual resources used to perform the batch activities. This is an example of where activity-based costing and activity-based budgeting can help managers more accurately determine costs and budget figures.

Similarly, as we go farther up the hierarchy of activities, we find product-sustaining activities such as testing for quality or developing new products, and customer-sustaining activities such as providing individual customers with service. We can relate these activities to the current products, but we can't measure their resource expenses in terms of units produced or direct labor hours. Here again, assessing the resource costs for each activity gives a clearer picture of the overall costs of production.

Developing Cost Drivers

The real power behind ABC lies in understanding the cost drivers for each activity. The activity cost driver is a quantitative measure of the output of that activity. For example, for the activity of "setting up the machines," the cost driver is the number of setup hours. For the "schedule production tasks" activity, the cost driver is the number of production runs.

There are three basic types of cost drivers. By identifying which type of cost driver is associated with a particular activity, we can measure the real resource expenses required for that activity.

- **Transaction cost drivers:** These drivers measure how often an activity is performed; for example, the number of machine setups or production runs or materials receipts.

- **Duration cost drivers:** These measure the amount of time an activity takes. For example, labor hours or setup hours may be the most accurate measure for activities related to producing a certain product.

- **Intensity cost drivers:** These drivers charge for the resources used by an activity. If, for example, a customer service call requires a specialized technician to be available, then the real cost lies with the technician as a resource rather than the time involved for the call.

Once you've determined the cost drivers for each activity, you know what the activity truly costs. You can then use this information for efficient operations, for efficient allocation of resources, and for planning ahead—in other words, for budgeting.

From Activity-Based Costing to Activity-Based Budgeting

Derived from ABC methods, *activity-based budgeting* concentrates on the cost of resources required for producing and selling products and services. ABC starts with the cost of resources, allocates these costs to activities, and then allocates the cost of these activities to products. Moving in the opposite direction, ABB starts with the planned product, sales volume, and mix and comes up with the required activities to produce that mix and volume. From these activities, budget planners can estimate the resources required and the cost of those resources. Thus, to use an ABB process, an organization needs to have historical data derived from an ABC system. The information is then used to project the required cost of resources based on the anticipated product, volume, and mix.

The primary advantage of ABB is that costs can be more accurately associated with activities, making the planning process more precise and corrections more effective. The disadvantage is that ABB can be costly and complex to establish—it may not be worth the trouble for a small company with few products or services. It also has to be adopted by and embedded into the whole organization; one division alone can't decide to develop its own ABC or ABB system. But when the circumstances are right, activity-based approaches to understanding the economic dynamics of an organization provide long-term planning benefits.

Balance-Sheet Template

Assets

Cash and marketable securities $_____

Accounts receivable $_____

Inventory $_____

Prepaid expenses $_____

    Total current assets $_____

Gross property, plant, and equipment $_____

Less: accumulated depreciation $_____

Net property, plant, and equipment $_____

    Total assets $_____

Liabilities and Owners' Equity

Accounts payable $_____

Accrued expenses $_____

Income tax payable $_____

Short-term debt $_____

    Total current liabilities $_____

Long-term debt $_____

    Total liabilities $_____

Contributed capital $_____

Retained earnings $_____

    Total owners' equity $_____

    Total liabilities and owners' equity $_____

Source: HMM Finance.

Income Statement Template

Retail sales	$_____
Corporate sales	$_____
Total sales revenue	$_____
Less cost of goods sold	$_____
Gross profit	$_____
Less operating expenses	$_____
Depreciation expense	$_____
Earnings before interest and taxes	$_____
Less interest expense	$_____
Earnings before income tax	$_____
Less income tax	$_____
Net income	$_____

Source: HMM Finance.

Cash Flow Statement Template

Net income	$_____
Operating Assets and Liabilities	
Accounts receivable	$_____
Finished-goods inventory	$_____
Prepaid expenses	$_____
Accounts payable	$_____
Accrued expenses	$_____
Income tax payable	$_____
Depreciation expense	$_____
Total changes in operating assets and liabilities	$_____
Cash flow from operations	$_____
Investing Activities	
Sale of property, plant, and equipment	$_____
Capital expenditures	$_____
Cash flow from investing activities	$_____
Financing Activities	
Short-term debt increase	$_____
Long-term borrowing	$_____
Capital stock	$_____
Cash dividends to stockholders	$_____
Cash flow from financing activities	$_____
Increase in cash during year	$_____

Source: HMM Finance.

Cash Budget Template

	Jan.	Feb.	March	April	May
Cash inflows					
Sales revenues					
Other revenues					
Interest income					
Total inflows					
Cash outflows					
Purchases					
Salaries					
Hourly wages					
Health-care payments					
Retirement contributions					
Interest payments					
Taxes					
Utilities					
Total cash outflows					
Cash surplus or deficit					
Beginning balance					
Ending balance					

HR Department Budget Template

Labor

Salaries, wages and benefits	$_____
Labor total	$_____

Operating Expenses

Materials and supplies	$_____
Office supplies	$_____
Printing and binding	$_____
Telephone	$_____
Postage	$_____
Travel and training	$_____
Equipment rental	$_____
Contractual services	$_____
Operating expense total	$_____

Capital Outlay

Machinery and equipment	$_____
Capital outlay total	$_____
Total for department	$_____

Notes

Chapter 1: Finance and the HR Professional

1. This section draws substantially from Julie Cook, "Money Matters," *Human Resource Executive* (April 2003), and Bill Thomas, "Minding Your Own Business," *Human Resource Executive* (May 16, 2003).

2. SHRM (Society for Human Resource Management) News to Use, press release, December 2, 2003.

3. Jack J. Phillips, *Return on Investment in Training and Performance Improvement Programs* (Woburn, MA: Butterworth-Heinemann, 1997), xiii.

4. Steve Bates, "Accounting for People," *HR Magazine,* October 2002.

5. Valerie E. Pike, "Balanced Scorecard Basics on Implementation," SHRM White Paper, December 2000.

6. This example was described in H. David Sherman and S. David Young, "Spinning the Numbers," *HR Magazine,* November 2002.

7. Frank Z. Ashen, "Corporate Ethics: Who Is Minding the Store?" SHRM White Paper, July 2002.

8. Sherman and Young, "Spinning the Numbers."

9. H. David Sherman and S. David Young, "Tread Lightly Through These Accounting Minefields," *Harvard Business Review Enhanced OnPoint Edition* (October 2002).

10. Sherman and Young, "Spinning the Numbers."

11. Jonathan A. Segal, "The 'Joy' of Uncooking," *HR Magazine,* November 2002.

12. Robert J. Grossman, "Holding Back Bankruptcy," *HR Magazine,* May 2003.

Chapter 3: Finding Meaning in Financial Statements

1. Our discussion of financial ratios leans heavily on William J. Bruns Jr., "Introduction to Financial Ratios and Financial Statement Analysis," Class Note 9-193-029 (Boston: Harvard Business School Publishing, 1996).

Chapter 4: From Financial Measures to a Balanced Scorecard

1. Robert S. Kaplan and David P. Norton, "The Balanced Scorecard: Measures That Drive Performance," *Harvard Business Review* (January–February 1992).

2. Robert S. Kaplan and David P. Norton, *The Balanced Scorecard: Translating Strategy into Action* (Boston: Harvard Business School Press, 1996), 278–279, appendix.

3. This section draws significantly from Brian E. Becker, Mark A. Huselid, and Dave Ulrich, *The HR Scorecard: Linking People, Strategy, and Performance* (Boston: Harvard Business School Press, 2001).

4. Ibid, pp. 64–72.

Chapter 5: Important Accounting Concepts

1. Our discussion of accounting for inventory is partly based on William J. Bruns Jr., "Accounting for Property, Plant, Equipment and Other Assets," Case Note 9-193-046 (Boston: Harvard Business School Publishing, 1996).

2. This section is adapted from ibid.

3. H. Thomas Johnson and Robert Kaplan, *Relevance Lost* (Boston: Harvard Business School Press, 1987).

4. Lianabel Oliver, *The Cost Management Toolbox: A Manager's Guide to Controlling Costs and Boosting Profits* (New York: AMACOM, 2000), 211–215.

Chapter 6: Taxes

1. This section relies heavily on Michael J. Roberts, "The Legal Forms of Business," Class Note 9-898-245 (Boston: Harvard Business School Publishing, 2001).

Chapter 7: Financing Operations and Growth

1. For the complete story of eBay's evolution, see David Bunnell (with Richard Luecke), *The eBay Phenomenon* (New York: John Wiley & Sons, 2000), 17–30. All financial information about the company described here is from eBay's 2001 10-K form.

Chapter 8: Money and Capital Markets

1. Marcia Stigum and Frank Fabozzi, *The Dow Jones-Irwin Guide to Bonds and Money Market Instruments* (Homewood, IL: Dow Jones-Irwin, 1987), 6.

Chapter 9: Budgeting

1. These steps were adapted from Lianabel Oliver, *The Cost Management Toolbox: A Manager's Guide to Controlling Costs and Boosting Profits* (New York: AMACOM, 2000), 91–99.

Chapter 11: Measuring and Reporting Human Capital

1. Leslie A Weatherly, "Human Capital: The Elusive Asset," *SHRM Research Quarterly* (2003): vol. 1.

2. This list of the forms of value that human capital can generate is derived from Lisa M. Aldisert, *Valuing People: How Human Capital Can Be Your Strongest Asset* (Chicago: Dearborn Trade Publishing, 2002), chapter 1, and Weatherly, "Human Capital: The Elusive Asset," 3–4.

3. Weatherly, "Human Capital: The Elusive Asset," 3.

4. Ibid.

5. Adapted from Aldisert, *Valuing People,* 7–10.

6. Leslie A. Weatherly, "The Value of People: The Challenges and Opportunities of Human Capital Measurement and Reporting," *SHRM Research Quarterly* 3 (2003): 7.

7. Weatherly, "Human Capital: The Elusive Asset," 4–5.

8. Steve Bates, "The Metrics Maze," *HR Magazine,* December 2003.

9. Adapted from Aldisert, *Valuing People,* 81–84.

10. Ibid., 71.

11. Ibid., 84.

Chapter 13: Business Valuation Concepts

1. This chapter has material adapted from Michael J. Robert, "Valuation Techniques," Class Note 9-384-185 (Boston: Harvard Business School Publishing, 1988).

Chapter 14: Developing and Using Your Financial Know-How

1. Richard F. Stolz, "Human Capitalists," *Human Resource Executive,* June 16, 2003, 17.

2. Mark Huselid, quoted in Steve Bates, "Business Partners," *HR Magazine,* September 2003.

3. Stolz, "Human Capitalists," 24.

4. List adapted from ibid., and Bates, "Business Partners."

5. This section draws extensively from Michael W. Mercer, *Turning Your Human Resources Department into a Profit Center* (New York: AMACOM, 1989), chapter 1.

Appendix A: Activity-Based Budgeting

1. The material in this appendix is from the "Budgeting" module of Harvard ManageMentor, Harvard Business Online Enterprise Solutions, Harvard Business School Publishing, available at <http://elearning.hbsp.org>.

Glossary

ACCOUNTS PAYABLE   A category of balance-sheet liabilities representing moneys owed by the company to suppliers and other short-term creditors.

ACCOUNTS RECEIVABLE   A category of balance-sheet assets representing moneys owed to the company by customers and others.

ACCRUAL ACCOUNTING   An accounting practice that records transactions as they occur, whether or not cash trades hands.

ACID-TEST RATIO   The ratio of so-called quick assets (cash, marketable security, and accounts receivable) to current liabilities. Inventory is left out of the calculation.

ACTIVITY-BASED BUDGETING (ABC)   A budgeting method in which planners start with the planned product, sales volume, and mix and comes up with the required activities to produce that mix and volume. From these activities, budget planners can estimate the resources required and the cost of those resources.

ACTIVITY-BASED COSTING (ABC)   An approach to cost accounting that carefully quantifies the links between performing particular activities and the economic demands those activities make on the organization's resources.

ADJUSTED BOOK VALUE   A refinement of the book value method of valuation that attempts to restate the value of certain assets on the balance sheet according to realistic market values.

ALLOCATIONS   See *indirect costs*.

ASSETS   The balance-sheet items in which a company invests so that it can conduct business. Examples include cash and financial instruments, inventories of raw materials and finished goods, land, buildings, and equipment. Assets also include moneys owed to the company by customers and others—an asset category referred to as *accounts receivable*. Another way to think of an asset is as something a company owns that has an agreed-on trading or exchange value.

AVERAGE COST   The average cost of inventory items is determined by adding the value of the beginning inventory and the total purchases made during the accounting period and dividing by the number of items.

BALANCE SHEET   A financial statement that describes the assets owned by the business and how those assets are financed—with the funds of creditors (liabilities), the equity of the owners, or both. Also known as the statement of financial position.

BOND   A debt security usually issued with a fixed interest rate and a stated maturity date. The bond issuer has a contractual obligation to make periodic interest payments and to redeem the bond at its face value on maturity.

BOOK VALUE OF SHAREHOLDER EQUITY   A balance-sheet valuation method that calculates value as total assets less total liabilities.

BREAKEVEN ANALYSIS   A form of analysis that helps determine how much (or how much more) a company needs to sell in order to pay for the fixed investment—in other words, at what point the company will break even on its cash flow.

BUDGET   A document that translates strategic plans into measurable quantities that express the expected resources required and anticipated returns over a certain period. A budget functions as an action plan and presents the estimated future financial statements of the organization.

BURDEN   See *indirect costs*.

CAPITAL MARKETS   The financial markets in which long-term debt instruments and equity securities—including private placements—are issued and traded.

CASH-BASIS ACCOUNTING   An accounting practice that records transactions only when cash changes hands.

CASH BUDGET   A budget that predicts and plans for the level and timing of cash inflow and outflow.

CASH FLOW STATEMENT   A financial statement that details the reasons for changes in cash (and cash equivalents) during the accounting period. More specifically, it reflects all the changes in cash as affected by operating activities, investments, and financing activities.

CHAPTER 11 BANKRUPTCY   A federal protected legal status that offers some financial breathing room while a struggling company attempts to stabilize its operations and survive.

COLLATERAL   An asset pledged to the lender until such time as the loan is satisfied.

COMMERCIAL PAPER   A short-term financing instrument used primarily by large, creditworthy corporations as an alternative to short-term bank borrowing. Most paper is sold at a discount to its face value and is redeemable at face value on maturity.

COMMON STOCK   A security that represents a fractional ownership interest in the corporation that issued it.

CONTRIBUTION MARGIN   In cost accounting, the contribution by each unit of production to overhead and profits, or net revenue less direct cost per unit.

COST-BENEFIT ANALYSIS   A form of analysis that evaluates whether, over a given time frame, the benefits of the new investment, or the new business opportunity, will outweigh the associated costs.

COST OF CAPITAL   The opportunity cost that shareholders and lenders could earn on their capital if they invested in the next-best opportunity available to them at the same level of risk, calculated as the weighted average cost of the organization's different sources of capital.

COST OF GOODS SOLD   On the income statement, what it costs a company to produce its goods and services. This figure includes raw materials, production, and direct labor costs.

CURRENT ASSETS   Assets that are most easily converted to cash: cash equivalents such as certificates of deposit and U.S. Treasury bills, receivables, and inventory. Under generally accepted accounting principles, current assets are those that can be converted into cash within one year.

CURRENT LIABILITIES   Liabilities that must be paid in a year or less; these typically include short-term loans, salaries, income taxes, and accounts payable.

CURRENT RATIO   Current assets divided by current liabilities. This ratio is often used as a measure of a company's ability to meet currently maturing obligations.

DAYS RECEIVABLES OUTSTANDING   The average time it takes to collect on sales. Also called days sales outstanding.

DEBT RATIO   The ratio of debt to either assets or equity in a company's financial structure.

DEPRECIATION   A noncash expense that effectively reduces the balance-sheet value of an asset over its presumed useful life.

DIRECT COSTS   Cost incurred as a direct consequence of producing a good or service—as opposed to overhead, or indirect costs.

DISCOUNT RATE   The annual rate, expressed as a percentage, at which a future payment or series of payments is reduced to its present value.

DISCOUNTED CASH FLOW (DCF)   A method based on time-value-of-money concepts that calculates value by finding the present value of a business's future cash flows.

DIVIDEND   A distribution of after-tax corporate earnings to shareholders.

EARNINGS BEFORE INTEREST AND TAXES (EBIT)   See *operating earnings*.

EARNINGS PER SHARE (EPS)   A company's net earnings expressed on a per-share basis.

ECONOMIC VALUE ADDED (EVA)   A measure of real economic profit calculated as net operating income after tax less the cost of the capital employed to obtain it.

ENTERPRISE VALUE   The value of a company's equity plus its debt.

EQUITY BOOK VALUE   The value of total assets less total liabilities.

FINANCIAL BUDGET   A budget that includes a company's capital budget, cash budget, budgeted balance sheet, and budgeted cash flows.

FINANCIAL LEASE   A lease that typically covers the entire useful life of the asset. The lease cannot be canceled unless the lessee makes all the scheduled payments. The lessee typically is required to pay for insurance, taxes, and the maintenance of the asset.

FINANCIAL LEVERAGE   The degree to which borrowed money is used in acquiring assets. A corporation is said to be highly leveraged when its balance-sheet debt is much greater than its owners' equity.

FIRST-IN, FIRST-OUT (FIFO)   A method of accounting for inventory that attributes the cost of goods sold to the cost of the oldest units of inventory.

FIXED ASSETS   Assets that are difficult to convert to cash—for example, buildings and equipment. Sometimes called plant assets.

FIXED BUDGET   A budget that covers a specific time frame—usually one fiscal year. At the end of the year, a new budget is prepared for the following year. A fixed budget may be reviewed at regular intervals—perhaps quarterly—so that adjustments and corrections can be made if needed, but the basic budget remains the same throughout the period.

FLEXIBLE BUDGET   A budget whose revenues and costs can be adjusted, or flexed, according to the variances calculated between the budgeted amounts and actual product output and revenues.

FUTURE VALUE (FV)   The amount to which a present value, or a series of payments, will increase over a specific period at a specific compounding rate.

GENERALLY ACCEPTED ACCOUNTING PRINCIPLES (GAAP)   In the United States, a body of conventions, rules, and procedures sanctioned by the Financial Accounting Standards Board, an independent, self-regulating body. All entities must follow GAAP in accounting for transactions and representing their results in financial statements.

GOODWILL   An intangible balance-sheet asset. If a company has purchased another company for a price in excess of the fair market value of its assets, that "goodwill" is recorded as an asset. Goodwill may also represent intangible things such as the acquired company's excellent reputation, its brand names, or its patents, all of which may have real value.

GROSS PROFIT   Sales revenues less the cost of goods sold. The roughest measure of profitability.

HUMAN CAPITAL   The collective skills, knowledge, life experiences, energy, and enthusiasm that a firm's people choose to invest in their work.

HURDLE RATE   The minimal rate of return that all investments for a particular enterprise must achieve.

INCOME STATEMENT   A financial statement that indicates the cumulative results of operations over a specified period. Also referred to as the profit-and-loss statement, or P&L.

INCREMENTAL BUDGETING   A budgeting practice that extrapolates from historical figures. Managers look at the previous period's budget and actual results as well as expectations for the future in determining the budget for the next period.

INDIRECT COSTS   Costs incurred that cannot be attributed to the production of any particular unit of output. Often referred to as overhead, allocations, or burden.

INITIAL PUBLIC OFFERING (IPO)   A corporation's first offering of its shares to the public.

INTELLECTUAL PROPERTY   A firm's marketable products and services that are proprietary and that can be trademarked or patented.

INTERNAL RATE OF RETURN (IRR)   The discount rate at which the net present value of an investment equals zero.

INVENTORY   The supplies, raw materials, components, and so forth, that a company uses in its operations. Inventory also includes work in process—goods in various stages of production—as well as finished goods waiting to be sold or shipped, or both.

INVENTORY TURNOVER   The cost of goods sold divided by the average inventory.

IPO   See *initial public offering.*

KAIZEN BUDGETING   A budgeting method that incorporates continuous improvement into the budgeting process. Cost reduction is built into the budget on an incremental basis so that continual efforts are made to reduce costs over time. If the budgeted cost reductions are not achieved, then extra attention is given to that operating area.

LAGGING INDICATORS   Measures that show how a company has performed in the past, such as net income for a specific period.

LAST-IN, FIRST-OUT (LIFO)   A method of inventory accounting that attributes the cost of goods sold to the most recently acquired units of inventory.

LEADING INDICATORS   Measures that indicate how a company might perform in the future, such as the amount invested in training for a particular period.

LIABILITY   A claim against a company's assets.

LIQUIDITY   The extent to which a company's assets can readily be turned into cash for meeting incoming obligations.

MARGINAL TAX RATE   The percentage rate of tax paid on the next or last dollar of income.

MASTER BUDGET   A budget that brings all the operating budgets and the financial budget of an organization into one comprehensive picture. The master budget summarizes all the individual financial projections of an organization for a given period.

MONEY MARKET   The network of issuers and dealers through which large borrowers raise short-term money by selling their debt instruments. This network represents both new issues and secondary market trading.

NET EARNINGS   See *net income.*

NET INCOME   The "bottom line" of the income statement. Net income is revenues less expenses less taxes. Also referred to as net earnings or net profits.

NET PRESENT VALUE (NPV)   The present value of one or more future cash flows less any initial investment costs.

NET PROFITS   See *net income.*

NET WORKING CAPITAL   Current assets less current liabilities; the amount of money a company has tied up in short-term operating activities.

OPERATING BUDGET   A projected target for performance in revenues, expenses, and operating income.

OPERATING EARNINGS   On the income statement, gross margin less operating expenses and depreciation. Often called earnings before interest and taxes, or EBIT.

OPERATING EXPENSE   On the balance sheet, a category that includes administrative expenses, employee salaries, rents, sales and marketing costs, as well as other costs of business not directly attributed to the cost of manufacturing a product.

OPERATING LEASE   A lease whose term covers a portion of the asset's anticipated useful life. The lessor (the asset's owner) must typically renew the lease one or more times to recoup the cost of the asset and make a profit.

OPERATING LEVERAGE   The extent to which a company's operating costs are fixed versus variable. For example, a company that relies heavily on machinery and very few workers to produce its goods has a high operating leverage.

OPERATING MARGIN   A financial ratio used by many analysts to gauge the profitability of a company's operating activities. It is calculated as earnings before interest and taxes (EBIT) divided by net sales.

OPPORTUNITY COST   What shareholders could earn on their capital if they invested in the next-best opportunity available to them at the same level of risk.

OVERHEAD   See *indirect costs*.

OWNERS' EQUITY   What, if anything, is left over after total liabilities are deducted from total assets. Owners' equity is the sum of capital contributed by owners plus their retained earnings. Also known as shareholders' equity.

PARTNERSHIP   A business entity with two or more owners and particular legal and tax characteristics.

PAYBACK PERIOD   The length of time it will take a particular investment to pay for itself.

PLANT ASSETS   See *fixed assets*.

PREFERRED STOCK   An equity-like security that pays a specified dividend and has a superior position to common stock in case of distributions or liquidation.

PRESENT VALUE (PV)   The monetary value today of a future payment discounted at some annual compound interest rate.

PROFIT-AND-LOSS STATEMENT (P&L)   See *income statement*.

PROFIT MARGIN   The percentage of every dollar of sales that makes it to the bottom line. Profit margin is net income after tax divided by net sales. Sometimes called the return on sales, or ROS.

REPLACEMENT VALUE   A valuation approach that estimates the cost of reproducing an asset, rather than the more common reliance on an asset's book value.

RETAINED EARNINGS   Annual net profits left after payment of dividends that accumulate on a company's balance sheet.

RETURN ON ASSETS (ROA)   Relates net income to the company's total asset base and is calculated as net income divided by total assets.

RETURN ON EQUITY (ROE)   Relates net income to the amount invested by shareholders (both initially and through retained earnings). It is a measure of the productivity of the shareholders' stake in the business and is calculated as net income divided by shareholders' equity.

RETURN ON SALES (ROS)   See *profit margin*.

REVENUE   The amount of money that results from selling products or services to customers.

ROLLING BUDGET   A plan that is continually updated so that the time frame remains stable while the actual period covered by the budget changes. For example, as each month passes, a one-year rolling budget is extended by one month, so that there is always a one-year forward-looking budget in place.

SALE AND LEASEBACK   A leasing arrangement in which an entity sells an asset to another (usually a financing company) to raise capital and then leases back that same asset.

SHAREHOLDERS' EQUITY   See *owners' equity*.

SOLE PROPRIETORSHIP   A business owned by a single individual.

SOLVENCY   The ability to pay bills as they come due.

STATEMENT OF FINANCIAL POSITION   See *balance sheet*.

TAX CREDIT   A dollar-for-dollar reduction of tax liability.

TIMES INTEREST EARNED RATIO   Earnings before interest and taxes divided by interest expense. Creditors use this ratio to gauge a company's ability to make future interest payment in the face of fluctuating operating results.

VALUE CHAIN   The sequence of activities by which a company creates and delivers products or services to customers and increases shareholder value. The value chain consists of outside suppliers and customers, as well as internal activities and individuals.

VARIANCE   The difference between actual results and the results expected in the budget. A variance can be favorable, when the actual results are better than expected—or unfavorable, when the actual results are worse than expected.

VENTURE CAPITALIST (VC)   A high-risk investor who seeks an equity position in a start-up or an early-growth company with high potential. In return for capital, the VC typically takes a significant percentage ownership of the business and a position on its board.

WORKING CAPITAL   See *net working capital.*

ZERO-BASED BUDGETING   A budgeting practice that begins each new budgeting cycle from a zero base, or from the ground up, as though the budget were being prepared for the first time. Each budget cycle starts with a critical review of every assumption and proposed expenditure. The advantage of zero-based budgeting is that it requires managers to perform a much more in-depth analysis on an annual basis of each line item—considering objectives, exploring alternatives, and justifying their requests.

For Further Reading

Accounting Concepts

For a discussion of accounting for inventory and the various approaches to depreciation, see William J. Bruns Jr., "Accounting for Property, Plant, Equipment and Other Assets," Case 9-193-046 (Boston: Harvard Business School Publishing, 1996).

For any question on cost accounting for managers, see Charles T. Horngren, George Foster, and Srikant M. Datar, *Cost Accounting: A Managerial Emphasis* (Upper Saddle River, NJ: Prentice-Hall, 1997).

On the subject of activity-based cost accounting, see Robert S. Kaplan, "Introduction to Activity-Based Costing," Case 9-197-076 (Boston: Harvard Business School Publishing, 2001). This class discussion note tells you what most managers need to know about ABC. Another useful and highly readable article on this subject is Robin Cooper and Robert S. Kaplan, "Profit Priorities from Activity-Based Costing," *Harvard Business Review* (May–June 1991).

Balanced Scorecard

The following books explain the balanced scorecard methodology and its power to help organizations analyze leading indicators of financial performance: Robert S. Kaplan and David P. Norton, *The Balanced Scorecard: Translating Strategy into Action* (Boston: Harvard Business School Press, 1996); Brian E. Becker, Mark A. Huselid, and Dave Ulrich, *The HR Scorecard: Linking People, Strategy, and Performance* (Boston: Harvard Business School Press, 2001); Robert S. Kaplan and David P. Norton, *The Strategy-Focused Organization: How Balanced Scorecard Companies Thrive in the New Business Environment* (Boston: Harvard Business School Press, 2001); Robert S. Kaplan and David P. Norton, *Strategy Maps: Converting Intangible Assets into Tangible Outcomes* (Boston: Harvard Business School Press, 2004). You can also find numerous case studies of how successful companies have used the balanced scorecard methodology in the *Balanced Scorecard Hall of Fame Report 2004*, available from the Balanced Scorecard Collaborative, at 1-800-668-6705 or 1-617-783-7474.

Bankruptcy

See Robert J. Grossman, "Holding Back Bankruptcy," *HR Magazine,* May 2003, for a detailed look at the bankruptcy filing process and ways in which HR professionals can help their companies avoid or prepare for bankruptcy filing and recovery.

Budgeting

Robert S. Kaplan and David P. Norton, "Linking Strategy to Planning and Budgeting," *Harvard Business Review* (May–June 2000), shows how traditional budgeting practices can be made more responsive to a company's rapidly changing needs. The authors urge managers not just to focus on the operational budget, but to pay attention to the strategy budget as well, because the strategy budget is what finances the initiatives that facilitate company growth. Managers also need to avoid falling into the trap of thinking that initiatives are ends in themselves. Rather, initiatives are the means by which a company accomplishes its strategic objectives.

Charles T. Horngren, George Foster, and Srikant M. Datar, *Cost Accounting: A Managerial Emphasis* (Upper Saddle River, NJ: Prentice-Hall, 1997), is a classic textbook on cost accounting. The book describes budgeting as a concept, a strategic tool, and a planning process in detail, with examples and exercises. Not only is the treatment of budgeting thorough, but the topic is fully integrated into other cost accounting and planning material.

Embezzlement and Theft by Employees

Robert J. Grossman, "The Five-Finger Bonus," *HR Magazine,* October 2003, sheds additional light on the conditions that encourage stealing—and the strategies for decreasing embezzlement and theft by employees.

Financial Statements

For a concise treatment of ratio analysis, see William J. Bruns Jr., "Introduction to Financial Ratios and Financial Statement Analysis," Class Note 9-193-029 (Boston: Harvard Business School Publishing, 1996).

For the subject of the balanced scorecard, go right to the source: Robert S. Kaplan and David P. Norton, "The Balanced Scorecard: Measures That

Drive Performance," *Harvard Business Review* (January–February 1992). For a fuller discussion of the balanced scorecard and its implementation, see Robert S. Kaplan and David P. Norton, *The Balanced Scorecard* (Boston: Harvard Business School Press, 1996).

HR as Profit Center

For more detail about how to position and operate your HR department as a profit center rather than a cost center, see Michael W. Mercer, *Turning Your Human Resources Department into a Profit Center* (New York: AMACOM, 1989). Mercer describes thirty-five specific techniques HR professionals can implement to enhance their company's bottom line through HR programs and initiatives.

Also see Lianabel Oliver, *The Cost Management Toolbox: A Manager's Guide to Controlling Costs and Boosting Profits* (New York: AMACOM, 2000), for strategies and tools related to two important profitability levers.

Intangible Assets

To learn more about various aspects of measuring intangible assets such as human capital, see the following resources: Steve Bates, "Accounting for People," *HR Magazine,* October 2002 (measuring the contributions of people to organizations); Steve Bates, "The Metrics Maze," *HR Magazine,* December 2003 (selecting metrics for measuring human capital); Lisa M. Aldisert, *Valuing People: How Human Capital Can Be Your Strongest Asset* (Chicago: Dearborn Trade Publishing, 2002) (measuring and enhancing the value of your firm's strongest asset); Jac Fitz-enz, *The ROI of Human Capital: Measuring the Economic Value of Employee Performance* (New York: AMACOM, 2002); and Jack J. Phillips, *Return on Investment in Training and Performance Improvement Programs* (Woburn, MA: Butterworth-Heinemann, 1997) (calculating the financial return of training and other HR programs).

Money and Capital Markets

Marcia Stigum and Frank Fabozzi, *The Dow Jones-Irwin Guide to Bonds and Money Market Instruments* (Homewood, IL: Dow Jones-Irwin, 1987), remains one of the most accessible introductory sources on fixed-income securities and money market instruments. Stigum has written the authoritative volume on money market calculations (yields and pricing), and Fabozzi has produced several landmark books on fixed-income securities, but these are highly technical and suited to the interests of investment professionals.

For a straightforward description of various debt and equity securities, and the investor's perspective on them, Herbert B. Mayo, *Investments:*

An Introduction, 6th ed. (Fort Worth: Harcourt/Dryden Press, 1999), is hard to beat.

Samuel L. Hayes III and Philip M. Hubbard, *Investment Banking: A Tale of Three Cities* (Boston: Harvard Business School Press, 1990), provides a highly readable history of investment banking and the development of money and capital markets in the three epicenters of global finance: New York, London, and Tokyo. The authors describe the historic role that investment banks have played in financing governments and industry and how that role has changed over the years.

Not-for-Profit Organizations

Edward McMillan, *Not-for-Profit Budgeting and Financial Management* (Hoboken, NJ: John Wiley & Sons, 2003), and Edward McMillan, *Not-for-Profit Accounting, Tax and Reporting Requirements* (Hoboken, NJ: John Wiley & Sons, 2003), provide helpful information on the financial standards required and the terminology used in financial statements for not-for-profit organizations.

Sarbanes-Oxley Act of 2002

See Jonathan A. Segal, "The 'Joy' of Uncooking," *HR Magazine,* November 2002, for detailed information on the Sarbanes-Oxley Act of 2002 and how you can ensure that your firm complies with the act's various employment-related provisions.

H. David Sherman and S. David Young, "Tread Lightly Through These Accounting Minefields," *Harvard Business Review Enhanced OnPoint Edition* (October 2002), and H. David Sherman and S. David Young, "Spinning the Numbers," *HR Magazine,* November 2002, provide additional information on the dangers of overly aggressive accounting practices.

Taxes

Weighing in at less than eight hundred pages of text, the *U.S. Master Tax Guide* (Chicago: CCH, 2002) is a good source on individual and business taxes. Revised annually, it has the most up-to-date information on tax rules and rates.

The Time Value of Money

Time-value concepts are among the most important you can master in becoming a better analyst and decision maker. We've presented the very basics in this book, but there's much more to learn. Any modern textbook on the principles of finance will include a chapter on this subject, with many examples and exercises. Pick up one of these books, study the time-value chapter, and gain practice through the examples and exercises.

Also see Steve Bates, "Accounting for Time," *HR Magazine,* September 2003, for a detailed example of how one hypothetical company used time-value-of-money techniques to evaluate the relative benefits and costs of three proposed HR initiatives.

Valuation

The current bible on valuation is Tom Copland, Tim Koller, and Jack Murrin, *Valuation: Measuring and Managing the Value of Companies,* 2nd ed. (New York: John Wiley & Sons, 1995). This volume describes the valuation process and explains the differences between valuation and accounting practice. It illustrates how to maximize shareholder value, demonstrates how value-based management contributes to improved strategic thinking, and indicates how managers and different levels can add value.

For a short but less complete take on the subject, see Timothy Luehrman, "What's It Worth? A General Manager's Guide to Valuation," *Harvard Business Review* (May–June 1997). As Luehrman indicates, managers need to be able to value operations, opportunities (real options), and ownership claims. His article addresses all three. A reprint can be ordered directly from the Harvard Business School Publishing Web site at <http://www.hbsp.harvard.edu/home.html>.

Index

About the Series Adviser

WENDY BLISS, J.D., SPHR, has experience as a human resource executive, attorney, senior editor, and professional speaker. Since 1994, she has provided human resource consulting, corporate training, and coaching services nationally through her Colorado Springs-based consulting firm, Bliss & Associates.

Ms. Bliss is the author of *Legal, Effective References: How to Give and Get Them* (Society for Human Resource Management, 2001) and was a contributor to *Human Resource Essentials* (Society for Human Resource Management, 2002). She has published numerous articles in magazines and periodicals, including *HR Magazine, Employment Management Today, HR Matters,* and the *Denver University Law Review.*

Ms. Bliss has a Juris Doctor degree from the University of Denver College of Law and has been certified as a Senior Professional in Human Resources (SPHR) by the Human Resource Certification Institute. Since 1999, she has conducted human resource certificate programs for the Society for Human Resource Management. Previously, she was an adjunct faculty member at the University of Colorado at Colorado Springs and at the University of Phoenix, where she taught graduate and undergraduate courses in human resource management, employment law, organizational behavior, and business communications. Additionally, Ms. Bliss has served on the board of directors for several professional associations and nonprofit organizations and was a President of the National Board of Governors for the Society for Human Resource Management's Consultants Forum.

National media including *ABC News, Time* magazine, the *New York Times,* the *Associated Press,* the *Washington Post, USAToday.com,* and *HR Magazine* have used Ms. Bliss as an expert source on workplace issues.

About the Subject Adviser

SAMUEL L. HAYES holds the Jacob H. Schiff Chair in Investment Banking, at the Harvard Business School, Emeritus. He has taught at the school since 1971, prior to which he was a tenured member of the faculty of the Columbia University Graduate School of Business. He received a B.A. in Political Science at Swarthmore College in 1957 and an M.B.A. (with Distinction) and a D.B.A. from Harvard Business School in 1961 and 1966, respectively.

His M.B.A. teaching assignments have included the second-year courses in Investment Banking, Management of Financial Services Organizations, and Corporate Financial Management, as well as the first-year Finance course (where he served as Course Head). He has also chaired Harvard's International Senior Managers Program in Vevey, Switzerland. He taught in the summer Corporate Financial Management Program for senior finance executives for a number of years and chaired that faculty during six of those years. He has also taught in the Advanced Management Program and the Corporate Finance component in the school's Owner-President Management Program.

Professor Hayes's research has focused on the capital markets and on the corporate interface with the securities markets. He has written numerous working papers and articles on related topics in journals such as the *Harvard Business Review,* the *Accounting Review,* the *Financial Analysis Journal, The Economic Review,* and *Financial Management* and has contributed chapters to a number of books. Two articles that he coauthored on real estate finance won the Shattuck Award for the best article on real estate in 1967 and 1972.

Professor Hayes is the coauthor or editor of seven books, including *Competition in the Investment Banking Industry* (Harvard University Press, 1983), *Investment Banking and Diligence* (Harvard Business School Press, 1986), *Wall Street and Regulation* (Harvard Business School Press, 1987), *Investment Banking: A Tale of Three Cities* (Harvard Business School Press, 1990), *Managing Financial Institutions* (Dryden Press/HBJ, 1992), *Financial Services: Perspectives and Challenges* (Harvard Business School Press, 1993), and *Islamic Law and Finance: Religion, Risk, and Return* (Kluwer Press, 1997).

Professor Hayes has consulted for a number of corporations, financial institutions, and government agencies, including the Justice Department, the Treasury Department, the Federal Trade Commission, and the Securities and Exchange Commission, where he served on the Tully Commission in 1994–1995 to examine compensation arrangements for stock brokers. For twelve years, he was Chairman of the Finance Advisory Board of the Commonwealth of Massachusetts. He now serves on the Board of Managers of Swarthmore College (where he is Chair of the Investment Committee), the Board of Trustees of the New England Conservatory of Music (where he is Chair of the Finance Committee), and the Boards of the Eaton-Vance mutual funds, Tiffany & Company, Kobrick mutual funds, and Telect, Inc.

About the Writers

LAUREN KELLER JOHNSON has contributed to several volumes in the Business Literacy for HR Professionals series. Based in Harvard, Massachusetts, Ms. Keller Johnson writes for numerous business publications, including the *Harvard Business Review* OnPoint Series, *Harvard Management Update, Sloan Management Review*, and the *Balanced Scorecard Report*. She has ghostwritten several books and online training modules for managers. She has a master's degree in technical and professional writing from Northeastern University.

RICHARD LUECKE is the writer of several books in the Harvard Business Essentials series. Based in Salem, Massachusetts, Mr. Luecke has authored or developed more than thirty books and dozens of articles on a wide range of business subjects. He has an M.B.A. from the University of St. Thomas.

About the Society for Human Resource Management

THE SOCIETY FOR HUMAN RESOURCE MANAGEMENT (SHRM) is the world's largest association devoted to human resource management. Representing more than 170,000 individual members, the Society's mission is to serve the needs of HR professionals by providing the most essential and comprehensive resources available. As an influential voice, the Society's mission is also to advance the human resource profession to ensure that HR is recognized as an essential partner in developing and executing organizational strategy. Visit SHRM Online at www.shrm.org.

The Results-Driven Manager

The Results-Driven Manager series collects timely articles from *Harvard Management Update* and *Harvard Management Communication Letter* to help senior to middle managers sharpen their skills, increase their effectiveness, and gain a competitive edge. Presented in a concise, accessible format to save managers valuable time, these books offer authoritative insights and techniques for improving job performance and achieving immediate results.

These books are priced at US$14.95.
Price subject to change.

Title	Product #
The Results-Driven Manager: **Face-to-Face Communications for Clarity and Impact**	3477
The Results-Driven Manager: **Managing Yourself for the Career You Want**	3469
The Results-Driven Manager: **Presentations That Persuade and Motivate**	3493
The Results-Driven Manager: **Teams That Click**	3507
The Results-Driven Manager: **Winning Negotiations That Preserve Relationships**	3485
The Results-Driven Manager: **Dealing with Difficult People**	6344
The Results-Driven Manager: **Taking Control of Your Time**	6352
The Results-Driven Manager: **Getting People on Board**	6360
The Results-Driven Manager: **Becoming an Effective Leader**	7804
The Results-Driven Manager: **Managing Change to Reduce Resistance**	7812
The Results-Driven Manager: **Motivating People for Improved Performance**	7790

How to Order

Harvard Business School Press publications are available worldwide
from your local bookseller or online retailer.
You can also call

1-800-668-6780

Our product consultants are available to help you
8:00 a.m.–6:00 p.m., Monday–Friday, Eastern Time.
Outside the U.S. and Canada, call: 617-783-7450
Please call about special discounts for quantities greater than ten.

You can order online at

www.HBSPress.org